CHALLENGER 2
MAIN BATTLE TANK

1998 to present

First published in October 2018
Reprinted February 2023

A catalogue record for this book is available from the British Library.

ISBN 978 1 78521 190 4

Library of Congress control no. 2018938897

Published by J H Haynes & Co. Ltd.,
Sparkford, Yeovil, Somerset BA22 7JJ, UK.
Tel: 01963 440635
Int. tel: +44 1963 440635
Website: www.haynes.com

Haynes North America Inc.,
859 Lawrence Drive, Newbury Park,
California 91320, USA.

Printed in India.

Senior Commissioning Editor: Jonathan Falconer
Copy editor: Michelle Tilling
Proof reader: Penny Housden
Indexer: Peter Nicholson
Page design: James Robertson

CHALLENGER 2 MAIN BATTLE TANK

1998 to present

Owners' Workshop Manual

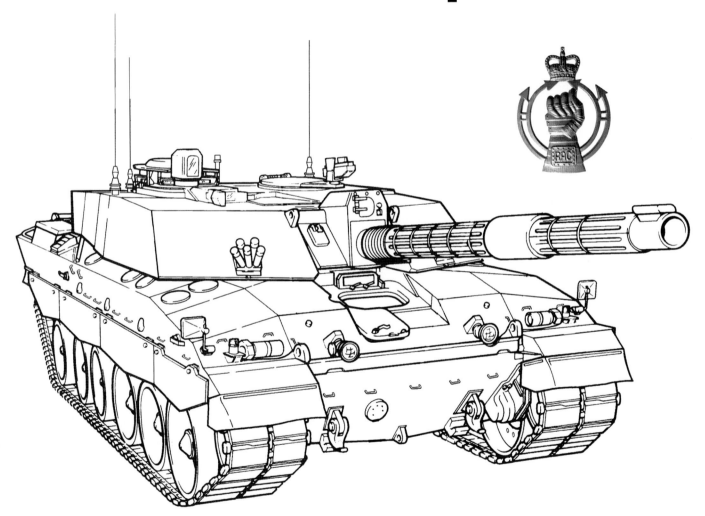

An insight into the design, construction, operation and maintenance of the British Army's Main Battle Tank of the 21st century

Dick Taylor

Contents

OPPOSITE Challenger 2 (CR2) has been the British Army's Main Battle Tank for the last two decades and is expected to remain in service until 2035, but with many updated systems. This is MEGATRON of the Armour Trials and Development Unit.

(Crown Copyright Open Licence)

Acknowledgements

Organisations: HQ RAC Bovington, HQ Armour Centre Bovington, The Regiments and Home Headquarters of the RAC, AFV Technical Training School Bovington, Armoured Trials & Development Unit Bovington, The Tank Museum Bovington Archive and Library, *Tank Magazine*, Cook Defence Systems.

Individuals: Maj (Retd) Cliff Allum MBE, Mike Angwin, Maj (Retd) Nigel Atkin, WO2 (SSMI) Stew Baird KRH, Lt Col Paddy Bond QDG, Neil Boston, Andy Brend, Richard Brown, Cpl Chez Cherrett KRH, Col Guy Deacon OBE, Simon Dunstan, Jim Elgar, Maj (Retd) Jamie Erskine, Lt Col John Gregory RWxY, Cpl Matthew Hatfield RTR,* Lt Gen (Retd) Sir Robert Hayman-Joyce KCB CBE DL, S/Sgt Keith Hendron KRH, Dr Mark Helliker, Nathan Johnson, L/Cpl Nathan Keys RTR, Dennis Kirby, Bryan Maddams, Maj (Retd) Colin Macintyre RWxY (ex-Scots DG), Capt William Montgomery QOY (ex-Scots DG), Ian Nicholson, Maj Gen (Retd) Roland Notley CB CBE, WO2 Chris Pavelin RWxY, SSgt Ian Pearson QRH, Maj (Retd) Steve Penkethman, Lt Col (Retd) Andrew Phillips, Cpl Ilaitia Ratuqalovi Scots DG, Richard Rawlins, Lt Col (Retd) Norrie Robertson MBE BEM, Matt Sampson, Maj Gen (Retd) Alan Sharman CBE, Capt (Retd) Allan Smith, Padre Andrew Totten MBE QHC, Maj (Retd) Joe Toward MBE RWxY (ex-Scots DG), Les Tyler, L/Cpl Greg Underhill QRH, Lt Col (Retd) Mark Williams, Lt Matt Winters RTR.

* Cpl Matthew Hatfield was tragically killed in a CR2 accident in June 2017, just after having assisted greatly with the research for this book. He is sadly missed.

BELOW MEGATRON of the Armour Trials and Development Unit in full Operational Entry Standard fit, including additional hull and turret armour packs. *(Courtesy Andy Brend)*

Foreword

Colonel G.H.J. Deacon OBE ADC

Colonel Commandant RAC, 2015–18

When I joined the army, Challenger (1) was about to enter service. As a troop leader destined for a reconnaissance regiment, I can recall looking on in envy as it was put through its paces at Bovington and Lulworth. It was a step-change in capability compared with Chieftain, particularly in terms of mobility, and it seemed that I was destined to miss out on it. In fact, my regiment later changed role from reconnaissance to tanks and so I did get to serve on Challenger 1 as a squadron leader and got to know it – and love it – as all tank soldiers do. Then, when I was working back in Bovington in HQ RAC, I became closely engaged in the fielding of Challenger 2 and so lived through the testing (in both senses of the word) and then delivery of the first batch of new tanks; I experienced the same sentiments again, knowing that my regiment would retain Challenger 1 for some while yet. But I also witnessed its first demonstration to representatives of the Warsaw Pact, which saw the tank destroy six targets in less than a minute as a consequence of its superior target acquisition capability and, from that moment on, I have been in awe of it. The fact that this tank has been able to hold its own against its competitors for the last 20 years and, with the forthcoming life extension programme, is destined to remain the ultimate battlefield predator in the British Army's inventory for a further 20, speaks volumes for the designers and builders of this unique piece of equipment. By the time it is retired (to be replaced by who knows what), it will have served for at least 40 years as one of the most tangible demonstrations of the nation's commitment to defence.

This outstanding book covers a period of change in Europe and the UK's defence posture, which saw significant adjustments in the size, shape and role of the RAC. But above all it tells the story of Challenger 2 and its development and service, in a depth that has not before been possible. Ultimately it is dedicated to the men who designed and built it, and to the thousands of soldiers who devoted their working lives to ensuring it was ready for whatever crisis unfolded.

All the royalties from this book are being donated to the soldiers and officers of the Royal Armoured Corps by way of the RAC Benevolent Fund, and it remains for me to thank the author for his generosity, and all the staff at Haynes for their continuing support and assistance.

**Colonel G.H.J. Deacon OBE ADC
(late 1st The Queen's Dragoon Guards)**

Introduction

Lt Gen Sir Robert Hayman-Joyce

Colonel Commandant RAC, 1995–99

The Main Battle Tank (MBT) that so dominated the Cold War strategic thinking has appeared to have been relegated to the background in recent years. The commitment of the Western powers to countering the insurgencies in Iraq and Afghanistan has led to a perceived need for lighter, mine-protected vehicles, though it has to be said that where tanks have been deployed in those theatres, the effect has been salutary. Those campaigns are now over and military minds are contemplating new realities and how to respond; once again the MBT is being seen as a key component of this response.

OPPOSITE CR2 seen in its training configuration without the additional armour that makes such a difference to its appearance and weight. *(Courtesy Andy Brend)*

ABOVE Conqueror was a stop-gap tank designed specifically to counter the threat posed by new Soviet heavy tanks.

I have watched the development of British tank technology from the business end since the early 1960s. Centurion came into service after the Second World War and its successful design owed much to the equipment fielded by the other combatant nations, notably the Germans. The tank fought in Korea and was not superseded until the late 1960s. Centurion was powered by a modified Meteor petrol engine developed for the Spitfire and it had a habit of catching fire: many are the apocryphal stories of quartermasters rushing old blankets

on to a fire in order to straighten their inventory accounts. It was also thirsty: before the days of bulk refuelling, replen was a major task. The Cent initially fielded the 17-pounder gun based on the effective 17-pounder anti-tank gun in the ground role. Later it was equipped with a 20-pounder and then the 105mm L7 which gave that tank a capability to at least match any other in the world at the time. Upgraded periodically during its life – the last was the Mark 13 – by the 1960s it was clear that it was going to be outmatched by Soviet armour developments.

This was the cue for the Conqueror, hastily fielded to counter the perceived threat and was armed with a US-designed 120mm rifled gun. A veteran was overheard remarking that 'the sound of the Conqueror engine was music to an armoured soldier's ears'. Despite its powerful gun it was never seen as more than a stop-gap: it was too heavy for many bridges, too large to meet the rail gauge without much disassembly, and woefully unreliable.

LEFT A 6 RTR Centurion practices beach landings prior to the 1956 Suez operation. Centurion gave sterling service for over two decades. *(Courtesy Paul Brewer)*

The Chieftain, meanwhile, was about to come into service. The first Chieftain arrived in theatre in the mid-1960s, and was hailed as the tank to meet the threat for some years to come. Newly designed frontal armour and mounting the UK-designed 120mm rifled gun with three ammunition natures gave the British Army a step-change in effectiveness . . . that is, if you could rely on the tank to be where you needed it when you needed it! To achieve the necessary high power-to-weight ratio in the restricted space allowed for the engine, Leyland had designed a brilliantly compact engine, using horizontally opposed cylinders. Throughout its life Chieftain was dogged by the problem of oil starvation in the upper cylinders, causing the liners to fail. Efforts to replace the Chieftain were attempted several times in subsequent years with little success. By the mid-1980s that need had been sharpened by further armour developments in the USSR. MBT 80 and various attempts to jointly develop a tank with other European nations all fell by the wayside. The ambitious requirements for MBT 80 were

ABOVE This is possibly the only surviving Chieftain Mk 2 still in its original configuration. At the time of writing this tank stands guard at the vehicle depot, Ashchurch.

LEFT Chieftain went through numerous upgrades and modifications. It is shown here in 1987 carrying the new Stillbrew armour package. Despite this, the ageing design clearly needed replacing with a new tank.

technically unachievable at the time and the difficulty of reconciling British requirements with the other nations proved impossible.

In the background Vickers had been developing a new tank, the Shir Iran, ordered in large numbers by the Shah of Persia. The events of 1979 stopped that programme dead. The obvious solution for Vickers and for the British Army was to redirect the Shir Iran to British service, hence after some modification Challenger was born. Four regiments were initially re-equipped with Challenger which represented a considerable uplift in the Royal Armoured Corps' effectiveness: the 120mm was retained with ammunition compatible with the Chieftain, and a new 1,200bhp powerpack and Chobham armour were major improvements. On the debit side the fire control system and internal electrical systems were still based on 1960s technology and were in dire need of a rethink.

BELOW Challenger 1 (CR1) was not what the Army wanted to replace Chieftain, but through a combination of circumstances it began to enter service in 1983. *(Courtesy Andy Brend)*

By the mid-1980s the backbone of the British armoured formations remained the Chieftain; fewer than half of the nearly 1,100-strong tank fleet had been replaced by Challenger, itself dated technically. After so many abortive efforts to field a tank that could outmatch the rapidly developing Soviet threat, it became clear that Britain desperately needed to develop a new national MBT. The Master General of the Ordnance, Sir Dick Vincent, visited Vickers in 1986 and tasked the company to come up with proposals to replace the ageing Chieftain for the British Army. By then the Challenger 1 was in service and the expectation was that the new tank would be a derivative . . . 'And the rest is history'. But that history has never been properly documented until now. Intimately involved over the decade that it took to field Challenger 2, I have been conscious that the full story ought to be told; this meticulous study answers

that need. It will appeal not only to the reader interested in general armour matters, but also to the enthusiast who wants to delve more deeply into armoured warfare, and anyone interested in the development process for a major weapons system will find this work both absorbing and useful.

Challenger 2 came into service in 1998. By then the need for these formidable fighting machines appeared to be over: throughout its history the survivability and usefulness of the tank in warfare has been questioned as more and better anti-armour weapons are fielded and the vehicles have become more and more complicated and expensive. Despite this, recent developments in world politics have reawakened the realisation that the pundits who dismissed the tank as outmoded may have been wrong. Challenger 2 and the people who crew and support it could well be needed again in the 21st century.

ABOVE CR1 still used the same L11 120mm gun and fire control equipment as that on its predecessor, which meant that lethality was not much improved.

BELOW CR2 entered service in 1998 and has proved to be a popular tank with its crews, being both fast across country and extremely well protected. *(Courtesy Andy Brend)*

Chapter One

Design and development

The development of Challenger 2 represented the next evolutionary chapter in British MBT development that had seen Centurion, Chieftain and then Challenger 1 designed and produced both for the British Army and for export customers. Indeed, the tank can be said to have derived its DNA from no fewer than three parents: Challenger 1, MBT 80 and the Vickers Mk 7/2. Now intended to remain in service until 2035, it may be that Challenger 2 will eventually have the dubious distinction of being the last British-designed and -built battle tank, ending over 100 years of development and production in the country that invented the tank.

OPPOSITE A dusty Challenger 2 of A Sqn 1RTR moves at high speed on exercise on the Salisbury Plain Training Area, playing the part of an enemy tank as denoted by the red cross on the turret. This tank is carrying the full suite of Tactical Engagement Simulation equipment, which allows realistic – and very competitive – force-on-force training.

Introduction

As the Berlin Wall was being dismantled in 1990, the British Army was still operating a reasonably large fleet of MBTs, with no fewer than 1,072 in service in 13 tank regiments, plus in the training fleet and repair pool. The most obvious problem with this was that two different types of tanks were in service: 646 of the older Chieftains, plus 426 of the newer Challengers. Although there was some commonality between the two, particularly with turret systems, it is never a good idea to operate a mixed fleet, as it causes both logistic and training burdens. However, the real issue went beyond the types of tanks, in that both were based on 1950s/60s technologies, and a select group of scientists and senior officers realised that they were no longer capable of defeating the latest generation of Soviet battle tanks, let alone anything that might be faced in the future. The Soviets were fielding a new tank roughly every seven years, and the British Army needed to find a way to regain at least technical parity, if not superiority. A new tank was needed, and fast.

Before looking in some detail at how that new tank, the Challenger 2, came into being, it is worth starting by reviewing the preceding three generations of battle tank development by Britain in the decades after the Second World War. In that time, Britain had used three MBTs as the spine of the fleet: Centurion, Chieftain and Challenger, with the heavy tank Conqueror also being used during the life of Centurion to fill a specific capability gap. Each of these, rather than being the simple replacement that the lineage implies, actually overlapped in service with the preceding tank to a significant degree: Centurion remained operational for nearly eight years after Chieftain entered service, and Challenger overlapped Chieftain for no less than 13 years! The story of those three tanks is told in much more detail in their own respective dedicated Haynes Manuals, but in order to set the scene for what came next, their key development milestones from the Second World War to 1985 can be summarised in table form.

BRITISH MBT DEVELOPMENT TIMELINE, 1943–85

YEAR	DATE	EVENT	REMARKS
1943	October	Development starts for new A41 medium tank.	Designed by the Directorate of Tank Design.
1944	May	Wooden mock-up of A41 produced.	20 prototypes built, 10 at ROF (Royal Ordnance Factory) Woolwich and 10 at ROF Nottingham.
1945	April	First prototype completed in Woolwich.	
	May	A41, now named Centurion, enters limited service with 6 tanks on Operation Sentry in Germany.	The tanks miss operational service by a few days, but undergo extensive testing by experienced tank crews.
	November	Full-scale production of Centurion commences.	c2,000 eventually serve as gun tanks with British Army in 13 marks.
1948		Production of Centurion Mk 3 armed with new 20-pounder (83.4mm) gun.	Built at Vickers Newcastle and ROF (Leeds).
1951	September	War Office proposal to scope development of Centurion replacement.	As a result of increased tensions and vulnerability concerns arising from the Korean War.
1953	September	Treasury agreement to fund development of Centurion replacement.	
1954	15 March	War Office Policy Statement No 1 issued for a new 'Medium Gun Tank No 2' as the Centurion replacement.	
1955		Production starts of FV 214 Conqueror armed with US-made 120mm L1 gun.	Designed as stop-gap solution for defeating new Soviet heavy tanks. 185 built 1955–9.
1957	16 April	Contract issued to Leyland for six prototype Medium Gun Tanks No 2, now called FV4201.	Contract also included 2 × FV4202 '40-Ton Centurions'
	November	Detailed design work on FV4201 under way.	
	December	War Office considers co-operating with France over new tank design.	Decision later made not to co-operate.

YEAR	DATE	EVENT	REMARKS
1958	August	War Office Policy Statement No 2 issued for FV4201.	Superseded WOPS No 1.
	September	Vickers-Armstrong (V-A) asked to design turret for FV4201.	
1959		Up-gunning of Centurions with new 105mm L7 gun.	
	May	Provisional Development Specification for FV4201 issued.	Superseded WOPS No 2.
	June	Contract issued for six FV4201 prototypes.	3 from ROF (Leeds) and 3 from V-A.
	December	FV4201 wooden mock-up on display to RAC Conference, Bovington.	Hull of P1 prototype also displayed in an incomplete state.
1960	18 January	P1, first prototype FV4201 completed by Leyland.	
	April	FV4201 is named Chieftain.	
	March	W1, first development Chieftain completed by ROF (L).	
1961	June	General Staff Requirement (GSR) 1008 for Chieftain replacement issued.	Over five years *before* Chieftain enters service.
	24 October	First public demonstration of Chieftain at Chertsey.	
1962	April	Sixth Chieftain prototype P6 completed.	
	December	Two development Chieftains begin troop trials in Germany.	1 each to 1RTR (W1) and 5RTR (W3).
1963	10 October	First production order for 571 Chieftains.	39 × Mk 1, 532 × Mk 2. 381 made at ROF (L), 190 at V-A.
		Dr Gilbert Harvey takes out patent on what will be developed into Chobham armour.	Subsequently developed into Dorchester Armour.
1965	June	First Mk 1 Chieftain completed at ROF (L).	First V-A Mk 1 completed in February 1966.
1966	April	First Mk 2 Chieftain completed at ROF (L).	First V-A Mk 2 completed in January 1967.
	11 November	Initial issue of six Mk 2 Chieftain to BAOR (11th Hussars).	Official entry into service of Chieftain.
	December	Last Conqueror leaves service.	
1967	27 February	Production order for 152 Mk 3 Chieftains.	All to be made by ROF (L).
	24 March	11th Hussars completely equipped with Chieftain.	
1970		FV4211 development tank built at Chertsey. Ten turrets also made.	Based on Chieftain but with Chobham armour and extensive use of aluminium. Cancelled 1972.
		British Army considers purchasing a half-fleet of Chieftain Mk 5/2 with Chobham armour from 1975 onwards.	Not proceeded with.
1971		Final production order placed for Mk 5 Chieftains.	
		General Staff Target for Chieftain replacement circulated.	
		Iran orders 707 Chieftain Mk 3 and 5 MBT. Subsequently, Iran orders 193 FV 4030/1 Improved Chieftain Mk 5 MBT.	
1972		Future MBT (FMBT) conceived as Anglo-German collaborative project to replace Chieftain.	
1973	19 April	Final British Army Chieftain MBT completed.	

YEAR	DATE	EVENT	REMARKS
1974	22 July	Last Centurion gun tank withdrawn from British Army service.	
	December	Iran orders 125 FV 4030/2 (Shir 1) MBT, plus 1225 FV4030/3 (Shir 2).	Shir 1 is improved Chieftain MBT; Shir 2 is new MBT with Chobham armour.
1976	June	913 Chieftains are in British Army service.	941 Chieftain MBT produced in total for British Army in 11 marks.
	17 June	Existence of Chobham armour revealed.	
1977	January	First 3 Shir 1 prototypes produced.	
	March	FMBT collaborative project cancelled.	
	4 April	Feasibility study for new MBT to replace Chieftain commences.	To become MBT 80.
	12 October	GSR 3572 for Main Battle Tank for the 1980s (MBT 80) issued; endorsed January 1978.	Sometimes referred to as Project 5880.
1978	1 July	Two-year project definition study for MBT 80 commences.	£63.8m allocated for the phase.
	September	Full development costs for MBT 80 estimated at £127 million.	15 prototypes planned, P1 to be delivered September 1983. In-service date (two complete regiments operational) expected to be 1989.
	1 December	GSR 3572 for MBT 80 developed into more detailed MVEE Specification 762.	
1979		Two Automotive Test Rig hulls for MBT 80 produced.	
	6 February	Iran repudiates all outstanding MBT orders, including Shir 1 and 2.	In same month the Royal Jordanian Army expresses interest in a Shir 1 derivative to be known as Khalid.
	March	British Army considers option to operate c250 Shir 2 tanks.	Decision deferred pending further studies.
	5 September	GSR 3574 for FV 4030/4 issued in draft.	FV 4030/4 is British Army derivative of Shir 2.
	24 September	Decision to part-equip British Army with FV4030/4 made (but not announced).	
	28 November	Royal Jordanian Army orders 274 Khalid.	
1980	14 July	British government announces decision to order 243 FV 4030/4. On the same day the decision to cancel MBT 80 is announced.	Sufficient to equip only four armoured regiments in the British Army of the Rhine (BAOR) plus some training vehicles. FV 4030/4 subsequently named Challenger (and later still Challenger 1).
	October	DGFVE report into possibilities of buying non-British MBT in future.	Conclusion is that foreign tanks offer no significant operational, cost or resource advantages.
1982		Production of Challenger under way in ROF (L).	
	14 December	Challenger officially accepted into service.	
1983	1 February	First pre-production Challenger completed.	
	16 March	Official handover ceremony of first Challenger.	In Mk 1 configuration.
	12 April	First Challenger tank goes into operational service with Royal Hussars in Fallingbostel, BAOR.	Total of 427 Challenger 1s built for British Army. Final mark used is Mk 3.
1984		Consideration given to replacing rifled gun in Challenger with smoothbore.	Not proceeded with.
1985	June	Vickers Defence Systems (VDS) awarded contract to develop the Challenger Armoured Repair and Recovery Vehicle (CRARRV).	Included new TN 54 transmission, later used on CR2.

A number of important points can be extrapolated from this information. Firstly there is the issue of developmental timescales. Centurion, built during wartime conditions, took only 18 months from specification to the first tanks being fielded. The specification for its successor, Chieftain, was issued in March 1954, but it did not make its appearance in prototype form until January 1960, an initial gestation period of nearly six years, and taking another six before starting its operational life. Challenger 1 entered service in early 1983, seemingly only 3½ years after the British specification was issued, but it was actually closer to eight as it derived from the Shir 2 specification agreed in the mid-1970s. Developing modern tanks takes a lot of time, money and effort, and as tanks become increasingly more complicated, timescales naturally lengthen too. This was not a purely British problem: work on replacing the American M60 tank started in 1965, but fielding a replacement tank was delayed because the proposed solution, the collaborative MBT 70, took longer than expected and eventually failed, meaning that the new M1 tank did not start to enter service to replace the M60 until 1982, no fewer than 17 years later. It will be explained shortly that Challenger 2 benefited in many ways from being based upon an existing tank, but still took around 11 years to get the first tank into service.

Secondly, it can be seen that in parallel with the development of those tanks which came into being (eventually) as service vehicles, numerous other studies and projects were pursued, mostly with extremely demanding aspirations to produce the 'wonder tank' of the future. These were not limited to Britain, and included FMBT, the proposed Anglo-German tank of the 1970s; the German/US MBT 70 which was intended as the replacement for both the M60 and the Leopard 1; and the purely British MBT 80. None of these tanks came to fruition, due in large part to mounting development costs, unrealistic expectations of immature and novel technologies, and ever-more-distant dates for the tanks to enter service. And collaborative projects added a further layer of problems, as the collaborating nations found it difficult (meaning impossible) to do just that – to agree on how to compromise.

ABOVE In order to counter the Soviet JS3 and T10 heavy tanks, the British introduced the Conqueror heavy tank into service alongside Centurion, where its L1 120mm gun provided long-range punch. *(TM 8530D5)*

It is, however, worth exploring a little of the history of the British MBT 80 project, as although at first sight it does not appear to be directly related to Challenger 2, there were a significant number of overlaps between the two projects, and lessons were learned that would be used when putting Challenger 2 together in a relatively short period.

MBT 80

MBT 80 was a British-only project initiated in 1977[1] to design the replacement tank for Chieftain, which was meant to be made easier by avoiding the known pitfalls of becoming immersed in the politics of a collaborative project, however desirable that seemed from the NATO standardisation perspective. The project title indicated when the tank was required to enter service: the 1980s. As we know, the MBT 80 project was cancelled in July 1980 after only just over three years, the cancellation being announced at the same time that the decision to buy a part-fleet of Challenger tanks was made public, making the development of another tank seemingly unnecessary. There was much more to the cancellation than this, however, and MBT 80 was kicked into the long grass mainly because of constant changes to the required in-service date, which the project definition study kept pushing further and further into the future; the realisation had dawned that the so-called tank of the 1980s was never going to appear in that decade at all. One of the main reasons was that the project revolved around building the first eight prototypes in a number of different configurations in order to discover, through testing, which systems worked best. The second batch of seven prototypes would only be built, to a common standard, once the results of this experimentation were known, and this prevented the development timescale from being shortened. An example of this was the intention to test the AGT1500 gas turbine engine alongside the diesel-fuelled CV12. This, combined with the timing of the Iranian repudiation, the existence of an advanced tank design mounting Chobham armour (Shir 2) and the political/economic need to keep ROF (L) – as well as a large number of mainly British sub-contractors – in operation with orders on the books, made the decision to only partially replace Chieftain more palatable. It was certainly not done on the understanding that the Challenger was going to be anything like as good a tank as MBT 80 promised: mathematical studies had predicted that MBT 80 would be twice as effective in a variety of battlefield scenarios as Challenger, whereas Challenger was only slightly more effective than Chieftain.

Cost was also a major factor: excluding the spiralling development costs (estimated as £127 million in 1978), over a period of ten years, MBT 80 was likely to be 37% more expensive to operate than Challenger, which would have the effect of limiting the number of tanks that Britain could afford to buy – the argument deployed was that you could have either 22 MBT 80s or 30 Challengers! However effective an individual tank was, the argument went, it could not be in two places at once, and when fighting a numerically superior opponent, numbers mattered.

The specification for MBT 80 is to be found in GSR 3572 (final draft, endorsed 1 December 1977) and MVEE Specification 762 (of December 1978). These documents define in some detail what MBT 80 was expected to be capable of, and which systems must be used, as at those dates; of course, some things would have been refined as the project matured. However, from these documents we can state that MBT 80 was expected to have these main features:

■ Mass not to exceed MLC 60 (62 tonnes)
■ Maximum use of aluminium to save weight
■ Bespoke high-velocity high-pressure 120mm rifled gun

■ Probability of a kill (PK) against T72 @ 2,000m to be at least 70%
■ 45 (min), 55 (desirable) rounds of main armament to be carried, with 4,000 rounds of MG
■ Co-ax MG to be Hughes Chain Gun
■ Thermal Imaging (TI) night-fighting equipment
■ Powerpack to be 1,500bhp CV12 with 'suitable' transmission[2]
■ Powerpack life of 4,000km
■ 65kph on road
■ Overall reliability in excess of 70%
■ Four-man crew.

Project timelines defined in 1978 were extremely optimistic for such a revolutionary tank, envisaging the first prototype being finished in April 1983, the ninth in October 1984 and the first production vehicle being completed in January 1986. MBT 80 had always been intended as the tank to replace the Chieftain fleet in its entirety, and so introducing a half-fleet of Challengers made the continuation of an expensive development project to be viewed as an avoidable luxury, and so it was easier for the government to simply cancel it, and put off the headache on how to replace the Chieftain/Challenger fleet for another day (and probably another government), while ignoring the arguments over effectiveness. Despite this, the project documentation makes it clear that there was going to be a considerable degree of overlap between areas of the development of MBT 80 and Shir 2, with a single official at MVEE being responsible for both tanks. The main areas of overlap, which were to feed into the eventual Chieftain/Challenger replacement known as Challenger 2, were as follows:

■ Nationally designed and produced at Leeds
■ Conventional design with turret and four-man crew
■ New 120mm rifled gun with separated ammunition, capable of defeating 640mm (minimum) to 690mm (preferred) of Rolled Homogeneous Armour (RHA)
■ Hands-on control philosophy for the commander and gunner
■ CV12 diesel engine
■ Hydrogas suspension
■ Detachable armour packs

- A driver training variant, plus other common hull derivatives
- Requirement for a suite of modern high-fidelity training simulators
- Derivative versions able to be built around the hull design, particularly for REME and RE.

But the biggest and most important difference between MBT 80 and Challenger 1, and which most concerns us as it would be used on CR2, was how the fire control system was set up. On CR1, as with Chieftain, the Gun Control Equipment responded to inputs from the gunner or commander and moved the gun and turret accordingly; the sights were mechanically linked (slaved) to the gun and turret which was both inefficient and inaccurate. On MBT 80, however, it was the other way around – the gun was slaved to the sights. The main advantage of this was that all the gun operator (either gunner or commander) had to do was to keep his aiming mark on target, operate the laser rangefinder and then the computer would do the rest: offset the gun for the lased range taking into account the various outputs from the ballistic sensors. When the gun was pointing in the right direction so that the predicted point of impact was where the target would be (after the time of flight in the case of a moving target), a coincidence relay was activated to close the firing circuit and, provided that the safety switches had all been set to live, the gun would fire.

It is important to note that this system was specifically designed for the 1(BR) Corps battleground of the North German plain, where attrition rate was a vital consideration, thus the rapid handover of targets from commander to gunner was a key requirement. The overall design aim was to be able to be 'twice as good and twice as fast' and this led directly to the adoption of the hunter/killer philosophy used on CR2, and first thought of, although not using that terminology, on Conqueror and then Chieftain using contra-rotation gear on the commander's cupola. The Ordnance Board, the body responsible for approving guns and ammunition for use, found it very difficult to come to terms with a firing circuit that was controlled directly by software rather than by a crewman's physical control – a description used was that

the Board 'freaked out' at the concept![3] The hands-on controls were also configured for automatic target tracking in the future, once computing advances made this possible: the system architecture anticipated future stretch. Also included in the design was a proper information management system, anticipating the use of future battlefield information systems. Both gunner and commander would have had decent-size displays that could also be used for 'relaxed viewing' of the thermal scene with a genuine silent watch capability.

No actual MBT 80s were ever built; the first prototype was scheduled to be completed in September 1983. The closest to a real tank that the project ever produced was the two (of three planned) Automotive Test Rigs (ATR) made in 1979 and based upon the Shir 2 hull. These were built in order to develop the automotive components and systems. The real tank, if ever built, may have differed significantly from the ATRs, although it is likely that the final hull design would have been very similar, and thus the FV4030/3 (Shir 2) design on which the ATRs were based.[4] The turrets that were placed on the ATRs are not really indicative of the MBT 80 in its final form; for example, the FCR or Fire Control Rig turret was produced in December 1979 and based upon an available 'fire-at' FV4211[5] turret shell – itself a derivative of Chieftain – and was used to develop systems integration. The FCR featured a 'classic star' architecture with a Ferranti F100L-based fire control computer; it also had a conventional commander's cupola based on the No 15 with a stabilised sight/aiming mark, with the cupola ring being electrically driven in azimuth. The gunner used a Barr & Stroud laser rangefinder sight with a stabilised sight head. Several different thermal sights were considered for FCR, and the design was able to accommodate either a fully independent panoramic TI or one fixed to the turret in azimuth á la CR1.

Gun control was digital and was made by Marconi Radar Systems. Intriguingly, because of the complexity and novelty of what was being tried, skills and techniques not easily found within the AFV world were needed, and so assistance was gained from the Multi-Role Combat Aircraft (later renamed Tornado) programme. This represented a genuinely revolutionary advance in building tank systems. The STR or Systems Test Rig was due to consist of two turrets and one hull, to be completed between December 1980 and December 1981, but these were never fully built due to the programme being cancelled – they would, however, have been much closer to the final turret and hull configurations. The systems design for STR was completed just before the cancellation and featured an advanced architecture based upon distributed processing, the first time this had been considered for use on a military vehicle. STR also evolved from the experience gained on the FCR, and made use of newly available microprocessors to handle data processing and sub-system intercommunications. From this it became clear to the design team that a central computer unit was unnecessary, and indeed if one was used it could also become a single point of failure for the whole system. STR featured the MilSpec1553 databus that had been first envisaged for use on fast jet aircraft and which had only became available in 1978, indicating just how cutting-edge the engineering was. Although not built, Prototypes 1 to 8 were intended to allow the design to evolve and to be altered as experience was gained; the actual finalised design would not have been revealed until Prototypes 9–15 were built, intended for the summer of 1985. It is almost certain that the main difference in appearance between Shir 2 and MBT 80, where the hulls would have been

a similar design, would have been in the turret configuration, which might have been radically different in the latter tank – and which is another area of similarity with Challenger 2.

As with almost every other tank ever built, the original intention – stated in GSR 3572 – was to build a tank that was as light as possible; in the case of MBT 80, the target figure was MLC 60 (62 tonnes) in training configuration. This was to be achieved by putting 480mm of armour on the turret front and 430mm on the hull front, to which eight removable appliqué Chobham panels weighing an additional 5½ tonnes in total could be added for warfighting. However, the RAC, as the users, rejected this approach as unrealistic due to the time needed to mount the packs in a crisis . . . an interesting decision that would be overturned a decade later in order to up-armour Challenger.[6] In December 1978 three options were on the table for the name by which MBT 80 was to be known: Gladiator, Lion and Cavalier. This was as close as the tank came to entering service, as events in Iran were already under way that would lead to the project being cancelled. In summary, MBT 80 provided a great deal of useful conceptual work that eventually fed into Challenger 2 via a somewhat roundabout route, but it was generally viewed, even while the project was active, as unlikely ever to produce a service tank. One progress report referred to 'that hardy annual, MBT 80', and workers on the project joked that MBT stood for 'meetings before tanks'.

The Vickers Mk 7

The other tank that was critical – in many ways more so – to the later development of Challenger 2 was the private-venture Vickers Mk 7. This was built by VDS (Vickers Defence Systems) for export markets as a cheaper alternative to the top-end MBTs on offer, but nevertheless contained many innovative and high-tech features. Vickers had a long history of building relatively cheap but more-than-cheerful tanks for exporting, with the first such examples being made in the early 1920s, and which allowed many nations to begin or develop their tank design skills, including Japan, the USSR and Germany. In the late 1950s

BELOW **The turret and mantlet of the MBT 80 that survives in the Bovington Tank Museum. The front of the turret is cast steel and was designed to be upgraded with the application of Chobham armour panels which would give it an angular appearance. The design also did away with Chieftain's mantlet-less design, and used instead a conventional mantlet.**

Vickers reinvigorated their export aspirations, and eventually developed the Vickers Mk 1 (aka Vickers 37 Ton), in many ways a simplified and lighter Centurion, which was exported to India under the name Vijayanta, as well as to Kuwait. This success led Vickers to develop a family of private-venture MBTs, including the Mk 3, sold to Kenya and Nigeria in the late 1970s, and the Mk 4 or Valiant, which incorporated Chobham armour in a 43-tonne tank with an aluminium hull. VDS were certainly not afraid of incorporating new technologies in these vehicles, and one of their features was a menu of optional extras, allowing a potential customer to choose just how simple or sophisticated they wanted their version to be. The successor to the Valiant was the Mk 7, the development of which started in 1984, and so benefited from being able to include technology that had been too immature to use in the Challenger 1, bearing in mind that it had been rushed into service and was largely based upon the FV 4030/3 design intended for Iran. The 54.6-tonne tank boasted an impressive 27.45bhp per tonne, and had a quoted top speed of 72kph. Only one model of the tank was made, bearing the military sales registration 68MS46. Although the tank was never exported, Egypt looked carefully at the design in late 1985 and Abu Dhabi expressed a lot of interest in mid-1989.

The turret design from the Valiant was revised for the Mk 7 and thus modified was called the 'Vickers Universal Turret', which could mount either the L7 105mm or the L11 120mm guns. The second version, the Mk 7/2, was introduced in 1987 and incorporated a host of novel features, including many that were far in advance of those mounted on the in-service Challenger 1 tank. These were mainly to be found within the turret systems, as the hull was built around a Krauss-Maffei chassis based on Leopard 2. The turret systems included Marconi solid-state fire control equipment known as Centaur 1. This incorporated a fully stabilised SFIM commander's panoramic sight with an integral laser rangefinder, allowing the commander to acquire and establish the range to a target, before handing it over to the gunner to engage, thus freeing the commander to acquire the next target, and so on, as well as speeding up the overall engagement time. This technique came to be known as 'hunter/killer' and was successfully incorporated into the Challenger 2 design. In September 1987 a so-called 'mini CAT' competition, based on the out-of-favour (with the British at least) NATO competition, was staged at Lulworth between a Challenger 1 and the Mk 7/2. The latter won hands down, hitting all its targets in an average engagement time of about half that

ABOVE The second tank that contributed greatly to the development of Challenger 2 was the private-venture Vickers Mk 7/2 tank, designed to attract export customers. This possessed many features, particularly in terms of sights and the fire control system, that would later see service on CR2.
(Courtesy Steve Woods)

of the in-service tank. This must have gone a long way to convince the decision-makers that Vickers might just be able to come up with the system design that they wanted. The turret also featured a panoramic day/night sight for the gunner on the left roof, a feature that was not carried forward on to CR2.

Additionally, a lot of work went into cleaning up the turret – compared to the horrendous 'plumbing' and cable nightmare of Chieftain and Challenger 1 – and modernising the ergonomics to make the crew more comfortable and efficient. The secondary armament was a 7.62mm chain gun, a departure from the conventional gas-operated machine guns used in other British AFVs, and again a design that found its way on to CR2. The tank was also designed with the intention of reducing the signature, both visual and in parts of the electromagnetic spectrum including surveillance radars, in order to make it more difficult to acquire.[7] Again, this approach found favour when CR2 was developed, leading to a very clean external turret, with the maximum of flat surfaces and the majority of tools and stowage under armour.

Replacing Chieftain – the options

By 1987 it was clear that any hopes of introducing a new MBT built around truly revolutionary new technologies – new gun, armour, fire control, engine, transmission, etc. – was simply unrealistic in the timescales required, and that the in-service date for such a tank was not getting closer; in fact the opposite was true. It was assessed that the earliest such a tank could be fielded was in 2015, over 28 years away. Therefore a replacement tank for Chieftain using only those technologies which were mature enough to exploit in the immediate future could be contemplated. In May 1987, a report entitled 'Options for the Replacement of Chieftain' looked back on a critical decision made at the start of the decade:

By mid-1980 the MBT 80 project was seen to involve unacceptable costs and a slipping in-service date. It was therefore cancelled and the decision was taken to procure up to half a fleet of Challenger 1, with the expectation that the remaining Chieftains would be replaced in the late 1990s by an improved Challenger, or a new collaborative tank.

As a result of this an outline Staff Target Land (known as ST (L) 4004 Future Tank) was written. The key characteristics called for in this document were:

- Much improved firepower over that currently fitted to, or projected for, Challenger 1. The weapon system had to be able to defeat not only the frontal armour of any Soviet tank in service or scheduled to be introduced by 2000, but also have the stretch potential to defeat the next generation out to 2015, at ranges of up to 2,000m in all weather conditions. Additionally, helicopters were identified as the most important secondary target and the weapon was to be capable of countering them out to 3,000m.
- Improved survivability against both Direct Fire weapons (kinetic and chemical energy) and top-attack munitions.
- Mobility was to be as good as that achieved by the German Leopard 2, at a maximum weight not to exceed that of CR1.
- Operational availability had to be at least as good as that achieved by CR1.
- Interoperability with the main (but not specified) NATO allies was desirable; as a minimum this was to include the same main armament, ammunition and fuel.

These characteristics were placed into an order, not intended to be an absolute priority but rather indicative of the initial degree of emphasis, which could be 'traded' against each other as the design matured:

- Firepower
- Survivability
- Mobility
- Reliability and maintainability
- Interoperability
- Fightability
- Simplicity
- Command and control.

The ST (L) was forwarded to industry, asking

a number of interested private companies to submit their ideas for a concept for a future tank that met the requirements, and at the same time in parallel the government-operated armaments experts Royal Armament Research Development Establishment (RARDE) developed the so-called Product Improved Challenger (PIP Challenger). Only one of the industry proposals plus the PIP tank was found to be acceptable: both were to be three-man tanks fitted with an autoloader for a 120mm gun. Buying an existing (the leading contender at this stage was Leopard 2) tank off-the-shelf was also considered, including the possibility of building the tank under licence in the UK – more of which later. The PIP Challenger featured the Challenger 1 hull mounting a new three-man turret, plus a new gearbox, a completely new electronic architecture called SAVE (Systematic Approach to Vehicle Electronics), BICS (Battlefield Information Control System), plus increased protection from top-attack weapons. SAVE was seen as particularly important, as Challenger 1 had no fewer than 290 different electronic harnesses, with the interconnecting cables alone weighing in at around half a tonne!

Unfortunately for the proposals, despite the advantages that an autoloader system appeared to offer, previous work had provided evidence that weighed against the use of one. During spring 1985, and again a year later, 2RTR had provided

a squadron of Challengers for Exercise Endura. This series of exercises was an experiment into the long-term efficiency and effectiveness of three-man tank crews (using Challenger 1 without loader/operators) deprived of sleep and subjected to a barrage of physical and mental tests. It found, not surprisingly, that the effectiveness of the crews deteriorated rapidly as fatigue set in, and it was concluded that the four-man crew model still represented the best overall way for tanks to operate over extended periods of time. That tended to add weight to arguments not to develop an autoloader-based turret, which was also seen as a huge technological challenge. (Other nations tried different methods of solving the same problem: France experimented with allocating more than one crew to each tank, allowing a fresh crew to be rotated through the tank for specific missions in a manner similar to military aircraft, and Russia, operating three-man tanks with autoloaders, had the sheer numbers to be able to 'echelon' complete units through exhausted ones.) Other components of the exercise also investigated other technological changes that might offer advantages on a modern

BELOW Challenger 2 eventually replaced two British MBTs – the Chieftain Mk 11 (left) and the Challenger (right), which was later renamed Challenger 1 when no one could come up with a more original name than Challenger 2! *(Tank Museum)*

tank, including: compact powerpack, gas turbine engine, panoramic TI sight for the commander, signature reduction and an automated target detection and tracking system – ATDT.

While this was going on normal military life continued. In 1990 the British Army tank fleet comprised seven regiments of Challenger 1 (CR1) and six of Chieftain (CH). Including the war maintenance reserve (WMR), the repair pool and training tanks, this totalled 1,072 MBTs: 426 CR1 and 646 CH. The shortcomings of Chieftain were listed in a document used to explain why a new tank was urgently needed; as many of these applied to Challenger as well, such arguments were used to deflect the possibility of simply buying more Challengers:

- **Ammunition**. With the CHARM project (see page 86) the ammunition could be improved up to the same standard as other competitor tanks, but the speed of target acquisition and engagement was too slow at an average of c15 seconds, and needed to be reduced to around 8 seconds.[8]
- **Mobility**. This was lacking in terms of raw power and speed, affecting both tactical and operational mobility. With the latter, this meant that armoured reserves had to be committed early in combat, and were difficult to redeploy if the situation changed. Better mobility allowed deployment to be delayed, giving tactical operational advantages.
- **Survivability**. The Stillbrew appliqué had improved the turret protection on Chieftain to nearly the same level as the Chobham on CR1 when faced with a KE attack, but not against chemical energy (HEAT) or from top attack.
- **Availability**. Chieftain had only a 55% chance of completing the specified Battlefield Day (BFD) without breaking down. A BFD was defined as driving 60km per day, 27km on roads and 33km cross-country, plus 8 hours of static running of all systems, and firing 34 120mm rounds and 1,000 rounds from the co-ax. Changing the powerpack took about 8 hours, compared to about 1½ hours on Challenger 1 and less than 1 hour on Leopard 2.
- **Fightability**. The turret design made it difficult to operate efficiently, which affected the crew and degraded overall capability.

Replacing Chieftain – the Soviet threat

During the Second World War Britain had learned a lesson that by the 1980s was ingrained into the DNA of its tank experts: that however good a tank might appear on paper or on an exercise, its effectiveness could only be truly assessed when compared to the capabilities of its enemy. For much of the Cold War period, it is fair to say that the crewmen operating Britain's tanks had no real idea of how well their own (generally much-loved) tank would perform in the real test of battle, with the Soviets being the obvious enemy. Tank crewmen, whether they were on Centurion, Chieftain or Challenger, had great confidence that they were operating a tank which had well-thought-out survivability features – thick armour, fire extinguisher systems, protected ammunition, smoke dischargers, etc. – which were superior to those of the enemy. They were also convinced that their regularly practised tactical skills were of a high standard, and frequent gunnery training including field firing exercises using live ammunition allowed them to be confident that they could hit their intended target.

But what none of them really knew (myself included), was whether their weapon system was capable of defeating the enemy tank's armour protection. We all assumed it would, thinking that Soviet tanks were relatively thin-skinned, while also believing that our thicker armour would provide something approaching invulnerability to the Soviet weapons. However, in the upper echelons of the military machine, such assumptions were not shared. The reason for this was that soldiers' assumptions – known to the army colloquially as SWAGs, or scientific wild-arsed guesses – were not good enough, and a lot of effort was expended in assessing the Soviet capabilities and comparing the results with our own. For example, within the Group of Soviet Forces Germany (GSFG), the formation which the British Army of the Rhine (BAOR) would fight, it was thought that around half (2,000) of the GSFG tanks would be in action against the two British armoured divisions, and that the Soviet doctrine of massed attack on the perceived weakest point would mean that a Soviet numerical advantage of 5:1, and sometimes as many as 10:1 could be expected.

But what really worried the senior leadership was not so much the simple numerical superiority but rather the increasingly capable tanks that the Soviets were fielding, on average putting out a new, much-improved tank every seven years. From the days of the relatively unsophisticated T55, a whole range of new technologies were developed and quickly put into service – night-fighting equipment, NBC protective systems, larger guns, better ammunition, increased armour, autoloaders, laser rangefinders and the ability to launch missiles through the barrels. Sometimes these features would be fitted as upgrades to existing tanks, in other cases they appeared when a brand new tank was produced. This applied to the introduction of the T62, T64, T72, T80 and T90. In those cases when successor tanks were known to be in development but not yet in service, they were referred to as FST, or Future Soviet Tank. FST1 would be the tank that would be fielded next, FST2 the one after that, and so on. It was initially assessed that FST1 (later to be designated T72) would not be deployed to GSFG, so the main concerns were FST2 and FST3.

A very important part of the conundrum was the increasing amounts of armour and other protective systems being added to the hitherto lightly armoured Soviet tanks. The introduction of Explosive Reactive Armour (ERA) packs used as appliqués was a particularly worrying development, as it called into question the ability of the Chieftain and Challenger's 120mm L11 gun to defeat Soviet tanks at battle ranges, which up to that stage was always taken as guaranteed. An expert report on Soviet protection had this to say on the subject:

The Soviet tank is now, and will increasingly in the future be, a tough target to defeat. Assessment is that half of all attacks on a tank occur in the frontal 60° arc, with the others in the remaining 300°; this frontal arc is where the Soviet tanks have their thickest armour. It is therefore essential that our own Kinetic Energy projectile attack is capable of defeating at battle ranges the frontal arc of the enemy. In order to defeat Soviet tanks the following performance is required:

T64B ERA	*530mm*
T80 ERA	*600mm*
FST2	*700mm*
FST3	*750mm+*

Such reports set out the requirements for our own tank guns and ammunition – using gun/ammunition systems that could not destroy the enemy at battle ranges (in effect meaning at 2,000m) would condemn the British crews to fighting in less capable tanks in a manner akin to the worst experiences of the Second World War, and this could not be allowed to happen.

Another critical aspect was that of Soviet firepower. The new 125mm smoothbore gun on the T64 introduced in 1976, with autoloaded BM23 APFSDS ammunition, was assessed by the experts to be capable of penetrating 430mm of RHA angled at 0° at a battle range of 2,000m. The development of the next-generation BM85 ammunition in the same gun would probably increase this to 480mm, and it was further assessed that subsequent ammunition developments had the potential to take this to a maximum of 540mm, which equated to defeating about 600mm point-blank. Knowing what the enemy could do to your protection is of course critical when deciding how much armour to put on to your own designs, and where. Once the armour-defeating and protection characteristics of a Soviet tank was known (or calculated, or estimated), it was possible to compare its performance against one's own vehicle in a variety of tactical settings. Shortly after T64 was introduced in January 1978, the following comparison was constructed to show how each tank fared against the other in static shoots: head on, Chieftain would defeat T64 at 2,500m using APDS, whereas T64 defeated Chieftain at 2,700m. At an oblique angle of 30°, Chieftain only defeated T64 at 380m, but T64 was able to defeat Chieftain at 930m.[9] Such understanding, reinforced by the mixed experiences of Chieftain in the Iran–Iraq war, led to the introduction of the Stillbrew appliqué armour package.

Such comparisons were important in assessing vulnerabilities, not only those of armour thickness and position, but also those based on typical tactical situations. It was hoped that the British, fighting a defensive battle from well-chosen, prepared and camouflaged hull-down positions, could negate a lot of the numerical advantages held by the Soviets by destroying them in numbers at range while they were still moving, making it more difficult for them to observe and engage our own static tanks. This of course required a high rate of fire and a high single-shot kill probability (SSKP), allowing the defenders to whittle down the strength of the enemy before they had the chance to use their excellent mobility to close the gap. Unfortunately, such theories tended to come crashing down under the weight of Soviet artillery doctrine, which would be directed in huge concentrations at the point that the tanks were attacking. And in any case, ignoring such tactical considerations, it was clear that the potential enemy now possessed a tank with superior protection and firepower to Chieftain, not to mention mobility and agility, which called these assumptions into serious doubt. A new tank was urgently needed, not just to address the current problem, but which would be capable of being 'grown' or 'stretched' to keep up with future threats.

Birth of a tank

In October 1986 VDS acquired the Royal Ordnance Factory (Leeds) for the surprisingly small sum of £15 million. The acquisition enabled the company to bring together their talented Newcastle-based commercial tank design team, responsible for their innovative commercial Mk 7 design, with the experienced tank producers at Leeds who had built both Chieftain and Challenger 1. The company then spent another £14 million building a brand-new factory on the Manston Lane site in Leeds – a replica of the existing tank production facility at Newcastle – which was open by the end of 1987. All that was needed now was a full order book. However, when they took over Leeds they only had orders for one regiment's worth of Challenger 1s on the books, and so were taking a great deal of risk. A contract for about 20[10] Challenger training tanks placed in early 1988 was due to be complete by September 1990, but beyond that there was nothing . . . this affected not only the 1,600 personnel directly

employed at Leeds, but at least also another 6,000 or so around the country working for sub-contractors.

Although there is a widely held belief that the first proposal by VDS for a new British Army tank eventually called Challenger 2 was unsolicited and was all their idea, certain facts indicate that the springboard for the project did in fact stem from the MoD. In December 1986, the Master General of the Ordnance (MGO), responsible for army equipment, visited the offices of VDS in order to deliver a briefing on the options under consideration for a replacement tank for Chieftain. General Sir Dick Vincent must have had candid discussions with the senior VDS leadership, as only a few weeks later the company was able to put forward a mature proposal which was to form the basis of the eventual replacement – Challenger 2. VDS had consulted with RARDE following the MGO visit and on 30 March 1987 formally presented the Minister of Defence Procurement and the Chief of the General Staff with a solution that the company hoped would be attractive, having only started work on the design at the very end of the previous year. It was this date that VDS referred to as the birthday of the tank; although its design had started earlier, VDS documents invariably referred to this date as Day 1 of the Challenger 2 project. It might be more appropriate to think of it as the day of conception, as its entry into operational service, a better use of the birthday analogy, was to be over ten years later, representing a much longer gestation period than originally envisaged. At this stage there appear to have been two different versions on offer: what VDS referred to as 'Challenger 2', which was 70% the same as CR1 but with CHIP and CAIP[11] incorporated, and an upgraded version with much improved turret systems that Vickers confusingly referred to as 'Challenger 2/2'.[12] Despite the 2/2 being priced at £64k more per unit, it was a much more capable package and it was this tank that would eventually be selected as the Chieftain replacement and be named, wait for it . . . Challenger 2.[13]

A key selling point for the proposal was as much to do with the affordability as the technology, although it was always clear that the proposed tank would be significantly more

capable than the in-service Challenger; a fixed-price contract was on offer which it was known that the MoD were keen on sticking to and which limited VDS to some extent. The hull was an evolutionary development of the in-service Challenger using some systems including the transmission taken from the CRARRV,[14] and the turret took as its start point the most innovative features of the Vickers Mk 7/2 coupled to a new rifled gun being developed by RARDE and ROF Nottingham. VDS described the new tank thus:

Challenger 2 will be a vehicle which is a considerable advance on other vehicles in service, including the German Leopard 2 and the US Abrams. It employs 'new recipe' Chobham armour [and a] new suite of sights to provide reduced target acquisition and engagement times. The inclusion of the new CHARM[15] 120mm gun will ensure that the vehicle's firing power has growth capability. A great deal of effort is also being expended in providing the best ergonomic solution.

It was now critical to know how many tanks might be required; was the tank really only intended to replace Chieftain as the original discussions had indicated, or might it be used to replace the entire Chieftain and Challenger fleet? This was key, as costs would rise if fewer tanks were built, and economies of scale were a sensible way of forcing the overall price down, which of course was attractive to the Treasury. At this time serious consideration was being given to upgrading the existing Challenger tank with the same, new gun that would be fitted to the Chieftain replacement, whether this was the proven 120mm German smoothbore or the new in-development British rifled gun. The existing operational tank fleet[16] looked like this:

Chieftain

1 × Type 43 regiment   = 43 tanks
5 × Type 57 regiments = 285 tanks
Total   328

Challenger

3 × Type 43 regiments = 129 tanks
4 × Type 57 regiments = 228 tanks
Total   357

It was predicted that eventually all but one of the Challenger regiments would be authorised to adopt the Type 57 organisation, meaning that 399 (of the 420 produced) would be in operational use. Using these figures the

ABOVE A Challenger 2 of 1RTR fires its new 120mm L30 rifled gun at a long-range target. The enormous flash caused by the burning propellant is testament to the immense power of the weapon. *(Courtesy RTR)*

requirement might be for as many as 727 tanks (12 Type 57 regiments and only one Type 43), plus about 10% extra for the different non-operational roles, so around 800 in total. This was not to be, however. The fall of the Berlin Wall in November 1989 led to the so-called 'peace dividend' and the British Army was told to reduce the number of tank regiments it fielded. Under the Options for Change programme of 1990, manpower was cut by nearly 20% and many regiments were amalgamated, so that by 1993 there were only 11 operational regiments in the Household Cavalry and RAC, compared to the 19 of only three years earlier. Only six (and a bit) of these regiments were to be equipped with MBTs, and so the requirement for the new tank was much reduced; in the period from 1992 to 1999 the RAC reduced its number of operational MBT squadrons by exactly half, from 54 to 27.[17] Eventually only 386 Challenger 2s were built, replacing both Chieftain and Challenger – which had to be renamed Challenger 1 (CR1) once Challenger 2 entered the lexicon – with a brand new but much smaller fleet.

Until this became clear, however, the working total that most people were using when estimating costs in the late 1980s was for 590 (sometimes rounded up to 600) MBTs. The first VDS estimate of the total programme cost for 590 tanks plus 45 driver training variants, including design and development, long-term support, ammunition, etc. (though not a training package) was £1.178 billion. Cost inflation in the military sphere is notorious for spiralling upwards, and only 13 months later VDS had revised this estimate to £1.754 billion, an increase of nearly 49%. It must be realised that despite these extraordinarily high estimates, in 1987 the tank was still only being seen by some in the military as a stop-gap, providing a short-term capability until a future, high-technology and high-performance tank could be introduced. This had an important effect on the way that the tank came into service, as it meant that the most critical resource after money was time, and that anything that delayed an early in-service date could not be contemplated. This suited VDS, as they needed a quick decision from the MoD in order to keep their facilities in operation: they warned the decision-makers that 'any delay in the award of contract for

manufacture beyond 1 January 1989 will result in a gap in production and consequential costs to the MoD of £1.5 million per month in order to retain the skilled workforce and facilities at Leeds'. Internally, on 16 January 1989, VDS instructed its design and development (D&D) team that they were not to make any radical modifications to the design that would delay production, and that the emphasis was to be on making the existing design work. Despite this, the design was to include elements that would allow the tank to be improved easily in the future: these included fitting panoramic TI for the commander, an anti-helicopter capability, automatic target detection and tracking, increased armour and a defensive aids suite.

Back to the proposal: in April 1987 VDS formalised what they thought Challenger 2 would look like in their Specification VCS 1000. In October the MoD, having examined the VDS proposals, replied that aspects of the proposal were not acceptable and that VDS needed to conduct further work to remedy certain shortcomings. It seems that, as the result of this, the original Challenger 2 option was dropped and the revised Challenger 2/2 was taken forward (and referred to hereafter as Challenger 2!). About 10% of the tank had to be revised in light of the MoD criticism. In December 1987, after considering the details of the revised VDS bid, the MoD Equipment Procurement Committee (EPC) sought approval to procure a replacement for Chieftain to enter service in 1993, based upon SR (L) 4026 circulated in November. In the same month EPC also confirmed that it saw the VDS CR2 solution as the most attractive – or the most likely to become reality, which was not necessarily the same thing. But Challenger 2 was not the only option to be considered; far from it, in fact nine different options were examined by the MoD:

■ An improved Chieftain. This was quickly discarded as it was clear it could not meet the requirements without costing around £1.8 million per tank, the same as a brand-new vehicle, and it was no exaggeration to say that the name Chieftain stank in most military quarters.[18]
■ A full fleet of CR1 to the current build standard.

- CR1 improved with CHIP (Challenger Improvement Programme) and CHARM (Challenger Armament Programme).[19] This was referred to as option CR1-100.
- CR1 with a smoothbore gun in a new turret.
- CR2 with CHARM. This was assessed to be the cheapest overall option that met the requirement. This was sometimes referred to within the MoD as option CR1-400.
- CR2 with a smoothbore gun.
- Leopard 2. The price was estimated at (an unaffordable) £2.687 billion for the programme, and it did not meet all the requirements.
- M1A1 Block 2. This was a similar cost to Leopard, at £2.626 billion, and again did not meet the full requirement.
- The Challenger hull with either a Leopard 2 or M1A1 turret. This was technically difficult and simply placed the disliked turret features from both tanks on to a different hull.

Only two 120mm gun options were genuine contenders: the Rheinmetall smoothbore, or the new British L30 rifled gun, then under development. It was no surprise that Challenger 2 was always the favoured option, not because of any national pride or the political/economic desirability of keeping the Leeds factory in operation, but because the requirement document, SR (L) 4026 had to some extent been written with Challenger 2 in mind, and it also came out as the cheapest overall. The exercise of considering the options had the effect of firmly focusing many minds – military

ABOVE Some, but not all, of the tanks considered as competitors for the replacement of Chieftain (shown at extreme left): Challenger 1 armed with a new gun, the US M1, the Vickers Mk 7/2 and the German Leopard 2. *(TM 2134B2)*

BELOW A VDS image showing the main internal components of their proposed new 'Challenger 2 Mk 2'. The majority of the 120mm projectiles are stowed behind the loader in the turret, but all the potentially dangerous propellant charges are below the turret ring for enhanced safety. The actual design differed very little from this illustration.

and commercial – back on to the need for replacing Chieftain, which by now had been in service for over two decades. VDS then revised their CR2 proposal on 1 February 1988 to address some of the initial MoD concerns, suggesting that they could have the tank ready for acceptance in October 1991, with the first production tank being completed one year later and meeting a 1993 in-service date with two regiments operational. This was, as events were to prove, wildly optimistic and went against the grain of experience. It would only be realistic if the tank and all its systems and components demonstrated in trials that it met the performance claimed by VDS, and did not require any major changes – an unlikely scenario. In June 1988 VDS were able to estimate that the first 200 service tanks would each cost £1.745 million, £844k for the hull and £901k for the turret. By way of comparison, the MoD had paid around £975k per tank for the Challenger 1s built to equip regiments 5 and 6 only three years earlier.

By July 1988 in an internal memorandum VDS stated its belief that the MoD only had four viable options to replace Chieftain:

- A brand new 'Challenger 2' turret mounted on an upgraded CR1 hull, armed with the L30 rifled gun and which could be in service by 1995. This of course was the option favoured by VDS and which was to come to fruition as Challenger 2.
- The same as above, but mounting a 120mm smoothbore gun, which could also be in service by 1995. (This was an interesting statement, as VDS had already told the MoD that the SB gun would add up to two years to the in-service date!)
- The CR2 turret with smoothbore gun but mounted on a Leopard 2 hull, once again entering service in 1995. This option was thought to be attractive as it might persuade the Germans to use it instead of their proposed Leopard 3 programme.
- The M1A1 as it stood, which could enter service 'now'.

However, in the same year RARDE Chertsey (the technical and design authority for UK special armour) was tasked by the MoD to investigate putting Chobham armour on to the Leopard 2 turret, as the existing protection level was only assessed as being half that of Challenger 1. Their conclusion was that it simply could not be done, and that a complete new turret shell was required. Also in 1988 VDS were also asked to consider putting in a smoothbore gun (meaning a version of the German Rheinmetall 120mm) and answered that it was technically feasible, but the major redesigns needed would delay the project by 18–24 months and increase costs by around £56 million. Neither of these penalties were acceptable, and so the smoothbore question was shelved . . . for the time being at least. What we can deduce from the many options being looked at during 1988 was that all possibilities were open for investigation, and it was only by working out which ones were non-starters could the list be reduced to serious contenders only. Challenger 2, despite unease in some quarters, was always the front-runner.

In order to reduce the risks associated with such an ambitious undertaking, on 21 December 1988 the MoD officially awarded VDS a limited contract that required a 'Demonstration to Major Review' phase (sometimes referred to as proof of principle) to be successfully completed.[20] Many commentators at the time referred to this as VDS winning 'The Great Tank War!' Despite this, some were still hedging their bets; the previous day Peter Levene, the head of defence procurement, had written to the boss of Krauss-Maffei informing him of the decision, but also taking pains to inform K-M that the contract did not represent a final decision, and suggesting that if Leopard 2's survivability could be improved then the tank would be of interest to the UK should Challenger 2 not deliver. Some £90 million was allocated for the proof of principle phase, and VDS were required to achieve what later became known as 'The Ten Commandments':

1 Demonstrate overall performance using the nine prototype tanks.
2 Achieve successful proof firing of the main armament.

3 Demonstrate weapon system performance.

4 Demonstrate weapon system accuracy.

5 Demonstrate that improved ammunition could be successfully developed.

6 Demonstrate fightability.

7 Demonstrate armour performance.

8 Produce an acceptable risk assessment.

9 Produce an acceptable reliability analysis.

10 Specify the equipment and stores that the MoD might be required to supply should a full contract be awarded.[21]

The reliability of the tank was based around two main components: mission reliability using the specified BFD as the criteria, and logistic reliability. However, in February 1991 following the invasion of Kuwait by Iraq the previous August, all work on CR2 was halted in order to concentrate effort on supporting Operation Granby (the name given to British military operations during the 1991 Gulf War), and the decision on the selection of the new tank was postponed pending the outcome of the war and a review of the relative performances of CR1 and M1. However, in the interim, VDS, which had a lot at stake, continued to work on CR2 'in their own time and at their own cost', in order to address known areas of risk that were causing concern. This was in some ways fortunate for VDS as the reliability predictions were not being achieved and more work was certainly required. In June 1991 VDS were awarded a second contract, this time for the development and trials phase; 37% of these contract payments were related directly to the achievement of reliability, and were only

Foreign options

ABOVE This is the first official image released of Challenger 2 – note the early type of Commander's Primary Sight and the hull which is very similar to the Challenger 1 type, complete with full-depth bazooka plates. The tank does not yet bear a registration but is almost certainly V1. *(TM 3488D5)*

As well as directly collaborating with friendly NATO nations on future tank projects, periodically the British Army considered the viability and desirability of buying an off-the-shelf foreign tank, with the current US and German designs always the front-runners in such investigations. As well as looking at the merits of these tanks with a view to potentially buying them, such investigations also allowed the merits and weaknesses of current British tank design to be measured against modern competition. Although no foreign tank was ever bought as a result, there is no doubt that certain sectors of the British military and technical communities took these extremely seriously, and produced detailed 'warts and all' reports that were honest and open. At least two such reports were commissioned during the search for Chieftain's replacement in the late 1970s and early 1980s, which looked at not only the off-the-shelf options, but also the possibilities of modifying the tanks to a greater or lesser degree to better suit British doctrine. These included investigating putting the 1,500bhp MTU diesel powerpack from Leopard 2 into the Challenger hull, and replacing the high-torque but very thirsty gas turbine in M1A1 with a diesel engine. Such

paid as and when certain criteria were met. In November 1991 VDS were still predicting that they expected to meet all reliability targets within a year, allowing acceptance to take place in February 1993 on the completion of all trials.

RIGHT Defence Secretary Tom King looking over an early CR2 (V4) in about 1991, again featuring the early hull design and layout with single-pin 'dead' track. *(Courtesy Andy Brend)*

options were invariably found to be hugely complicated, and involved so much redesign that the conclusion was always that there was too much risk and cost involved. In 1988, after Challenger 1 had been in service for a few years allowing its vices and virtues to be better understood, another such investigation looked again at the two main foreign contenders by comparing them with what the VDS proposal being referred to as Challenger 2 should be capable of, and summarised them as follows:

Krauss-Maffei Leopard 2

'In terms of mobility, firepower, fightability and reliability it is the exemplar. [However] the turret is no better at protecting the crew than the emergency Chieftain Stillbrew armour, and redesigning the turret to include Chobham armour is likely to delay introduction by as much as three or four years.' The British also did not like the hydraulic gun control equipment as it was thought to increase crew casualties if the armour was penetrated, and for survivability reasons the stowage of ammunition in the rear turret bustle was disliked, as was the unsophisticated NBC protection system. In terms of armour protection, different turret designs proposed gave different levels: the Type B design was known to provide only about 350mm of RHA equivalent protection against KE attack, and 700mm against HEAT; Type C increased the former to around 420mm, but the

Germans refused to declare exactly how much the proposed Type D armour would increase this to, which was unhelpful.

General Dynamics M1A1 Block 2

The tank was described as falling short of the requirement 'in only a few respects'. The commander's station was assessed as poor, and the high fuel consumption was viewed with horror by the logistics experts. It was realised that any option of replacing the gas turbine engine with a diesel powerpack would be too expensive and time-consuming, and was not guaranteed to be successful. It was thought that the new depleted uranium (DU) armour would give it about 15% better protection against KE attack than Challenger 2's Dorchester base armour, but its performance against HEAT warheads (seen as the biggest threat) was not up to scratch, therefore Dorchester provided much better protection.[22] Similar to Leopard 2, the hydraulic turret drives, NBC system and turret ammunition stowage were viewed as markedly inferior to the British counterparts. It also lacked an auxiliary power unit, a much-treasured feature of British MBTs. In general terms, though, the M1A1 Block 2 design (later known as M1A2) was assessed as being superior to the Leopard 2, and met most of the desired requirements, the biggest stumbling block being the thirsty gas turbine engine which used about twice as much fuel

ABOVE Favoured by many within the British Army because of its reliability and ease of maintenance, the German Leopard 2 was ultimately discarded because its survivability levels were assessed as being too low. *(TM 2139B1)*

Lt Gen Sir Robert Hayman-Joyce

My links to CR2 began in 1987 when as the Brigadier Deputy Commandant RMCS, a request for comment on a draft staff target for the replacement of Chieftain arrived from Operational Requirements. The outline specification of the British MBT that OR had in mind clearly had received input from Vickers Defence Systems (VDS). We had some issues with the specification, mainly with respect to the gun-sight relationship, that we advised should be looked at again. Later that year Major General John Stibbon appeared in my office asking why I was resisting a posting to London to work for MGO, a post he was about to assume. The thought of leaving the rural life of Wiltshire to return to London did not appeal but what soldier can resist a direct order? I took over the role of Director Tanks in April 1998. The next nine months was to be a busy time. . . .Chieftain Replacement had by then become a key project, made more interesting by the intervention of the then Chief of Defence Procurement, Sir Peter Levene, who bluntly asked why we were not considering purchasing an MBT from another nation off the shelf. The German Leopard 2, the French Leclerc and the American M1A2 were first-class modern MBTs and might well meet (or even exceed) the specification set out in the Staff Requirement. Despite arguments that all had smoothbore guns which would entail a major upheaval in the logistic support for a foreign tank in British Army service, he directed that each of them should be examined in detail. And of course, unlike a British contender which at that time was no more than a piece of paper, they were already in production.

What had started as a process of developing a British-built tank based on CR1 now widened to a full technical review of the MBTs of three allied nations. The prime focus to begin with was on the US Abrams M1A2. The downsides of this tank were the thirsty gas turbine main engine and the lack of an auxiliary generator for silent watch. The turbine had roughly 50%

(and possibly higher) greater fuel consumption compared to a conventional diesel and if adopted would have major implications for our logistic fleet. Indeed, for this reason the Americans had studied the option of replacing the turbine with a more economical diesel but had decided not to proceed. On the plus side was the excellent turret protection afforded by their spaced armour. This was based upon a British invention (Chobham armour) that we had given to the USA for free, so there was much frustration in the British camp when we were told that under no circumstances were the Brits to be allowed to have access to the insides of the US version – the turret packs on a British Abrams were to remain sealed for US eyes only. Another handicap was that the performance of the Abrams main armament was a closely guarded secret, but unless we knew what it was capable of we could not possibly recommend the tank for British Army service. This provoked a high-level US visit and a highly classified briefing for a few key MoD players including representatives from RARDE. The outcome was clear: the Abrams' main armament performance would easily exceed our requirement – and also by some margin the latest RARDE figures for the new British rifled bore gun and ammunition. (Remarkably those RARDE estimates within a week or two had been upgraded and now matched the US performance!)

Meanwhile, we had also looked at the Leopard 2 and the French Leclerc. The latter was always going to be a difficult sell to the British because of its three-man crew. The four-man crew concept had stood the test of time and recent trials to test the resilience of a squadron of tanks with only three men in the crew had confirmed the British doctrine. To maintain the intensity of combat operations the French Army planned the use of Leclerc around the wholesale replacement of crews, a concept that the British would not entertain.

The Leopard 2 was more than just a derivative of Leopard 1. The Germans had built some 17 full prototypes with many different turret variations to arrive at the final specification for Leopard 2, a formidable new weapon system with the same smoothbore 120mm gun and ammunition as the US Abrams (although we discovered that they were not interoperable). Even so, our analysis identified some areas that we were concerned would not meet our Staff Requirement; we were later told by the Germans that the Leopard 2 was due an upgrade that would address some of these misgivings – we will return to that in a moment.

Our conclusion from all this work was that if we were to buy a foreign MBT it would have to be the M1A2 Abrams, even with the disadvantage of the high fuel consumption, restocking with smoothbore ammunition and the galling restrictions on access to the turret armour packs. This recommendation filtered up through the hierarchy to be discussed eventually at Cabinet. The Prime Minister, Maggie Thatcher, told us to go away and think again. The cost, the access to the armour packs and not least the fact that it was not British were the likely reasons for the rejection, but I had too little feedback from the meeting to be sure. I then had the painful task of telling the US government and General Dynamics of the UK decision not to buy their tank.

At this stage the British option of course was still on paper only; the Leclerc had been ruled out earlier because of the crew size so next we turned to Leopard 2, bearing in mind the proposed German plan to make improvements in the areas that had concerned us. However, this plan too was thrown out by Maggie Thatcher: her view was why can we not develop a tank of our own?

So we turned again to VDS. One of the great advantages of Peter Levene's excursion was that it had armed us with a lot of knowledge about the state of Western tank design and capabilities, and that was to stand us in good stead. With VDS we had tried to follow the German example of building a large number of prototypes but had to be satisfied with eight,

although after a brisk altercation with the Civil Service I managed to squeeze the funds for a ninth, which whilst better was still far short of the ideal. Tight money also meant we lost an important capability for the commander to fight the tank at night using the proposed panoramic TI sight. The new plan finally went through the Equipment Advisory Committee at the end of 1988. George Younger, who was the Secretary of State for Defence, announced in Parliament on 20 December that Vickers was to be given the opportunity over the next two years to demonstrate that it could meet the requirement. On 21 June 1989 Alan Clark, the Minister for Defence Procurement, announced that subject to satisfactory contract terms VDS would get the order to manufacture Challenger 2.

Issues that were discussed with VDS included a 1,500bhp engine and the installation of a smoothbore main armament. The engine idea foundered on cost and we agreed to retain the 1,200bhp Perkins diesel used in CR1. VDS later funded a private-venture Euro 1500 CR1 demonstrator that I tried when DRAC at Bovington, but the die was cast. No one could make a convincing case tactically for the extra 300bhp and so the funds were not released.

The rifled 120mm main gun was retained despite strong suggestions that we should go for the US version of the smoothbore 120mm; a major redesign of the turret and ammunition stowage would be needed were we to do this. VDS also resisted the suggestion on the basis of the impact on potential sales in the Middle East and the advantage to the UK of selling rifled bore 120mm ammunition there – as it turned out no sales were achieved. The MoD did not support the argument for smoothbore interoperability with our allies due to the costs of redesigning the tank, of buying (or making under licence) ammunition from abroad, the turmoil it would cause in the logistic supply chain, and the 'sunk costs' already used in developing the UK 120mm and its ammunition – which anyway matched the US gun and ammunition performance.

as the CV12. Had Challenger 2 been rejected, this was the tank that most likely would have replaced Chieftain, and which was always viewed as the fall-back plan.

Additionally, both tanks mounted the Rheinmetall 120mm smoothbore gun which was not in favour with many senior military and scientific decision-makers, partly because the two 120mm ammunition families were incompatible. Additionally, the British Thermal Observation and Gunnery Sight (TOGS) thermal imaging system was very much better than those mounted on either Leopard 2 or M1A2. The overall reliability of both foreign tanks against the standard BFD criteria was calculated as 70%, whereas the intention with CR2 was to deliver a tank that was at least 80% reliable.

As noted previously, in order to replace Chieftain with CR2, 590 tanks were required. However, to replace it with either Leopard 2 or M1A2 would require purchasing an additional 48 tanks, because of the requirement to replace the existing training tank fleets at both Bovington and in Canada. This added additional up-front costs of around 8% to an already expensive – bordering unaffordable – programme, and also meant that a lot of new logistic, training and support systems would be required, again adding cost. Another factor was the problems associated with the transitional period when a foreign tank was being introduced into service. This could conceivably lead to a few years when the army was operating a tank fleet of three different types with two different guns: Chieftain and Challenger 1 with 120mm rifled guns, and the newcomer with a 120mm smoothbore gun. VDS also added pressure to the 'buy British' argument, by stating that any suggestion to build foreign tanks under licence should consider that this would mean the loss of potential export markets, seemingly a specious argument but one which had appeal to the Treasury who liked the idea of an income generation scheme to offset the programme costs. It was also suggested that building tanks at the slow rate proposed –

BELOW The other foreign tank which had a large fan club in Britain was the American M1, but serious doubts remained about the thirsty gas turbine engine and the logistic burden that this would impose. *(TM 2139C5)*

only around 60 or 65 a year – would add about a third as much again to the cost. A further argument deployed was that even if the UK wanted such a deal, the US Congress would be unlikely to agree to it anyway, instead insisting that all tanks would be built in the USA.

It must be stressed that the British did not simply go through the motions of looking at Leopard 2 and M1A2 having already decided that the VDS Challenger 2 was the answer.[23] Rather, very serious consideration was given to the advantages offered by those tanks, which were both excellent in many ways and outperformed CR2 in a number of areas. Both Leopard 2 and M1A2 had many vocal supporters among the British military. Four separate project teams were eventually set up to look again at the four competitors: CR2, Leopard 2, Leclerc and M1A2. No team was allowed access to the findings of the others, and had to report on the tanks' performance in five main areas: lethality, survivability, mobility, fightability and availability. The bottom line seems to have been that the Leopard 2 lacked sufficient survivability, the Leclerc was innovative but the technology immature and the autoloader disliked, and the M1A2, despite its thirst, was the best foreign option mainly owing to its better armour. The reports from these teams also made it clear that the new British L30 rifled gun possessed certain advantages over the smoothbore rivals, and the turret of CR2 performed exceptionally well during the 'firing at' protection trials. But it should be remembered that VDS also had the advantage of being able to propose a tank which was designed specifically to meet the British requirement and doctrine, and it was this, plus the apparent affordability rather than any misplaced patriotism, that decided the argument. But to be fair there was also a political factor: the Prime Minister Margaret Thatcher and her successor John Major from 1990 were both hugely in favour of a 'buy British' approach, and in November 1988 the Overseas Policy and Defence Committee of the Cabinet had already ordered that VDS should be given every opportunity to prove that they could meet the required specification for the new tank before looking elsewhere.

Proving the capability

When the detailed specification (DGFVE Spec 630) was issued in May 1988, a lot of the content was written knowing what VDS were able or proposing to deliver, rather than what was required – this was of course because the company had submitted detailed proposals only a few months earlier. This can be interpreted as a pragmatic solution accepting financial and time constraints; an alternative and more cynical version is that it ensured that the VDS proposal was the one which was going to be selected, and thus guaranteed that the foreign competitors were doomed to failure. Whichever is closer to the mark, on 20 January 1989 VDS signed a contract with the MoD to develop Challenger 2 in order to meet the requirements of Spec 630. This included an ambitiously short 18-month demonstration phase lasting until 30 September 1990, intended 'to demonstrate that CR2 is likely to meet the requirements of Spec 630 with the minimum of risk'. What was not clear was that the real risk lay in trying to do things too quickly; the whole plan would become derailed as soon as a key milestone was not met.

Nine prototypes were to be constructed, with intended delivery dates as follows: 31 December 1989 × 1; 31 January 1990 × 3; 28 February 1990 × 2; 31 March 1990 × 2; 30 April 1990 × 1. Each of the hand-built prototypes was priced at £3.467 million, a total of £31.2 million out of the £90 million development budget. Three major performance milestones were specified, breaking the demonstration phase into three six-month periods: Milestone 1 was set at 30 September 1989, 2 was to be 31 March 1990 and Milestone 3 was to conclude the demonstration phase on 30 September 1990. Of the nine prototypes built, seven were constructed at Leeds and two at Newcastle, as follows:

- ■ **V1 (06SP87)** went to Kirkcudbright for systems trials and was used as a general trials vehicle. This tank was subsequently sold back to VDS and used to develop the modifications for the Oman variant. It was then further converted to Challenger 2E

RIGHT V1 in the standard UK green and black scheme; although the sides look to be in a three-colour style, this is simply where the edges of the black are better defined than the infill. The hull now reflects the later layout, with two-pin track, modified lights and scalloped bazooka plates.

standard for export and used in the Greek MBT competition. It is now a gate guardian at the BAES Telford site.

■ **V2 (06SP88)** went to ATDU Bovington for reliability trials, and with V3 and V4 put on a lot of the automotive mileage required. It is now in the Bovington Tank Museum.

■ **V3 (06SP89)** went to ATDU Bovington for automotive reliability trials. This tank was used in the 'drive to destruction' trial and is now on plinth display at the Armour Centre, Bovington, with all the internal components stripped out. Interestingly, because of the delays to the tank coming into service, this vehicle was actually placed on the plinth before any CR2s had entered service, surely the only time this has ever happened!

■ **V4 (06SP90)** went to ATDU Bovington for reliability trials, and was used on demonstrations in the Middle East. This tank

CENTRE 06SP89 at speed on the trials circuit at Bovington – the problem of dust ingress would come to the fore in 2001 on Exercise Saif Sareea II, but was solved before the Iraq invasion of 2003. *(Courtesy Andy Brend)*

LEFT A view of 06SP90 from the rear, with the gun in the crutch that was later moved on to the top of the engine decks. In the manner of CR1, only one stowage box is fitted to the hull rear. *(Courtesy Andy Brend)*

is now the gate guardian at the AFV Gunnery School, Lulworth.

■ **V5 (06SP91)** went to Chertsey for maintainability trials and was kept at near-production standard as a User Trials vehicle. This tank is now on display at the Tank Museum, Bovington, and is still a runner.

■ **V6 (06SP92)** went to Kirkcudbright for turret systems trials. It was used during the User Trials. After decommissioning by the Army Base Repair Organisation (ABRO) and with most of the internal and some external components removed, it is now on display at the British Army Training Unit Suffield (BATUS) in Canada.

■ **V7 (06SP93)** went to VDS and then

ABOVE Most of the prototypes are now preserved as plinth tanks; V4 is at the AFV Gunnery School, Lulworth. The house where the author used to live when he was seven can be seen immediately behind! *(Courtesy Peter Breakspear)*

Catterick for GCE development trials. This tank was initially mounted with a ballasted turret. It is now on plinth display at the D&M School, Bovington.

■ **V8 (06SP94)** went to Kirkcudbright for

BELOW V7 posing for the camera, again showing the earliest hull type and cylindrical Commander's Primary Sight, plus lacking the GAS flap demanded by the trials crews. *(Courtesy Andy Brend)*

ABOVE V8 was used on signature trials at Kirkcudbright, and is preserved in the Defence Capability Centre, part of the Defence Academy at Shrivenham. *(Courtesy Peter Breakspear)*

BELOW V9, the final prototype built, being removed from its first plinth position at VDS Newcastle, on its way to the Discovery Museum, Newcastle. *(Courtesy Peter Breakspear)*

toxicity, MEMIC and signature trials. This tank is now on display at the Defence Capability Centre, Defence Academy, Shrivenham.

■ **V9 (06SP95)** went to Chertsey for ease of maintenance assessment. This tank was subsequently sold back to VDS and converted to the Oman-build standard, on which the conversion of V1 to CR2E was based. It was on display as the gate guardian at VDS Newcastle, and is now on plinth display at the Discovery Museum, Newcastle, bearing the made-up registration MH14MB.

The use of the letter V has been variously interpreted as Variant, Version, Vehicle and Vickers – perhaps it was chosen as it stood for all four! A slight note of caution regarding these numbers is appropriate here – at one stage VDS

had all nine prototypes together in Leeds, the one and only time that this happened, and not surprisingly took the opportunity to line them up for a photo shoot. However, it was then noticed that the V numbers were all jumbled up, and someone commented that surely the photo would look better if the numbers ran consecutively from V1 on the left to V9 on the right? It was agreed that this was a great idea, and then it was suggested that it would be easier to simply repaint some of the numbers rather than spend hours moving all the vehicles, which was what was done. And so, for a short period, V1 became V9, and V4 was V5, and so on.

In addition to the nine prototypes, two complete turret assemblies were also built, to allow separate trials on the turret systems that did not require them to be mounted on hulls. These were known as TA1 and 2. TA1 was fitted to the VDS Traverse Axis Rig at Newcastle to test and refine turret components, especially the GCE and traverse gearbox, and was subsequently used as an instructional aid. TA2 was used for the attack on armour protection trials, where it was attacked with a wide variety of threats and calibres to prove its integrity ... which it did![24] It is believed that both turrets were later dismantled.

When Challenger 2 was selected, VDS became both the Design Authority (DA) and the Prime Contractor (PC). Among the approximately 250 sub-contractors who supplied components and systems to build the tank, the major supporting companies included Barr & Stroud, Royal Ordnance Factory (Nottingham), Blair Catton, Dowty Controls, CDC, SFIM, DB Transmissions, Perkins Diesels and Marconi – not all of these were British. Although the hull was based upon the existing Challenger 1 tank and looked very similar, the differences lay under the skin and in fact Challenger 2 shared only about 4% parts commonality with its namesake predecessor. However, using the same basic hull, powerpack and suspension design as the start point was seen as the lowest-risk option, which would help to control cost inflation and reduce development time and risk.

The trials phase lasted from the first prototype not only until the tank entered service but also for some time afterwards, and went

beyond what was originally envisaged, as well as extending the time it took to get the tank into service. Because the original three milestones were not fully met at the end of 1990, VDS took the lead in insisting that the tank be developed further until the MoD was fully satisfied that the requirements were met, an approach that the MoD were delighted to agree to as they would have insisted on it anyway. This was most unusual; in many cases companies involved in producing any type of military equipment try to sell their product to the MoD 'as is', and tend to push back against any modifications that, while improving the product, cost them time and money. In this case, it is clear that a genuine collaborative effort took place between the customer and the supplier, to the extent that many lifelong friendships that crossed the

ABOVE Getting the prototypes together was no mean feat, as they were extremely busy on trials held all over the UK. Here are five of the nine all with the early hull design, including V2, 3 and 4. *(Courtesy Andy Brend)*

LEFT A turret being assembled on the welding manipulator. The front of the turrets are cast, with flat plates welded to them. The Dorchester armour is not yet in place, and was added in a separate high-security part of the factory. *(TM 10354-002)*

LEFT V4 at high speed, now with the majority of the hull modifications added, but still using the full-depth bazooka plates and the old BCF fire extinguishers. *(TM 4141C1)*

WO2 Norrie Robertson BEM Scots DG

The Royal Scots Dragoon Guards (Scots DG) were selected to be the first regiment to be issued [with] CR2 when it was meant to come into service in 1994/95. As part of the planned introduction two Scots DG crews were sent to ATDU in Bovington to carry out Gunnery and Automotive User Trials and finally to take part in an All Arms Exercise on Salisbury Plain. I was, at that time, a Warrant Officer Class 2 and was selected to be the Troop Leader of the User Trial due to having had extensive experience, in all crew positions, on both Chieftain and Challenger 1, culminating in commanding a Troop of CR1 during Operation Granby in 1991. Having completed Gunnery and Driving and Maintenance training at Lulworth Gunnery School and ATDU the crews took over the two tanks, V5 and V6, which were to be used for the trial. The trial was run under the direction of ATDU with a Trials Officer, Major Mike Bullen, who also happened to be a Scots DG officer. Vickers Defence Systems were closely involved as they were responsible, under the MoD contract, for all aspects of introducing CR2 into service.

During the trial I was very pleased with the Gun Control Equipment and Fire Control System. The ability to use the hunter/killer mode for target engagements was seriously impressive. Hunter/killer mode involved the commander using his independent sight to bring the gunner into alignment with the target and handing the shoot over to him, whilst immediately scanning for the next target, producing a high rate of target acquisition and destruction. What was really frustrating, however, was the inability to do this at night due to the lack of an independent thermal sight for the commander. Given that one of the main contributing factors for the success of CR1 during Operation Granby was its Thermal Observation Gunnery System, I really felt strongly that this was a missed opportunity to enhance the tank's capability. Even more frustrating was the knowledge that this was a cost-based decision as the planned export version was to have just such an independent commander's thermal sight. The co-axial machine gun was the L94A1 Hughes Chain Gun and this initially failed to impress. Part of the problem was that the drag of the ammunition belt from the ready round bin caused continual stoppages and this was only rectified after a number of modifications to the feed bin and tray. The crews took some time to adapt to this gun as it was not an easy weapon to get firing again after a stoppage; this often required the gun to be field stripped, unlike the user-friendly and well-loved 'Jimpy' L8A2 General Purpose Machine Gun with its rate of fire of 750rpm. Personally I felt that the Chain Gun's low rate of fire (520rpm) compared to the faster L8A2, combined with a protracted stoppage procedure, was not worth the lack of gases emitted into the turret, a stated reason for employing the gun. Interestingly both the US Army and US Marine Corps trialled this weapon for use as a co-axial machine gun on the M60 MBT but did not select it.

Automotive performance was superb throughout the trial. We took the tanks to the test track at MVEE Chertsey where V5 was tasked to go round the track at top speed on a circuit of about 200 miles while V6 was to do the same but only at convoy speed. The commander of V6, Sgt Steve McQueen, was not impressed. His attitude changed however when, having blasted round our circuits, the crew of V5 paid for our fun by having to change all the track pads on both tracks! The left-hand-side pads were worn down to the metal and the track was so hot the rubber on the roadwheels actually smouldered! We shared the track that day with the Caravan Club, who were testing for the best towing car of the year, which resulted in the surreal sight of V6 overtaking a Citroën Xantia towing a caravan!

The crews then moved to Salisbury Plain where a hill-climbing test was run, which resulted in an embarrassing moment for V5 and V6. The test was conducted as a comparison hill climb with an aged Chieftain from the Demonstration Squadron in Warminster. The slope was a fairly typical steep and chalky Salisbury Plain hill; the Chieftain got to the top easily while V5 and V6, with our TR60 double-pin track, continually slid back down. The general opinion from VDS was that the track was designed for fighting on the plains of Northern Germany or the sands of the desert, not Wiltshire. I commented that I hoped we would never have to fight a war in the UK! We then joined an exercise run by the All Arms Tactics Wing in Warminster. The only comment worth mentioning from the exercise is that all those who came to see the inside of the turret were less than impressed that the MoD had not bought an integrated Gunner's Primary Sight (GPS). Again the success of armour in the Gulf was in part due to the issue of GPS, albeit on a scale of two per Squadron. Another opportunity missed due to cost. . . .

The success of all the acceptance trials carried out by ATDU, including the Reliability Growth Trials and the User Trial, ensured that the Royal Armoured Corps received a world class MBT from VDS. I was involved in the formal signing-over ceremony, when the MoD took official delivery from VDS in 1994. Nearly a decade later, in 2003, I was serving as Headquarters Squadron Leader, and was proud to witness CR2 deploy with Scots DG and 2RTR to Iraq where the tank performed superbly, conducting raids and finally supporting the Infantry entry into Basra. As an afternote, in November 2013 it was the Scots DG Quartermaster Technical, Captain Jamie Gardiner, who oversaw the last CR2 to leave Wessex Barracks in Fallingbostel. No doubt he had a tear in his eye, as in 1994 he had been a Trooper and my driver of V5. This was a fitting way to end 75 years of tank soldiering for Scots DG, the regiment which was the first to receive CR2 into service.

RIGHT V9 conducting firing trials on a range. As well as using all the different types of ammunition used in service, a special water shot was also used during the trials programme. *(TM 4345B5)*

public/private boundary were formed. Indeed, much of the information in this chapter came from those involved, who the author met at the annual Challenger 2 development team get-together. Thus the predominant flavour of all the trials was a genuine desire to develop the tank to its utmost, and a spirit of honesty and partnership was present throughout. This is not to say that disagreements did not occur; they did and at times became heated, but were always able to be resolved without detriment to either the team or indeed the tank.

The Reliability Growth Trial (RGT) was implemented to test and improve the reliability of individual components, sub-systems and systems. The RGT was concluded in spring 1994, after a total of 285 BFD were completed using three of the prototypes. In this time over 20,000km of running was clocked up, along with nearly 12,000 rounds of 120mm ammunition. After the RGT was successfully completed, the Challenger 2 was formally accepted into service on 16 May 1994. The User Trials involved crews from both ATDU and an armoured regiment, intended to put the tanks through a realistic workload, using mainly V5 and V6. As a result of these different trials CR2 was improved and made more reliable, but what remained to be seen was whether the tanks coming off a production line were able to meet and maintain the same standards of reliability and availability.

In autumn 1994 the MoD had conducted an examination of three of the first six production tanks, selected at random and subjected to an incredibly thorough testing. Any fault, no matter how small, was recorded, down to a missing washer or an incorrectly tightened bolt. This was known as the 'First Off Production' trial and it revealed numerous faults which indicated that the service tanks were not at the standard of reliability and availability that had been demonstrated previously on the prototypes. As a result the MoD declined to accept the tanks into service, and insisted that VDS adopt any

ABOVE The old and the very new: CR1 65KG03 was in the final production batch, being built in early 1989. She is alongside V8 at ATDU and offers us a good comparison of both tanks including the European and BATUS camouflage schemes. *(TM 4807F6)*

BELOW Chieftain, Challenger 1 and 2 taking part in comparative acceleration and speed trials at Bovington. *(TM 5933A3)*

Lt Gen Sir Richard Hayman-Joyce

I handed over the role of Director Tanks in early 1989 on promotion but as Director General Fighting Vehicles retained the tank programme in my portfolio. Then came the first Gulf War (Op Granby) in which we were heavily involved preparing the equipment for desert conditions. On a recent desert trial Challenger 1 had suffered severely from engine dust ingestion and that was sufficiently worrying that the British seriously doubted the wisdom of deploying it. I received a call from the ACGS General Richard Swinburn to brief the Secretary of State – 'Now!' The briefing was to be on the risks of sending Challenger to the Gulf. The government had pledged to support the US who had said that they had plenty of helicopters, they had no need for our offer of a lightly armoured brigade based on CVR, but had asked us to provide a heavy armoured brigade. The dilemma was how to field Challenger so we could respond positively to the US request. I had no time to prepare a brief so had to speak 'off the cuff'. My advice was that as long as we were prepared to support the inevitable high usage of main engines, the other capabilities of the tank would more than match up. I also undertook to see whether in the short time before deployment we could improve the filtration performance. Finally, I said that our tank crews were very well trained and would be able to take extra care to maintain the filters.

On the basis of this advice, the British offer was made and 7th Armoured Brigade was told to prepare for deployment. Meanwhile, I had one of the very few serious rockets that I received in my service. A week or so after the decision had been made I was summoned by the Vice Chief of Defence Staff [VCDS], General Sir Dick Vincent, who had as MGO a year or two earlier been scarred (his words not mine) by a disastrous Challenger demonstration in the Middle East in desert conditions. On return from leave he discovered not only that the British had committed to a second very much more significant potential disaster, but that I was the author of the advice! Fortunately, the current MGO and my boss, John Stibbon, realised what was about to happen and accompanied me to face the ire of the VCDS. As history will tell us the USA welcomed the support, the filtration was improved and the supply chain was able to supply many more powerpacks than usual. A second armoured brigade (4th) was then deployed to form a full armoured division under Major General Rupert Smith. In the event 1st (UK) Division 'in 66 hours wrecked the better part of three Iraqi armoured divisions and captured more than 7,000 prisoners in an advance of 180 miles'.

As the 'distraction' of Operation Granby subsided, we turned once more [to] the development of Challenger 2. VDS having been given the green light by the government, we let a development contract on the company that included a Reliability Growth Plan. Our civil servant muse failed to understand the importance of this process to building a reliable tank and swore that the £2.5m I had allowed for in the EAC paper would never be accepted. It was, and the eventual cost of reliability growth to [the] MoD exceeded £35m, excluding VDS costs. VDS were to be given sole responsibility for development and reliability growth and had to present evidence to show that the tank was ready for series production.

Summoned by the Military Secretary in early 1991 I was told that I was to take over as Director of the Armoured Corps [DRAC] in Bovington in May, a return to rural living after four years in London. As DRAC I was able to monitor the development and trials of the new tank that was based at ATDU. And I became uneasy. The information I was receiving informally led me to conclude that trials lacked the rigour that we had hoped for, and that we could potentially sign up to the contract only to regret it later. Despite being the director of the corps which would operate the new tank, I was then officially out of the acquisition loop, so I had no influence on the judgements being made by the MoD on the trial reports, even though I was of course seriously concerned at the outcome.

By mid-1995 I was Master General of the Ordnance and production was underway. I was getting worrying reports from the 'in-Inspections' conducted at the Ludgershall vehicle depot that the level of faults was not declining in accordance with the expected 'bath-tub curve', but remained consistently at a high level. It looked to me that the scepticism I had felt during the prototype trials was now becoming real. The faults were not minor in many cases. I invited the Minister for Defence Procurement (James Arbuthnot) to join me on a visit to Bovington and Lulworth to see CR2 in action (26 June 1995). During the trip down in the car I briefed him on the news coming out of Ludgershall and he was sufficiently concerned to ask me for a formal briefing the next month. This took place on 19 July. At that meeting he agreed with me that production should be halted while VDS sorted the problems out; I think 136 tanks had been delivered by that time. I then went to see the Chairman of Vickers, Sir Colin Chandler on 3 August and told him what we were doing. This was a heavy blow to the company and had implications for cash flow, employment during the production hiatus, management of VDS and not least the reputation of the company. There was also the problem of maintaining the tank fleet in BAOR. Scots DG, who were due to be equipped, had already back-loaded their Chieftains but had no MBT to replace them. Although the risk was acceptable in military terms (because by then the Berlin Wall had come down and the Russians were not the imminent threat that they were seen to be in the 1980s), the effect on the regiment can be imagined.

I talked to the (by then) new MD of VDS, Colin Clark, and we agreed a plan for recovery that required a systematic and detailed engineering exercise from the bottom up. Every single component of every sub-system had to be tested and verified before incorporation into the next level, where the process was to be repeated. The new MD was a really top-class engineer and I was confident that in time CR2 would be a reliable weapon system. Having been brought up on Chieftain and CR1 (as an 11th Hussar we introduced these tanks into service) I was determined that CR2 would not be another unreliable British tank.

That winter (1995) while VDS started the recovery programme, the hierarchy in the MoD was getting restive, particularly the Secretary of State, Michael Portillo. I was required to justify my actions and presented a paper to the Equipment Advisory Committee after which the Chairman recommended that I should go into the used car business, such were my persuasive powers! That was in February 1996 in the light of a projected meeting with Portillo in March. I revisited VDS on 23 March to get up to date and attended the meeting with Portillo on the 25th. He was angry that as he saw it the company had let him and the government down, having dismissed three worthy foreign MBT contenders to replace Chieftain in favour of the British company, and was all for cancelling the contract. Fortunately the Minister for Defence Procurement asked that I should speak (although not part of the EAC) as I was in attendance. The upshot was that Portillo withdrew his threat of cancellation but made it clear that my offer of putting my head on the block if things did not work out would be remembered. . . .

However, VDS were extremely thorough in their rescue operation to the extent that when the new deliveries were put through a very rigorous Reliability Growth Trial, CR2 passed the test. My son, who had joined KRH at the time CR2 was being handed over to the army and was a severe critic, had nothing but praise and enthusiasm for the reliability of the new tank. Production restarted, Scots DG got their new and reliable tanks, and VDS formally handed Challenger 2 over to me on the ranges on 30 June 1998.

measures necessary to resolve the problem. This uncertainty led to another innovation, the Challenger 2 Fielding Team. Under the command of a regular officer, Maj (later Lt Col) Ken Davies KRH, this small team of experienced tank crewmen and REME personnel examined four tanks from each batch of 38 as they came off the production line, allowing VDS to not only rectify all the faults found on individual tanks, but also to feed this back into the production line to resolve the problems at source. This was very successful and led to a better standard of production tank, as well as a greatly increased level of confidence from the crews, who never faced the levels of major and minor problems normally associated with the introduction of a new tank, where it was considered normal to

ABOVE V5 was nicknamed 'Terminator' by its trials crew, and wore an image from the film on the fume extractor, as well as a saltire on the TISH mantlet as would be expected from a Scots DG crew! *(Courtesy Norrie Robertson)*

BELOW V5 again, this time crossing a river obstacle using the M3 rig, with WO2 Norrie Robertson in the commander's seat. The crew nearly gassed the sappers when, as a joke, the driver switched on the exhaust smoke generation system. *(Courtesy Norrie Robertson)*

ABOVE Early firing trials were conducted by live crews wearing anti-flash gear and respirators in case of a flashback; note the breathing tubes leading out of the loader's hatch. If these were incorrectly positioned – as occasionally happened – the crews might find themselves breathing in engine fumes! *(TM 4132B2)*

ABOVE RIGHT L/Cpl Martin 'Fozzie' Forester RDG in the loader's side, with the breech closed and loader's guard to the rear, ready to fire.
(Courtesy Jim Elgar)

accept any number of teething problems when it first entered service.[25] Additionally, a series of Production Reliability Growth Trials or PRGTs was undertaken between November 1997 and June 1998; the planned final PRGT which was to take place in October 1998 was cancelled as the desired standard was fully achieved by PRGT 3. The final piece in the trials jigsaw was the In-Service Reliability Demonstration (ISRD) conducted in late 1998 (described in

CHALLENGER 2 USER TRIALS 1994/95

Sgt Joe Toward Scots DG

In 1994 and 1995 Scots DG had to supply crewmen for the Armoured Trials and Development Unit (ATDU) to conduct the First Off Production (FOP) trial and the User Trials. When I was given the opportunity to go to VDS in Newcastle with Sgt Hiscock, I jumped at the chance. In the early days the 1995 trials had gone well with the first nine [prototype] tanks. This was an ideal chance for us to see the tank we could expect to receive in Fallingbostel. Once we were familiar with the vehicle, each squadron in turn came to look at how the tank was built: one squadron that shall remain nameless went to the Leeds factory instead of Newcastle! Everyone's expectations were high, including those of VDS. The concept was simple: VDS would prove that they were able to transfer the same quality and reliability established on FOP and the User Trials by carrying out a Production Reliability Trial (PRT). This would be closely followed by an In-Service Reliability Demonstration (ISRD) and finally the regiment would receive its full quota of tanks in 1996.

Unfortunately PRT was not as successful as everyone would have liked and a rethink was required. I was one of the crew who were then selected to go to Bovington alongside an ATDU crew. These trials were run with what is called a battlefield day (BFD), a concept used in FOP. This consisted

of driving 33km cross-country, 27km on roads, firing 34 main armament rounds, 1,000 rounds from the chain gun, and much more. Seven BFDs would be used for all PRTs and Production Reliability Growth Trials, or PRGTs. Crews would start work at around 0600 and sometimes would stay up all night while a vehicle was being repaired. Four PRGT trials were planned, each six months apart. Each trial was to show that reliability was better than the last, with the end result that after all four had been completed the overall reliability would be even higher than had been demanded from PRT. True to their word, VDS produced the goods and CR2 has been improved to such a degree that it is the envy of most other nations, and has been tested more than any other tank in the world. PRGT 3 finished at the end of summer 1998 and it was a great success for all, VDS having proved all that has been asked of them in both quality and reliability. But in order to squeeze the last drop of reliability from VDS, the MoD then introduced Batch Testing and Fielding which basically continues with the theme of proving the reliability of every tank that comes off the production line. Conversion is now in full swing and we have received our first eight tanks. B Squadron will move to Bovington in August 1998 to start ISRD, and in 1999 we can look forward to helping with the deployment of CR2 to BATUS.

Chapter 3). This period can once again be best described from one who was integral to the discussions and decisions made at the very highest level, General Hayman-Joyce.

Another Scots DG soldier very heavily involved in the trials and early development work on CR2 but at a very different level to General Hayman-Joyce was Sgt (later Capt) Joe Toward MBE who, in 1998, wrote an insightful report into the trials process. Over to you Joe: (see opposite page).

ABOVE LEFT Joe Toward completing trials paperwork: every single fault, no matter how minor, was meticulously recorded and then examined in detail to determine how to prevent it recurring. *(Courtesy Nigel Atkin)*

ABOVE 61KK68 was the First Off Production (FOP) tank, the first Challenger built on the production line that would eventually deliver 386 tanks for the British Army. *(Courtesy Nigel Atkin)*

BELOW The main tanks and 'three strands of DNA' that were important in CR2's development.

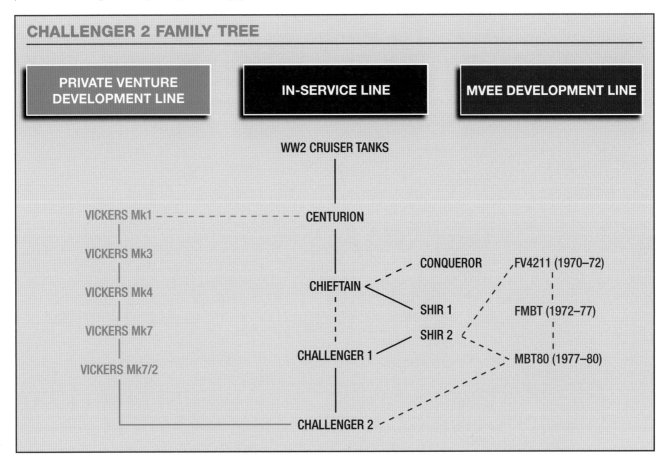

CHALLENGER 2 FAMILY TREE

| PRIVATE VENTURE DEVELOPMENT LINE | IN-SERVICE LINE | MVEE DEVELOPMENT LINE |

WW2 CRUISER TANKS

VICKERS Mk1 — — — — — — — — CENTURION

VICKERS Mk3

VICKERS Mk4   CONQUEROR   FV4211 (1970–72)

VICKERS Mk7   CHIEFTAIN   SHIR 1   FMBT (1972–77)

VICKERS Mk7/2   SHIR 2

                     CHALLENGER 1   MBT80 (1977–80)

CHALLENGER 2

Challenger 2 Development Timeline

YEAR	DATE	EVENT	REMARKS
1985	April–May	Exercise Endura I in BAOR.	Investigation into feasibility of three-man tank crews on extended operations. Endura II takes place April 1986.
1986	October	VDS purchases ROF (L) tank production facility for £15m.	
1986	December	General Sir Dick Vincent (MGO) briefs VDS on options for Chieftain replacement.	
1986	End	VDS start work on a private-venture concept for a new tank for the British army, to replace both CH and CR.	In consultation with RARDE.
1987	Early	Chieftain replacement envisaged as being a high-technology tank, possibly fitted with an electromagnetic main armament.	
1987	March	VDS proposes a new tank called 'Challenger 2 Mk 2' as Chieftain replacement.	Later simplified as Challenger 2, with Challenger renamed Challenger 1.
1987	May	Report 'Options for the Replacement of Chieftain' published.	Developed into Staff Target Land 4004 Future Tank and issued to industry.
1987	June	MoD EPC 'decouples' the Chieftain Replacement programme from the project to develop a longer-term Future MBT.	Replacement tank being referred to as Challenger 2 Mk 2 or 2/2.
1987	3 December	SR (L) 4026 endorsed as requirement document for Chieftain replacement.	Drafts written in autumn 1987.
1987	3 December	MoD EPC selects Challenger 2 Mk 2 as preferred solution for SR(L) 4026.	In-service version of Challenger now referred to as Challenger 1. Challenger 2 Mk 2 now referred to as Challenger 2.
1988		Nine tanks considered as potential Chieftain replacement.	Including Leopard 2 and M1A1.
1988		RARDE tasked to investigate putting Chobham on to Leopard 2 turret.	Not proceeded with.
1988	1 February	MoD receives revised VDS proposal for Challenger 2.	Based on SR (L) 4026.
1988	Spring	Consideration given to fitting Challenger 2 with a 140mm gun.	Not proceeded with, but turret designed to accept larger gun in future.
1988	5 April	VDS assure MoD that CR2 will 'embody almost all of the requirements of SR (L) 4026'	
1988	31 May	Detailed MoD specification for Challenger 2 issued.	DGFVE Spec 630, developed from SR (L) 4026.
1988	24 June	VDS forwards proposal and costs for development and production for 590/600 tanks, plus reliability plan.	Production costed at producing 65 tanks per annum.
1989	20 January	VDS signs contract to develop Challenger 2.	£90 million for the Demonstration (aka proof of principle) phase.
1989	30 September	Milestone 1 for Challenger 2 Demo phase.	
1990	31 March	Milestone 2 for Challenger 2 Demo phase.	

YEAR	DATE	EVENT	REMARKS
1990	August	Reliability Demonstration Growth Trial (RDGT) commences at ATDU.	
1990	August	Iraq invades Kuwait and Operation Granby implemented.	
1990	30 September	Milestone 3 for Challenger 2 Demo phase.	
1990	June	Challenger 2 publicly exhibited for first time at BAEE.	
1991	19 February	Decision on Chieftain replacement delayed due to Gulf War.	
1991	21 June	Order announced for 127 × Challenger 2 MBT, plus 13 DTT.	Worth £520 million. Decision made on 17 April, contract signed 28 June.
1993	June	Oman orders 18 Challenger 2, plus two DTT and four CRARRV, for around £140 million.	Deliveries commenced early 1995.
1993	10 August	DTT No 1 completed.	Built at Newcastle.
1993	6 October	CR1 fleet comprises 369 tanks: 300 BAOR; 39 UK; 30 BATUS.	
1994	16 May	CR2 formally accepted for service.	
1994	July	Order placed for 259 × Challenger 2 MBT, plus 9 DTT.	Worth £800 million including support and training package.
1994	25 July	First service Challenger 2 handed over to ATDU.	For testing and development, not operational.
1995	May	DTT No 13 completed.	
1996	22 March	Last Chieftain struck off strength of an operational unit (1RTR).	
1997	November	Oman orders 20 Challenger 2 for around £100 million.	Total orders for Oman 38 MBT. Final tank delivered late 2000.
1997	November	Production Reliability Growth Trial (PRGT) 1.	
1998	January	Scots DG receive the first eight operational CR2.	
1998	March	PRGT 2.	
1998	June	PRGT 3.	PRGT 4 scheduled for October 1998 cancelled as PRGT 3 achieved desired standard.
1998	30 June	Challenger 2 enters operational service when Scots DG receive their last (38th) tank.	ISD now defined as 1 complete regiment of 38 tanks.
1998	September to December	In-Service Reliability Demonstration (ISRD)	1 squadron of 12 tanks (B Sqn Scots DG).
1999	December	First use of CR2 on peace-keeping operations in the Balkans.	
2002	17 April	Last British Army Challenger 2 delivered to A Sqn 1RTR.	Total ordered for British Army 386 MBT plus 22 DTT.
2003	March	The Second Gulf War (Operation Telic) starts.	116 CR2 involved in invasion of Iraq; 1 destroyed in fratricide incident.

Chapter Two

Anatomy of Challenger 2

Challenger 2 follows the standard four-man crew layout that was first seen in Centurion, and many parts of it would be instantly recognisable to a crewman from that era. On the other hand, much of the technology used is very different and would seem alien and futuristic, particularly the extensive use of computers and digital displays.

OPPOSITE Challenger 2's impressive firepower being demonstrated by A Sqn 1RTR on a firing range, with the 120mm gun engaging a target at over 2,000m. The sophisticated fire control computer allows CR2 to rapidly and accurately engage targets even when the firing tank and the target are both moving at speed, using the renowned hunter/killer acquisition system. The sophisticated equipment used for this represents a large proportion of the tank's overall budget. *(Courtesy Andy Brend)*

General description

All descriptions of left/right and front/back in this volume are given as though the observer is standing behind the tank with the gun pointing to the front. The description here is of a tank in 2014, incorporating modifications made since the introduction into service. At the time of writing, for the first time ever female soldiers are able to serve on Challenger 2, and any references herein to either he or him, or indeed crewman/men, should be interpreted as gender-neutral.

Challenger 2 is an MBT with a crew of four. Three are located in the turret – commander, gunner and radio operator/loader, with the driver in the hull. The main armament is a 120mm rifled gun, stabilised in both traverse and elevation. A co-axially mounted 7.62mm chain gun and a 7.62mm GPMG on the turret roof form the secondary armament. Two banks of five-barrelled smoke grenade dischargers are mounted externally, one on each side of the turret front. The hull is made of welded MVEE 816 RHA armour plate. The front half of the turret is made of a one-piece casting of armour steel, with welded armour plates forming the rear half including the bustle. The tank is protected by Dorchester

armour, a development of the earlier Chobham armour system. Base armour is fitted during construction and is known as Dorchester Level 1 (DL1). Appliqué armour, added to the hull sides, toe and glacis plates for operational use only, is known as Operational Armour Packs (OAP) and increase the protection level to Dorchester Level 2 (DL2); this was based upon the system successfully used on CR1. Later upgraded versions of turret and hull-side packs and toe armour are known as Dorchester Level 2 Improved, or DL2i. The side packs on DL2 are of Dorchester construction, whereas the front hull toe/glacis packs are Explosive Reactive Armour (ERA); fitting the packs takes the crew approximately 5 hours, although this can be reduced significantly if extra manpower is made available. Bar armour to provide additional threat-specific protection can also be carried, as can an appliqué mine/IED protection panel fitted under the crew compartment floor. The crew are protected against the effects of nuclear, biological and chemical (NBC) agents by an air filtration and distribution pack contained within the armoured bustle at the turret rear. The Crew Temperature Control System or CTCS provides the means of controlling the internal temperature of the crew compartment.

ABOVE ATDU's so-called Megatron, fitted out on operational mode with additional armour, remote weapon station, ECM equipment and an early version of the mobile camouflage system. *(Courtesy Andy Brend)*

RIGHT The rear of a QRH tank prepared for operations in 2008, with bar armour used to provide protection from RPGs at the rear of the tank. *(Courtesy Jim Elgar)*

BELOW AND BELOW RIGHT The turret sub-structure, made up of a cast front and welded plate rear, over which the Dorchester armour panels are fitted and covered by a thin cosmetic armour which gives the turret its shape.

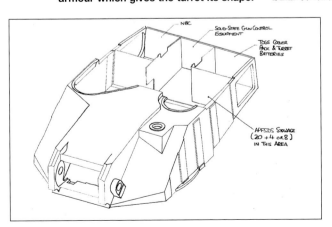

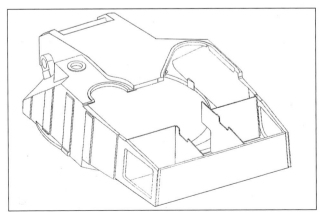

RIGHT The layout of the crew: commander (blue), loader/radio operator (orange), gunner (pink), and driver (yellow).

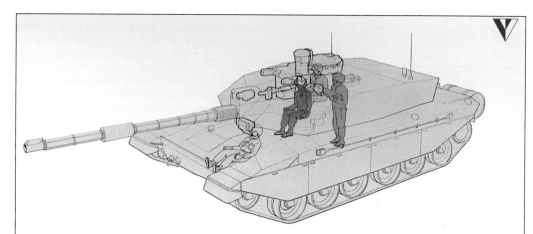

The crew of Challenger 2 occupies two of the vehicle's main compartments; the driver at the front of the hull, with the Commander, Gunner and Loader positioned in the fighting compartment within the rotating turret. Sights range from simple periscopes to highly sophisticated electro-optical devices, some of which are linked to the tank's computer.

Challenger 2's major sighting arrangements comprise:

Commander
Ring of eight x1 vision episcopes for observation.
Dual magnification telescope for engagement.
Monochrome TV monitor which displays the dual magnification thermal scene.

Gunner
An x1 episcope for orientation and gun husbandry.
A dual magnification telescope for engagement.
A monochrome TV monitor identical to the Commander's.
An emergency telescope for use if all other sights are damaged and for semi-automatic sights/gun alignment calibration.

All the telescopic sights are linked to the gun by computer and this ensures that the gun remains aimed at the target whatever the movement of the tank.

A significant proportion of the tank's value is accounted for by these systems.

BELOW The belly plates under the tank, which allow access for maintenance, drainage and so on. The 'bung' is removed when the dozer blade is fitted.

The tank layout is conventional, in that there is a forward compartment for the driver in the hull, with a partial bulkhead behind separating it from the central fighting compartment,

1 RH hull armour drain plug
2 Bung
3 LH hull armour drain plug
4 Driver's drain plug
5 Coolant drain access plate
6 GUE oil drain access plate
7 Fuel (base tank) drain access plate
8 Gearbox oil filters access plate
9 Gearbox oil drain access plate
10 ME drain access plate

consisting of the central portion of the hull, and the inside of the turret provides accommodation for the remainder of the crew. The rear compartment of the hull behind a sealed bulkhead houses the powerpack (engine and transmission), a generating unit engine, the final drives and the CTCS compressor. The driver's seat, access door (hatch) and periscopes are designed to enable the vehicle to be driven with the driver in the 'head out/opened up' position, or 'closed down' with the driver in the reclined position with the hatch closed.

The fighting compartment extends the width of the hull. A turret turntable is located on a system of roller bearings on the hull floor and rotates with the turret. The commander (upper) and gunner (lower) are located on the right side of the turret, with the operator/loader to the left. A fixed commander's cupola in the turret roof incorporates a rotatable panoramic sight, plus periscopes to provide all-round vision. The loader's station is equipped with a rotatable cupola that can be fitted with a machine-gun mounting. The turret can be rotated through 360° by electrical power or by hand; the turret carries the armament, electrical gun control equipment, communication systems, ammunition stowage, the TI and sighting systems and the NBC/ventilation equipment. A computerised fire control system in the turret integrates

RIGHT CR2 loader Cpl 'Parky' Park of 2RTR cradling an L27A1 APFSDS projectile during Operation Telic – as well he knows, he should be wearing his crewman's helmet! (*Courtesy RTR*)

the optical sighting system, the TI system, and the gun control equipment to form an effective weapon system for target acquisition, armament alignment and gun firing.

The rearmost compartment in the hull houses the powerpack beneath opening and removable armoured decking and louvres. The powerpack is a combined unit, designed to be rapidly removable for replacement and repair. The unit incorporates the main engine, transmission, the cooling and the lubricating systems. Located to the left of the powerpack is a generating unit engine (GUE), which may be operated independently of the main engine to provide electrical power. The TN54 transmission unit forms an integral part of the powerpack and is rigidly attached to the engine. The unit incorporates a torque converter, the change speed pack, the hydrostatic steering unit and the vehicle brakes. The gearbox is fully automatic and provides six forward and two reverse gears. A manual gear range selector is located in the driver's position. Steering is provided by a hydrostatic steering unit, controlled by linked steering levers (tillers) on either side of the driver's seat. The main brakes are applied by a hydraulically operated foot pedal when the tank is moving, and by a ratchet-operated handbrake lever as a parking brake. The functions of both the main engine and the transmission unit are controlled electrically by the Vehicle Integrated Control System (VICS).

The tank is supported on its double pin tracks by 24 rubber-tyred roadwheels, 12 on each side on the vehicle, arranged in pairs. Each roadwheel pair has its own independent hydrogas suspension unit, combining the functions of both a spring and a shock absorber; the damping rate is greater than that used on CR1. The latest pattern of roadwheels

RIGHT The turret turntable floor layout.

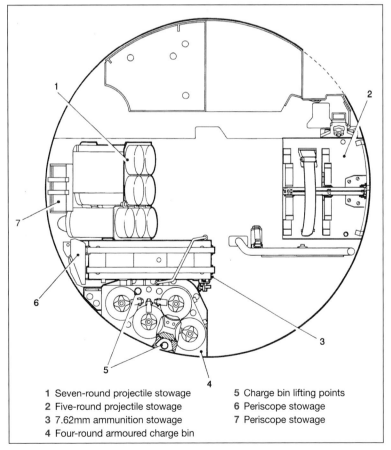

1 Seven-round projectile stowage	5 Charge bin lifting points
2 Five-round projectile stowage	6 Periscope stowage
3 7.62mm ammunition stowage	7 Periscope stowage
4 Four-round armoured charge bin	

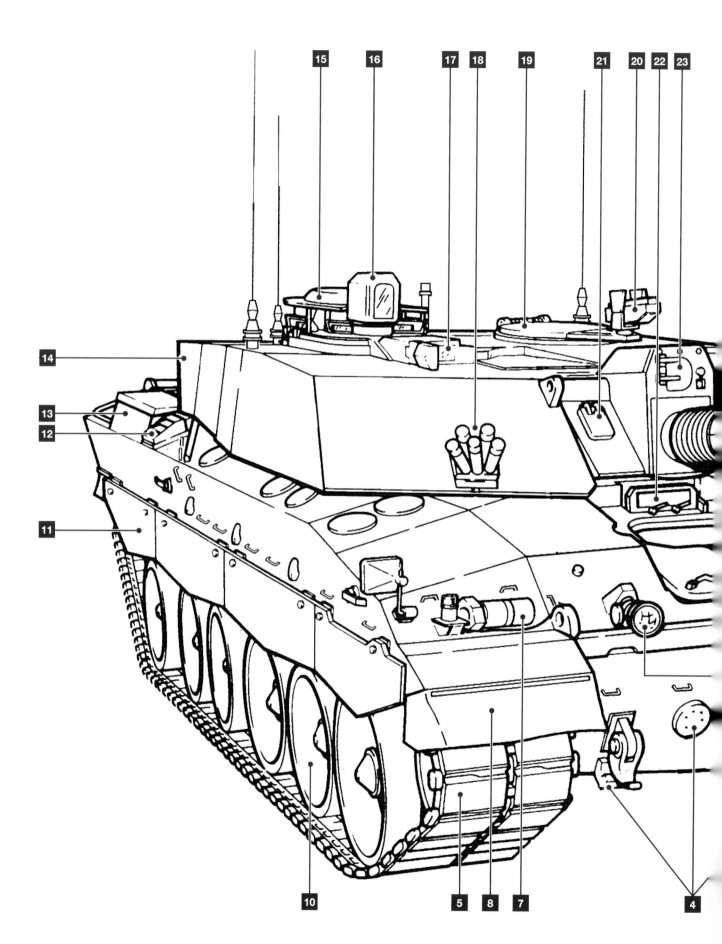

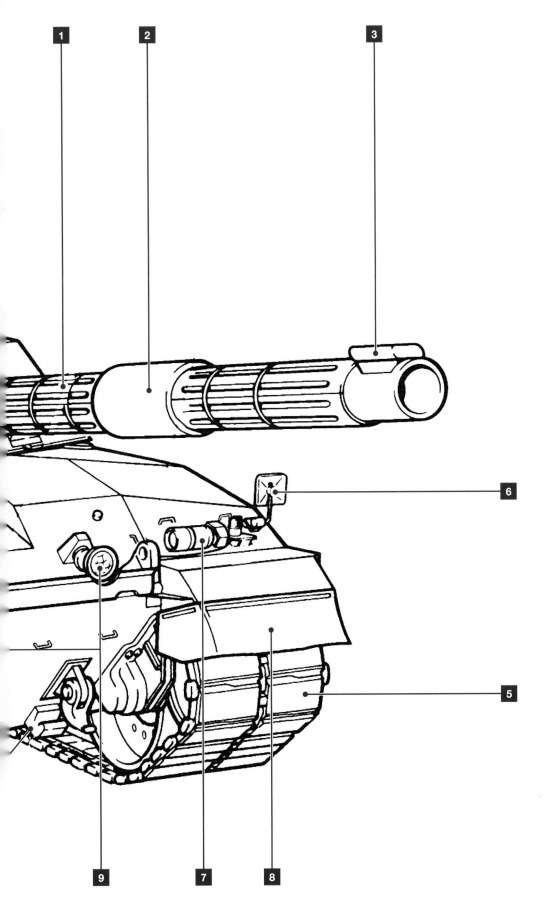

Challenger 2 Main Battle Tank.

1 L30 120mm gun
2 Fume extractor
3 Muzzle Reference System mirror and shroud
4 BEMA mounting points
5 Double-pin track
6 Rear view mirror
7 Rechargeable dry powder extinguisher
8 Front track guard
9 Headlamp
10 Road wheels
11 Bazooka plates
12 RHS main engine exhaust cowl
13 Driver's tools
14 Rear turret stowage bin
15 Commander's hatch
16 Commanders primary sight
17 Gunner's primary sight
18 Multi-barrelled smoke grenade discharger
19 Loader's hatch
20 Loader's GPMG pintle mount
21 Gunner's auxiliary sight
22 Driver's periscope
23 TOGS armoured cover

ABOVE Callsign 12 on exercise. Note the typical method of securing the rear skirting plate upside down; this stops the sprocket from getting clogged up when the ground is particularly muddy, and also makes sure that it does not get lost! *(Courtesy Andy Brend)*

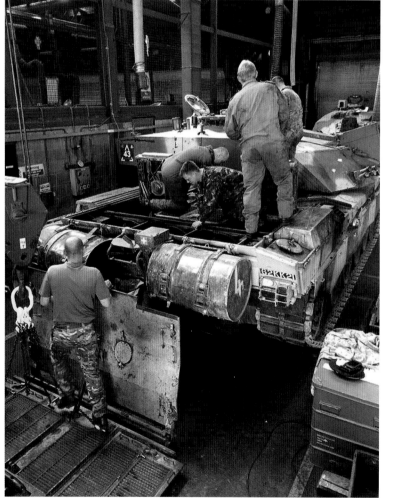

have 15 holes around the outside of the hub; these are designed not so much to lighten them, although it does help, but mostly to allow mud to escape through the holes thus relieving pressure, as previous versions were found to collect mud between the wheels. The tracks are adjustable from within the driver's compartment by a hydraulically operated track tensioning system. The tracks are supported along the top run by rubber-tyred top rollers. Removable skirting plates provide some protection to the wheels, suspension and hull side plates when the DL2 side packs are not fitted. The tank is 11.75m long with the gun front, or 9.8m long with the gun rear supported in the gun

LEFT In the hangars or workshop it is common practice to lift the decks off with a crane to make access to the powerpack easier, particularly for repairs or in-depth servicing. *(Courtesy RWxY)*

LEFT A King's Royal Hussars tank undergoing essential maintenance on exercise: the rubber on the roadwheels takes a real pounding in use, requiring the roadwheels to be replaced quite frequently. *(Courtesy Andy Brend)*

LEFT Replacing the top rollers can be done without splitting the track, as demonstrated here. Two jacks (each tank carries one) are placed on the roadwheels each side in order to lift the track off the roller that is to be replaced. The new item is on the ground ready to be fitted. *(Courtesy Andy Brend)*

clamp. Overall width without DL2 side packs is 3.55m, and the tank is 3.04m high to the top of the commander's sight hood. Fully loaded for combat with crew, stowage, ammunition and fuel, but without DL2, the tank weighs 64 tonnes and carries a bridge classification of 70. The bridge classification is increased to 80 when DL2 is mounted. Although the top speed on the road is officially listed as 60kph, it can comfortably exceed that, with 80kph being easily achievable.

LEFT The gun crutch (aka gun clamp) in the stowed position on the rear decks; the locating plunger is seen on the left side.

RIGHT The powerpack
front left, showing the
major components
with the radiators in
the lowered (operating)
position.

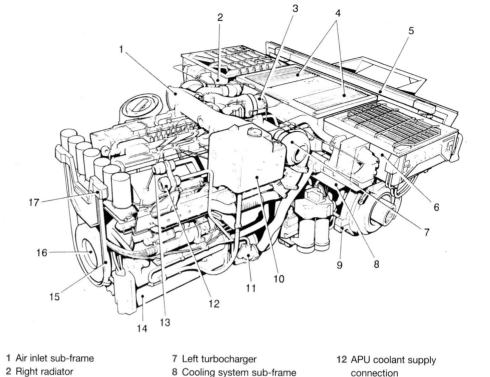

1 Air inlet sub-frame
2 Right radiator
3 Inlet Manifold Heater (IMH)
4 Charge air coolers and
  ACTOC
5 Fan frame
6 Left radiator
7 Left turbocharger
8 Cooling system sub-frame
9 Rear mount, left
10 Coolant header/expansion
   tank
11 Coolant pump
12 APU coolant supply
   connection
13 APU coolant return
14 Engine oil heat exchanger
15 'U' guide strap
16 Crankshaft damper
17 Front mounting bracket

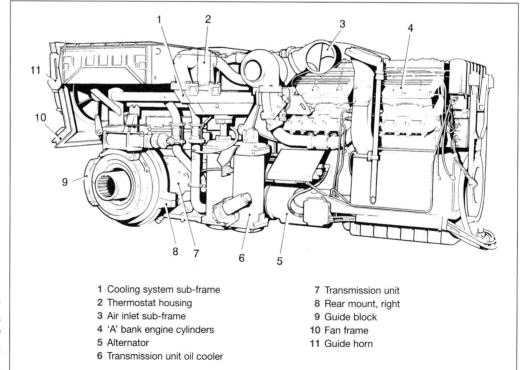

1 Cooling system sub-frame
2 Thermostat housing
3 Air inlet sub-frame
4 'A' bank engine cylinders
5 Alternator
6 Transmission unit oil cooler
7 Transmission unit
8 Rear mount, right
9 Guide block
10 Fan frame
11 Guide horn

RIGHT The pack from
the front right. The A
bank of cylinders of
the V12 engine are on
this side of the engine.

Mobility

The powerpack concept

The powerpack is installed as a single unit, and comprises the CV12 engine, the TN54 transmission and the associated attached components of the lubrication system and the cooling system. The engine and transmission are bolted together on prepared faces on the ends of the engine flywheel housing and the transmission input coupling housing. They are correctly aligned by means of dowels. The drive from the engine into the transmission is through a splined input coupling on the transmission unit, which fits into a matching ring bolted to the face of the engine flywheel. Changing a powerpack takes between 1 to 1½ hours. The powerpack is controlled by the VICS, which replaced the older Digital Automotive Systems Control Unit (DASCU), a carry-forward from the CRARRV and which was fitted to the first production models of CR2.

Main and generating unit engines

The engine – often referred to as the Main Engine or ME – is designated CV12TCA. This is decoded as: Rolls-Royce 'C' range of engines,

LEFT **A crewman samples engine oil as part of the procedures used to predict likely failure and conduct preventative maintenance and repair.** *(Courtesy RWxY)*

BELOW LEFT **A well-used powerpack on a maintenance stand in the RTR workshop. The connections are designed to be quick-release to allow rapid pack changes in the field.**

BELOW **The same pack from the left side. Crewmen used to the Chieftain will be amazed how little oil leakage there is on show (none), although the pack is still very dirty from the rough usage it gets in the back of a service tank.**

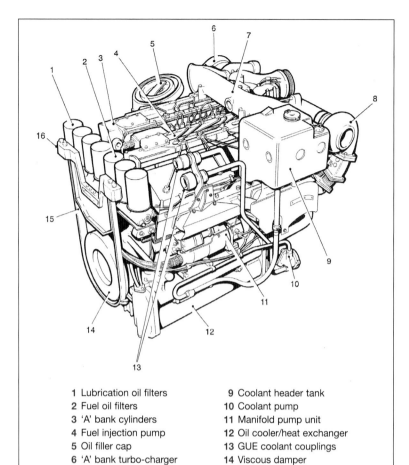

1 Lubrication oil filters
2 Fuel oil filters
3 'A' bank cylinders
4 Fuel injection pump
5 Oil filler cap
6 'A' bank turbo-charger
7 Air inlet trunking
8 'B' bank turbo-charger
9 Coolant header tank
10 Coolant pump
11 Manifold pump unit
12 Oil cooler/heat exchanger
13 GUE coolant couplings
14 Viscous damper
15 Damper guard
16 Powerpack front mounting

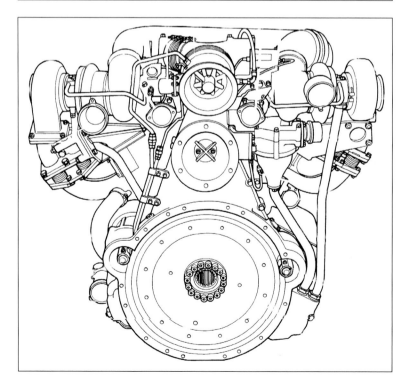

LEFT The CV12 left front, separated from the transmission and final drives. The viscous damper reduces engine vibrations.

Vee configuration cylinder block, 12 cylinder, turbo-charged, with charge-air cooling. The CV12 is a high-speed, high-output under-square diesel engine. It features cross-flow cylinder heads and high mounted camshafts inside the Vee of the cylinder block. The cylinders are arranged in two banks set at a 60° angle; the 'A' bank is on the right side, the 'B' bank on the left. Torsional vibrations caused by the engine configuration are taken up by a viscous damper positioned at the front of the crankshaft. The air supply is provided by two TV8110 turbo-chargers, each supplying one cylinder bank. Air cleanliness is provided by two-stage air filters within the air cleaner. The turbo-chargers draw air at ambient temperature and pressure via a triangular louvre in the front right engine deck, through the air cleaner, and then it is pressurised and passed from the compressor outlets through cast trunking, to the charge coolers. The turbo-chargers are driven by exhaust gases delivered from the respective exhaust manifolds. An inlet manifold heater system is fitted to facilitate easier engine starting and to reduce white smoke emission caused by running at light load. This is done by pre-heating the induction air in the inlet manifolds and is controlled by the VICS, so that it only operates when the inlet manifold temperature is between 128°C and 180°C.

Engine power output is dependent on the correct quantity of fuel being supplied (metered) to all the cylinder chambers at the right moment (phasing), regardless of the running conditions and throughout the whole power range. The Simms Maximec Fuel Injection Pump (FIP) provides both the metering and the phasing of the fuel. The fuel injection system comprises three fuel filters, the FIP (located on top of the cylinder block between the banks), a fuel shut-off valve, the pump-mounted equipment and 12 fuel injectors. Fuel is supplied from the

LEFT CV12 rear, with the Inlet Manifold Heater shown at No 9.

RIGHT The air route through the engine, showing the intake or air in red coming from the small louvre in the front engine deck (10), and the exhaust in blue. On operations the Thermal Exhaust Cowls (TECs) are often used to reduce the thermal signature created by the exhaust gases emerging from the sides of the hull.

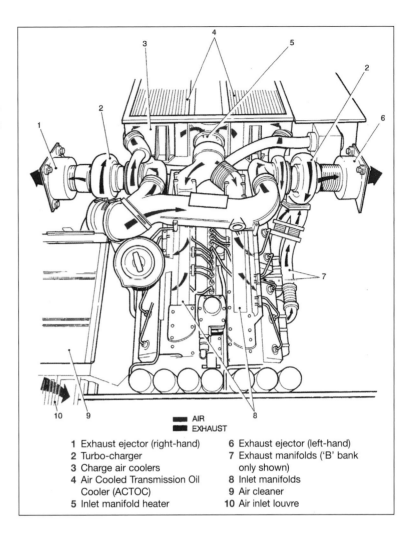

■	AIR		
■	EXHAUST		

1	Exhaust ejector (right-hand)	**6**	Exhaust ejector (left-hand)
2	Turbo-charger	**7**	Exhaust manifolds ('B' bank
3	Charge air coolers		only shown)
4	Air Cooled Transmission Oil	**8**	Inlet manifolds
	Cooler (ACTOC)	**9**	Air cleaner
5	Inlet manifold heater	**10**	Air inlet louvre

hull tanks to both the ME and the GUE by two identical electrically powered pumps running at half engine speed. Any fuel pumped which is excess to the requirement is returned to the tanks. The GUE fuel pump is also used to provide the fuel required by the engine smoke generation system. Should one pump fail, redundancy is ensured by the arrangement of the fuel lines which allow either pump to supply either engine.

Eight main fuel tanks are fitted in the rear of the hull, four either side, with two base tanks at the lower part of the hull, one for each engine. For identification purposes the tanks are numbered 1 to 4 from front to rear. Inside each main tank compartment is a flexible fabric reinforced rubber pannier which holds the fuel. Pipes allow fuel to flow between the four tanks in order to equalise the total fuel on each side when the vehicle is on level ground; fuel cannot travel easily from either side, however. The Explosafe or Safoam safety system fitted within the hull panniers adds to survivability but considerably slows down refuelling time compared with CR1; from empty to full takes around 22 minutes, and a 500-litre 'battle top-up' about half that. However, unlike its predecessor, CR2 has a refuel/defuel hydraulic pump system mounted on the right-hand No 4 (rear) tank, which allows the tank to refuel itself from the external drums, or to transfer fuel from itself to another, letting the crews top up from a broken-down vehicle, for example – a very useful tactical innovation. The refuel/defuel device on CR2 allows the contents of the two 205-litre external drums to be transferred to the main tanks in only about 5 minutes. Sender units are fitted to No 1 (front) and No 4 (rear) fuel tanks on either side allowing the driver to monitor fuel levels by means of a single gauge on the Driver's Instrument Panel (DIP).

BELOW On exercises the fuel drums are not always carried. Between the mountings for the drums are the infantry tank telephone, up to two D10 communication reels, a first-aid box and the small wire indicator (here with minetape attached) used by the commander to identify the centre of the hull rear to enable high-speed reversing. *(Courtesy RWxY)*

The controls for the refuel/defuel device are located within the infantry telephone box on the hull rear.

The main engine cooling system is an integral part of the powerpack cooling system; the ME centrifugal coolant pump circulates the cooling fluid (a mixture of water and anti-freeze to suit the environment) throughout the pack, including supplying the GUE coolant pump. The system employs liquid and air to absorb the excess heat generated within the powerpack compartment, and to expel it to

atmosphere through the louvred covers on the top engine deck. The liquid coolant circulates through the ME, GUE, the oil heat exchangers and the radiators. The airflow system works in conjunction with the liquid coolant. The three large fans at the rear of the powerpack draw air from outside through the radiator matrices, the Air Cooled Transmission Oil Cooler (ACTOC), the charge air cooler and through grilles in the rear top deck. The two outside fans are driven by a belt drive from the rear of the fan drive shaft which drives the centre fan. A condenser, part of the Crew Temperature Control System (CTCS), is mounted in the left-hand radiator; underneath the left-hand radiator is an electrically driven fan, used to cool the GUE when it is operating on its own. The main airflow through the radiators, about 90% of the total, reduces the temperature of the liquid coolant circulating within the radiators. The remaining 10% of the total airflow is drawn through the grilles in the rear compartment and ventilates the area between the cylinder banks on top of the ME. The liquid coolant is circulated around the system at 683 litres per minute by a centrifugal pump mounted on the ME; the pump is driven by an idler gear from the ME crankshaft. The GUE coolant circuit

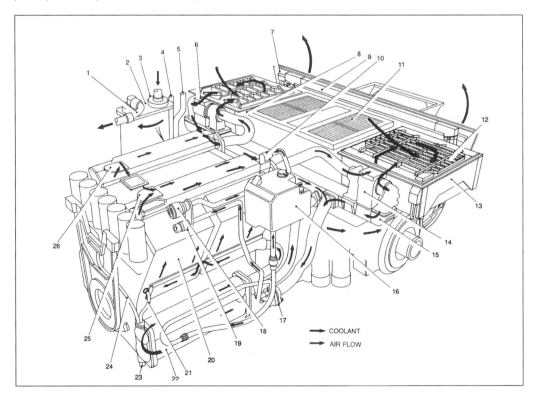

LEFT Two
Challenger 2s of
Badger 2RTR in
the hangars – the
large pipes hanging
from the ceiling are
used to extract the
exhaust gases from
the tank and out of
the hangars. On the
nearest tank the
mounting brackets
for the fuel drums
have been removed.
(Courtesy Andy Brend)

is coupled by flexible hoses fitted with quick-release self-sealing couplings to connect it into the ME circuit.

Two types of GUE have been used during the tank's service; early models used the Perkins P4.108, the same type as used on later marks of CR1, but this was superseded by the 404C-22.[26] This was because by 2006 a number of obsolescence issues with the P4.108 had come to light, and BAE were instructed by the MoD to source an alternative engine. This was developed from the Extel Systems Wedel (ESW) Auxiliary Power Unit based on the Perkins 404C engine, which was used to drive an ESW generator capable of delivering an output of 600A. This was seen as very useful, should future development require an increased GUE output. The GUE is located in the left front of the engine compartment. Both types of GUE are four-stroke, four-cylinder diesel compression-ignition engines, and are able to supply electrical power through a 350A generator even when the ME is not running.

LEFT Scots DG crews
working on their tanks
on the Alberta prairie
as part of the Medicine
Man exercises.
*(Courtesy Andrew
Totten)*

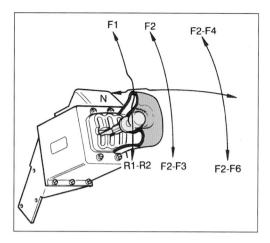

F1 F2 F2-F4
N
R1-R2 F2-F3 F2-F6

RIGHT The driver's gear selector in yellow, with the rubber gaiter shown sectionalised in grey and red.

Transmission and steering

The TN54 No 2 Mk 2 is a development of the transmission unit fitted to the CRARRV from 1990, and is a more capable and reliable unit than the TN37 gearbox used on Challenger 1. Final drive assemblies are mounted on either side of the hull rear, and transmit the drive from the gearbox to the tracks. Both assemblies are interchangeable. Each assembly comprises a single reduction gear, and uses a simple epicyclic gear train to give a reduction ratio of 4.875:1. A coupling assembly allows the drive from the gearbox to be disconnected from the final drive, to allow powerpack changes and to enable towing, and so on. Gear selection is by means of the selector mounted to the right-

hand side of the driver. Gears are selected in ranges according to the conditions: F1 (Forward first gear), F2, F2-3, F2-4, and F2-6. Reverse gear is selected as R1-2 only. First gear in forward is only normally used for tight and slow manoeuvring. The accelerator pedal is a conventional right-foot pedal; it provides a means of mechanically inputting desired vehicle speed via a transducer to the VICS, which transmits the information in digital form to the powerpack.

The steering control levers (tillers) are mounted on brackets welded to the cab floor, one either side of the driver's seat. The left-hand lever is mounted alongside the parking brake lever, and the right-hand lever is mounted next to the gear selector and emergency gear lever. The levers are configured in such a way that pulling back on one lever – causing the vehicle to turn in that direction – also causes the opposite lever to move forward, enabling one-handed steering if required. The brake foot pedal is mounted centrally forward of the cab, and consists of the pedal, a brake master cylinder, brake light switch, pedal return spring and the mounting bracket. Application of the pedal causes hydraulic fluid to move under pressure to a slave cylinder on the powerpack, operating the brakes. A parking brake lever mounted to the left of the driver applies the brakes mechanically by means of a ratchet action, and is locked 'on' by a button on the end of the brake lever handle. The button is pushed down and 'off' to release the brake.

Tracks and suspension

Forged aluminium alloy ventilated roadwheel discs are mounted in pairs on the wheel hubs which are on the end of stub axles. Each disc is fitted with a solid rubber tyre bonded to the wheel, and the roadwheels are secured in pairs to the wheel hub by ten roadwheel nuts. Two Hydraulic Track Tensioners (HTT) are fitted, one each side, at the front of the hull; correct track tension not only helps to prevent tracks being shed unnecessarily, it makes steering and turning easier and also affects both fuel consumption and track life. Each tensioner incorporates a cranked axle which mounts the idler wheel. Operation of the HTT causes the cranked axle to rotate, moving the idler

BELOW The layout of the driver's cab. The steering tillers (sticks) are in red, the gear selector in purple, the main brake is yellow and the accelerator is blue. The stowage for the driver's L85 rifle under the hull armour in front of his position is in green.

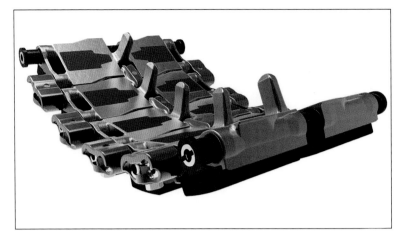

RIGHT CR2 track is a double-pin live track; here five links are shown connected. *(Courtesy Cook Defence Systems)*

wheel forwards, thus tensioning the track; this can only be done if either the ME or GUE are running and one of the generators is 'on-line'. Controls for the HTT are on the DIP and are operated by the driver from under armour; all the driver has to do is to select which side he requires on the directional control valve, and then hold the spring-loaded switch down (on) until the amber LED lamp underneath the switch illuminates. If the electrical system fails, a reversionary mode is provided using a hand-operated pump within the cab, but the vehicle speed is limited to 30kph until the fault is rectified. Supporting the top run of track are three guide rollers either side; the front roller is single- and the centre and rear rollers

BELOW Two members of Scots DG use a torque wrench to correctly tighten the bolts holding the sprocket ring to the hub. *(Courtesy Andrew Totten)*

BELOW RIGHT RTR crews track-bashing; even with the advent of power tools to help the crews, this activity still requires sweat, muscles and old-fashioned tools like crowbars. *(Courtesy Andy Brend)*

LEFT Tracks frequently have to be split on training exercises in order to conduct maintenance on the running gear; note how the front trackguard can be hinged up to make this easier. *(Courtesy Andy Brend)*

RIGHT A Challenger 2 requires an enormous amount of specialist tools and equipment, referred to as the CES or Complete Equipment Schedule.

are double-tyred. All have stub axles fitted on mounting brackets which are bolted on to the hull wall.

Unlike its predecessors, CR2 uses two-pin 'live' track; this means that the track links are sprung by the internal bushes, and prefer to curl rather than lie flat. The original track design for Challenger 2 was bespoke; it was initially hoped that the links could be made from aluminium to reduce weight, and which might make them longer-lasting than the steel alternative. The in-service tracks are made by Cook Defence Systems (formerly Blair-Catton) in Stanhope and are known as TR60 414FS, being authorised for use in December 2004. At least three slightly different versions have been used, although construction and maintenance is broadly similar. Normal track life is around 5,000km. Each link has two rubber track pads,

designed to protect European roads rather than having any function in combat; indeed, the pads are meant to be removed to improve grip before going into action. A number of different track designs have been tested on CR2 over the years in order to increase track life and improve grip, but as far as the crew – particularly the driver – are concerned, the biggest innovation was the provision of a set of power tools to use in 'track bashing', which make the work on the suspension and tracks much quicker and easier than on the predecessor vehicles, which all required the liberal application of muscle power and sledge hammers!

Electronics

The system is a nominal 24V DC, using six 100Ah low-maintenance batteries, two in the rear centre of the turret connected in series, and four in the hull connected in series/parallel. The vehicle (hull) batteries are fitted in pairs either side of the driver. All the batteries are charged when either the ME or GUE are running with their generators on-line. The hull battery master switchbox is one of the few direct carry-over items from Challenger 1 (and indeed Chieftain), modified and updated as required but visually almost identical; it is mounted to the right of the driver and includes the hull battery master switch.

The driver is provided with a Central Warning and Indicating system. This is based on the DIP and allows the driver to easily monitor changing conditions of both the powerpack and

BELOW Muscle power! A KRH trooper helps to guide the track off the idler wheel while the driver slowly edges the tank forward.
(Courtesy KRH)

GUE, and external lighting. The speedometer is a separate instrument, mounted to the right forward of the driver. The Driver's Warning Box (DWB) is mounted under the lip of the hatch and slightly left of centre within the driver's field of view when driving both opened up or closed down; the DWB lights up to show that there is an automotive warning on the DIP, to rapidly engage the driver's attention when he is busy. When an automotive system detects an alarm condition, it lights an individual fault-specific LED on the DIP, and also causes the master alarm LED on the DWB to flash red which is difficult for the driver to miss; the commander also receives the warning, which shows as the Hull Warning LED on the Commander's Control Panel. Once the driver has noticed the fault, and taken remedial action, he can cancel/reset the alarm using a switch on the DIP.

Starting the main engine

Two independent Butec 24V starter motors are fitted, designated 'A' and 'B', one for each cylinder bank. Prior to starting the ME, the GUE should be started and set to on-line, to prevent excessive load on the hull batteries. The starters are controlled by the Dual Starter switch on the DIP. If one of the starters is inoperative, the engine can still be started by isolating the faulty starter bank by setting the Dual Starter switch to the operating starter side only; periodically the operation of each individual starter should be confirmed by using this procedure.

To start the main engine (abbreviated procedure)
- Complete pre-start checks, AKA first parade. Rectify any faults.
- Start the GUE.
- Set the ME POWER ON switch to ON. Check that all relevant LED warning lights have illuminated.
- Set the IMH ON switch to ON. (If the engine is cold, set the RUN/START switch to START. Crank the engine for 30 seconds and set the switch to the central OFF position.)
- Set the ME FUEL/ON switch to ON.
- Set the RUN/START switch to START; crank the engine for up to 30 seconds or until it starts. If it fails to start wait 30 seconds

between attempts. If the vehicle does not start after five attempts report to REME.
- Once running, set the RUN/START switch to the central OFF position.
- Check that the LEDs for oil pressure, hyst boost and op brake have all extinguished.
- Reset the ALARM switch.
- A cold engine will fast idle between 725 and 875rpm for around 60 seconds until it reaches operating temperature, after which it will idle at 550–650rpm.

To stop the main engine
- Apply the parking brake, select neutral.
- Allow the engine to idle for two minutes.
- Set the RUN/START switch to the central OFF position.
- Set the IMH ON switch to OFF.
- Set the FUEL/ON switch to OFF.
- Set the POWER/ON switch to OFF.

Emergency starting and recovery

If the battery power is insufficient to start the tank, it can be easily slave-started using the issued slave lead connected to another tank; run the vehicle for at least two hours after slave starting to recharge the batteries. Alternatively it can be tow-started using another tank. It is important to tow-start in a straight line, without applying any steering, otherwise the transmission may be damaged. As soon as the towed vehicle starts, stop both vehicles immediately, and do not try to tow-start in reverse. The procedure is:

- Assemble and connect the rigid towing equipment from the items carried on both vehicles.
- Select gear range F2–F3 on the towing vehicle.
- Select emergency forward gear on the towed vehicle.
- Tow the casualty at a speed of about 12kph to start the engine.

Recovering a casualty vehicle can be done using either the rigid tow bars to form an A-frame, or the flexible hawsers carried on the hull sides; the latter is known as troop-level recovery. Where necessary, two recovery tanks

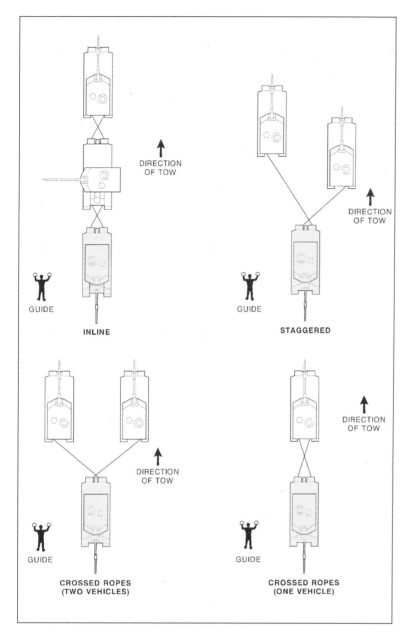

DIRECTION OF TOW

GUIDE

INLINE

DIRECTION OF TOW

GUIDE

STAGGERED

DIRECTION OF TOW

GUIDE

CROSSED ROPES (TWO VEHICLES)

DIRECTION OF TOW

GUIDE

CROSSED ROPES (ONE VEHICLE)

LEFT The towing illustration from the user handbook shows four different methods of conducting troop recovery using one or two other tanks.

can be used to maximise the recovery effort and the chances of a successful tow. These are shown in the accompanying diagram; note that for safety the guide positions himself where he can be seen by the crews of the vehicles involved, and far enough away from them to be safe should one of the hawsers snap and whiplash.

Emergency main engine stop

The commander can operate the stop button on the Commander's Control Panel (CCP) in an emergency. If the vehicle is stationary when it is operated, the main engine will switch off. If moving, the transmission will change down through the gears rapidly and bring the vehicle to an abrupt halt.

Fittings and ancillaries

The driver's sight mounting is another one of the rare items which is derived directly from Challenger 1; it can mount either the Driver's Unity Vision Periscope or, for night-time use, the L14A1 Driver's Night Vision Periscope, an image intensifier system. Changing from one to the other is the job of a few seconds, but cannot be done in an NBC environment as it would allow hazards outside to enter the crew compartment. External lighting and hull electrical services, controlled from the DIP and including blackout facilities, consists of head, side and tail lights, turn indicators, rear fog, brake, convoy light, a horn and a trailer socket. Internal lighting is provided for all crew members; this is a dimmable dual-colour system, which can be selected to either red or white light; five of these units are mounted within the turret. A gun breech light

LEFT The view through the driver's periscope as the mighty 120mm fires. The driver can often spot targets quickly as his low position allows targets to be silhouetted. *(Courtesy RWxY)*

is also mounted for the loader's use, and both commander and loader have flexible map lights. Externally, for road safety purposes, a flashing (rotating) amber beacon is fitted to the turret top alongside the meteorological sensor probe.

The Rotary Base Junction (RBJ) on the centre of the fighting compartment floor is the box by which permanent electrical connections are maintained between the hull and the rotating turret; ventilation (NBC and CTCS) for the crew is also routed through the RBJ. Spring-tensioned wire brush connectors within the outside rotating part of the RBJ are in contact with copper rings in the static part, allowing electrical signals to be maintained in both directions as the turret rotates.

Four skirting plates are fitted either side of the hull. These scalloped plates are primarily designed not to protect the hull – as these would almost always be replaced by DL2 appliqué side armour for operations – but rather to reduce the 'hot track' signature from the returning top run of track, as well as to reduce the amount of dust thrown into the engine air system. Early prototypes had a hull configuration that, externally at least, was not much changed from CR1, including full-depth bazooka plates, but these were quickly changed to reflect the in-service configuration.

Lethality

Turret and sighting systems

As noted, the hull was developed directly from that used on CR1, although the similarities are mainly visual and there is little commonality between CR1 and CR2.[27] The same cannot be said of the turret, which was designed using the Vickers Universal Turret from their Mk 7/2 design as the start point, and which looks very different from the CR1 turret. Two items which do directly carry forward from its predecessors are the ever-popular Boiling Vessel (BV), and the No 30 periscope fitted in the front turret roof for use by the loader; in essence, this is

LEFT **The 'met probe', shown in its raised position on the turret roof, gives local meteorological data to the fire control computer, making gunnery much more accurate.** (TM 10392-041)

BELOW **This tank is not carrying its fourth and rearmost bazooka plate – note also how spilled fuel has cleaned the rear quarter of the hull, and that the right-hand fuel tank is not fitted to allow an oil drip tray to be carried instead.** (Courtesy Andy Brend)

ABOVE **The business end. The muzzle of the rifled L30 120mm gun on a 2RTR tank in Iraq in 2003.** *(Courtesy RTR)*

the same design as that used on Centurion albeit in Mk 6 form. The TI system is still based upon the proven design used on Chieftain and CR1 in an updated TOGS 2 format, but otherwise, the turret is very different, with a new main armament, co-axial MG, sighting and fire control system, gun control equipment, muzzle reference system, and so on – even the method of mounting the 120mm gun is new, featuring a conventional mantlet with widely spaced trunnions which make shooting on the move more accurate. As the mantlet elevates and depresses, the spaces that appear above and below are protected from splinters and

fragmentation ingress by a combination of rigid and flexible sections.

The main sighting systems used are as follows:

■ **Commander's Primary Sight (CPS).** This is a roof-mounted stabilised sight positioned on the top of the turret in order to give full panoramic vision; it is used for visual engagements only, and does not incorporate a night-viewing capability. The commander can select between low and high magnification. Mounted within an armoured protective hood, it incorporates a laser rangefinder and is made by SFIM of France. To give the commander all-round vision without having to use the CPS, eight periscopes are mounted around his cupola.

■ **Gunner's Primary Sight (GPS).** This is mounted in front of the CPS, and provides the gunner with a gyroscopically stabilised sight picture. Made by SAGEM in conjunction with Barr & Stroud, it incorporates a laser rangefinder able to calculate ranges up to 9,995m, with an accuracy of ± 5m; the gunner can select between low and high magnification. The external part of the GPS is protected by an armoured hood. To the left of the GPS is the No 374 Mk 3 gunner's unity vision (×1) periscope. In order to allow the GPS to account for ballistic offsets, the line of sight can be moved left or right by up to 7°.

RIGHT **Firing! A HESH projectile speeds from the gun at nearly 700m/s. The large tube on the turret rear is part of the Live Firing Monitoring Equipment used on ranges.** *(Courtesy RTR)*

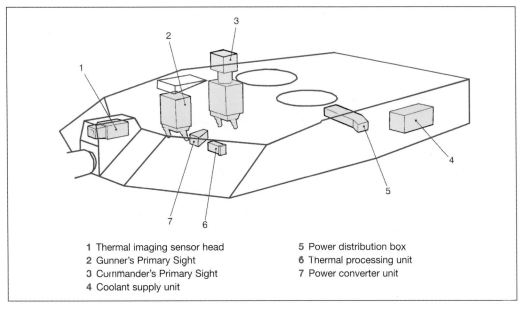

1 Thermal imaging sensor head
2 Gunner's Primary Sight
3 Commander's Primary Sight
4 Coolant supply unit

5 Power distribution box
6 Thermal processing unit
7 Power converter unit

■ **Gunner's Auxiliary Sight (GAS)**. In case the GPS is completely inoperative, a Vickers Instruments L30 telescope is mounted through the gun mantlet for emergency use. This uses a graticule pattern similar to that used in the gunner's sight of CR1, allowing the gunner to accurately engage targets using all natures of ammunition should the GPS be out of action. It is also used to check that the gun/sights relationship is still correct using the Muzzle Reference System (MRS).

■ **TOGS.** The thermal imaging sight is the TISH (Thermal Imaging Sensor Head) mounted in an armoured cover (known as a barbette) on the top of the mantlet; crews are constantly reminded that this is not just a night sight, but can – and should – be used throughout the day. On CR1 the TISH was offset to the right of the axis of the bore of the 120mm which caused technical difficulties in aligning the gun, laser rangefinder and TISH line of sight. By mounting the TISH above the gun on CR2 this is partially remedied.

■ **The Fire Control Computer (FCC) and Fire Control Panel (FCP)**. The computer is mounted on the turret turntable underneath the commander's seat; it is accessed via the FCP, located to the right of the CPS. It

allows the commander to input data and monitor outputs from the fire control system, including messages from the Built-In Test Equipment (BITE). At the top of the FCP is a large display window, with a keypad and control buttons underneath.

The solid-state GCE was made by Marconi and was developed directly from the Centaur 1 system used on the Vickers Mk 7/2 MBT. This is a responsive electrical system which is preferred by the British Army, as hydraulic systems can be damaged quite easily and high-pressure fluid can cause terrible injuries for the crew. The GCE controls the gun in both elevation and traverse, giving powered control of the turret for both the commander and gunner; the other two crewmen have safety switches to prevent dangerous gun and turret movement – one full rotation of the turret under power only takes around 12 seconds. During an engagement the GCE is also responsible for positioning the gun and turret in the correct position for firing in response to demands made from the fire control equipment. This is

ABOVE A close-up of the Commander's Primary Sight hood, with the washer nozzle which can only be used with the sight in the front position. Note the pinkish shade to the cupola periscope.
(TM 10392-034)

BELOW A Badger 2RTR tank shows off the turret sights as it fords through a water obstacle. The CPS and GPS sight covers are open, while the armoured flaps protecting the GAS and TISH remain shut.
(Courtesy RTR)

RIGHT The gunner's view using low magnification; the red circle around the aiming mark indicates the field of view once high magnification is selected.

known as coincidence firing, in which the gun controller (the commander at the start of a hunter/killer engagement, then handed over to the gunner) lays a moving dot of light on to the centre of the target, and the GCE is responsible for accurately aligning the gun and turret with this point of aim. This ensures that the gun will not fire due to the firing circuits being isolated until it is correctly positioned to hit the target, as determined by the Fire Control Computer. (This contrasts dramatically with previous fire control systems, in which the gunner physically controlled the GCE and thus the gun, and the sighting system was mechanically slaved to the gun.) This makes the firing sequence quicker, as the gun will fire as soon as coincidence is achieved, and also makes firing on the move much simpler and more accurate. Two other concepts are

important: Aided Lay and Align. The former assists the gun director (either commander or gunner) to maintain a constant track of a moving target prior to lasing and firing. The Fire Control System applies an automatic tracking rate to assist the gun director, and also desensitises the thumb controller to allow fine adjustments to be made. Align is used when the CPS is operating in independent mode as

BELOW An RTR tank firing at dusk using TOGS; the tracer element from the projectile has ricocheted off after striking the target. *(Courtesy RTR)*

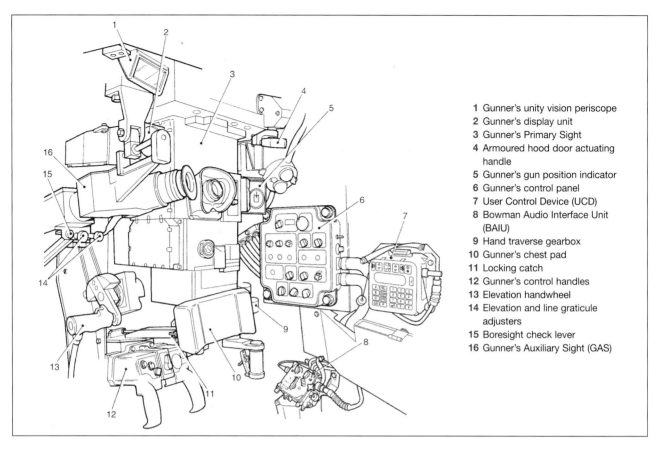

1 Gunner's unity vision periscope
2 Gunner's display unit
3 Gunner's Primary Sight
4 Armoured hood door actuating handle
5 Gunner's gun position indicator
6 Gunner's control panel
7 User Control Device (UCD)
8 Bowman Audio Interface Unit (BAIU)
9 Hand traverse gearbox
10 Gunner's chest pad
11 Locking catch
12 Gunner's control handles
13 Elevation handwheel
14 Elevation and line graticule adjusters
15 Boresight check lever
16 Gunner's Auxiliary Sight (GAS)

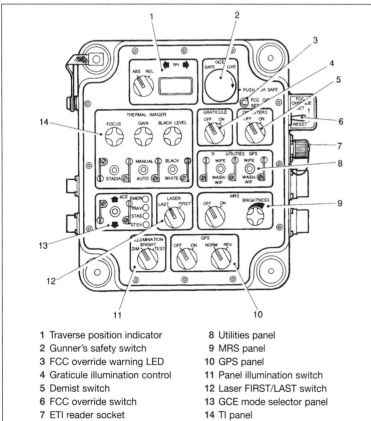

1 Traverse position indicator
2 Gunner's safety switch
3 FCC override warning LED
4 Graticule illumination control
5 Demist switch
6 FCC override switch
7 ETI reader socket
8 Utilities panel
9 MRS panel
10 GPS panel
11 Panel illumination switch
12 Laser FIRST/LAST switch
13 GCE mode selector panel
14 TI panel

ABOVE The major components in the gunner's station, with the gun control handles mounted underneath the GPS.

part of the hunter/killer technique; pressing the align switch on the commander's controller causes the gun and turret to move at high speed to align with the CPS and also switches the GPS to high magnification, in order to allow the gunner to take over the shoot.

The controllers used by both commander and gunner are often compared to those used on popular gaming controllers, and this is no surprise – much work has gone into deciding the best ergonomics for such items, and the efficiency, comfort and ease of use of these make the crewman's job so much easier. The earliest design had these flexibly mounted on a duplex (twin-axis) basis, but it was decided that this might be difficult to operate when moving

LEFT The layout of switches and controls on the Gunner's Control Panel.

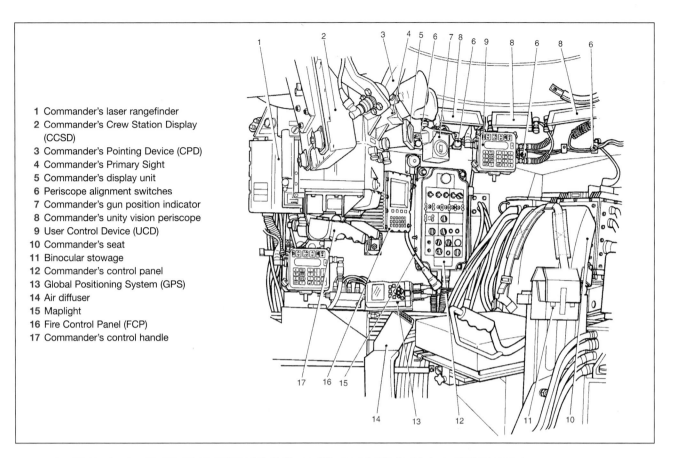

1 Commander's laser rangefinder
2 Commander's Crew Station Display (CCSD)
3 Commander's Pointing Device (CPD)
4 Commander's Primary Sight
5 Commander's display unit
6 Periscope alignment switches
7 Commander's gun position indicator
8 Commander's unity vision periscope
9 User Control Device (UCD)
10 Commander's seat
11 Binocular stowage
12 Commander's control panel
13 Global Positioning System (GPS)
14 Air diffuser
15 Maplight
16 Fire Control Panel (FCP)
17 Commander's control handle

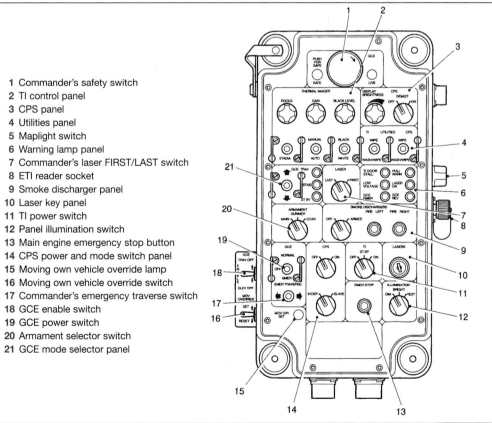

1 Commander's safety switch
2 TI control panel
3 CPS panel
4 Utilities panel
5 Maplight switch
6 Warning lamp panel
7 Commander's laser FIRST/LAST switch
8 ETI reader socket
9 Smoke discharger panel
10 Laser key panel
11 TI power switch
12 Panel illumination switch
13 Main engine emergency stop button
14 CPS power and mode switch panel
15 Moving own vehicle override lamp
16 Moving own vehicle override switch
17 Commander's emergency traverse switch
18 GCE enable switch
19 GCE power switch
20 Armament selector switch
21 GCE mode selector panel

ABOVE The layout of the commander's station; with the introduction of the Bowman communications system the amount of room was reduced, with a commensurate increase in the number of controls he has to be a master of.

LEFT A close-up of the CCP, similar but not identical to the GCP.

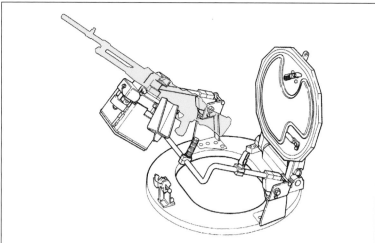

ABOVE The early and unloved D-ring mounting used on early tanks.

BELOW The D ring was replaced during production by the simpler pintle mount, which was later retrofitted to most of the early tanks.

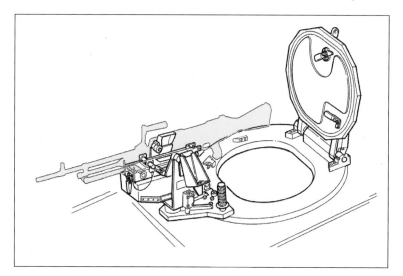

cross-country at speed, and fixed handles were fitted instead. The two controllers are not the same, as the controls and switches on them are used for different functions. However, both have the necessary controls to allow the commander or gunner to operate as gun director, moving the gun and turret, lasing the target and completing the engagement by firing and if necessary making corrections.

Unlike Chieftain or Challenger 1 and indeed Centurion and Conqueror, the commander's cupola on CR2 is fixed. There is no need for it to rotate as it is fitted with a 360° rotating (panoramic) sight. To provide all-round non-magnified vision for the commander when closed down, eight No 500 Mk 3 periscopes are mounted around the circumference.[28] The cupola hatch can be opened to an umbrella position, giving a 'peep out' facility while still well protected, as well as vertical and fully open positions.

The loader's hatch, unlike its predecessors, is rotatable, in order to make best use of the 7.62mm GPMG mounted on it. To prevent the MG being fired into the area occupied by the commander, an inhibit switch operates when it is pointing over the right side of the turret; this can be overridden in an emergency. Two types of mounting have been fitted: a D-ring tubular steel mounting, and a pintle mounting. The loader's MG mount was originally intended to be a simple pintle mount, but on early trials the users did not like it as it was difficult to use over a wide enough arc, and a D ring mounting made by Helio was substituted instead. Once in service, this in turn proved to be unpopular and a different type of pintle mount was designed to replace it, after around 50 or so tanks had been built with the D-ring mounting.[29]

Firepower

In early 1988, only a year or so after VDS had first proposed CR2 as the Chieftain replacement, questions were being asked as to whether a future 140mm smoothbore gun (known as FTMA or Future Tank Main Armament) could be mounted into the turret. This calibre was chosen as it had been assessed to be the maximum ammunition size that could be used within a conventional turret without an autoloader being necessary; it was also attractive in terms of the potential penetration that could be achieved from such a powerful gun, and was assessed as being necessary to deal with the estimated 750mm+ protection on FST 3. To mount this size of gun required raising the gun trunnions and hence the turret roof and overall height, and it was also thought that the only GCE system that could cope with such a heavy gun and turret would be hydraulic, which the British designers were doctrinally opposed to for survivability reasons.

Additionally, due to the sheer size of 140mm rounds, the majority of the ammunition would have to be stowed in the turret bustle, again something that the designers were not keen to do, as was the requirement for some form of mechanical assistance for the loader, complicating design and slowing down the rate of fire. As attractive as a 140mm gun was, for these reasons the project was halted, although it was hoped that in the future, such a gun, sometimes referred to as either the Lightweight Armament System (LWAS) or European Powder Gun (EPG), could be developed using an agreed common chamber profile allowing it to be adopted by the UK, USA, France and Germany. During the development phase, just in case the tank would be re-gunned at some later date, the gun rotor and cradle was designed with the intention of mounting a gun of up to 140mm calibre. At around 1996 or 1997 VDS would sometimes show visitors a scale model of a CR2 mounting a rifled 140mm gun firing three-piece ammunition from an autoloader and complete with a muzzle brake, but the idea remained as a wooden model only.

Developing the L30 gun

The L30 gun used in Challenger 2 is in many ways an evolutionary descendant of the L11A5 gun used on Challenger 1 and developed by ROF Nottingham. The L30 came via at least two experimental guns. These both featured a new split breech block and a different form

of obturation and were developed as the XL28M1 and then the XL32M1.[30] As noted earlier, MBT 80 never saw service and existed only in pre-prototype form used to evaluate concepts, but at least one of these mounted the experimental XL32 120mm rifled gun in 1979, although details of its development are scarce; it is known that another one was also mounted in Mk 1 Chieftain 02EB38, but externally it could not be distinguished from the in-service L11.[31] It is, however, reasonable to surmise that many features first tried out on the XL28/32 found their way on to the L30 gun on CR2, particularly the split breech design with a Crossley obturator pad, which was much safer than the twin-seal ring design used on the L11 (trials engineers deliberately tried to make the pad obturator fail by methods such as scoring it with abrasives and metal tools, but it remained serviceable).

The early versions of the new gun adopted on CR2 were designated as the XL30E1 to -E3, and these were seen as an evolutionary development of the successful L11 gun rather than as a revolutionary new system, and it can be assumed that the XL28/32 represented intermediate stages in the development line. The new split breech block design was seen as combining the virtues of a quick-firing sliding breech with the safety advantages of the Crossley pad obturation system. A crucial development, and one which is not immediately apparent, is that the L30 was designed to operate at significantly higher pressures than its L11 predecessor. Although

BELOW The experimental XL32 breech as fitted to the Bovington Tank Museum MBT 80 – this was an interim design that led to the adoption of the in-service L30 120mm gun.

the figures are classified, the percentage increase in chamber pressure is in the region of 25%, allowing much more powerful KE projectiles to be developed.

In January 1990 full safety approval was given to the new L30 high-pressure gun, allowing it to be confirmed as the main armament in CR2. (In mid-1988 investigations had been made into retrofitting the L30 gun on to CR1; this was estimated to cost £960k per tank, or over £400m for the fleet, which was just for the gun without any fire control enhancements. This was quickly and correctly discarded.) In June 1991 a number of pre-production guns along with just over 5,000 pre-production projectiles were delivered. In the same year a number of problems associated

with the design of the Tube Vent Electric (TVE) were encountered, as were problems with the chrome plating of the gun barrel, designed to greatly extend barrel life but which caused manufacturing difficulties that had to be overcome. By August 1992 140 guns from the initial production batch had been delivered, which was completed in December of the same year, allowing the trials programme to be speeded up as these guns could be fitted to other turrets or ground-mounted test rigs at various experimental establishments and ranges. By the middle of 1993 the use of an aluminium-copper base to the TVE in place of the problematic beryllium-copper had resolved the problems with TVE 'blowback' and toxicity.

The L30 gun described

The main armament (MA) of CR2 is the breech loading 120mm L30A1 gun, supported in a sophisticated mounting system. The gun is breech loaded with separate ammunition, meaning that the projectile is loaded first, followed by the fully combustible propellant charge, generally referred to as the bag charge. Bag charges are made more durable and water-resistant by enclosing them in a rigid cylinder of Nitro-Cellulose Kraft (NCK). The bag charge is ignited by an electrically initiated TVE, fed by an Automatic Tube Loader (ATL) from a ten-tube magazine on the rear of the breech ring. To prevent ejected vent tubes from damaging radio equipment and to stop them potentially jamming moving components, a TVE shield is fitted, hanging from the roof and behind the breech. This consists of a long padded shield made from an aramid fibre enclosing rope lagging, with a 3in-deep pocket at the bottom to catch the spent TVEs. Inside the top of the shield are two hooks; these are to allow the commander and gunner or loader to stow their crewman's helmets – a lot of thought has gone into this tank!

The L30 swage auto-frettaged rifled barrel and its plain chamber is made from a monobloc of Electro-Slag Refined (ESR) steel, with a screw thread externally at the rear for attachment to the breech ring. The chamber has a tapered seating at the front for the projectile, and a recess at the rear for the obturator pad on the breech block. Both the bore and chamber

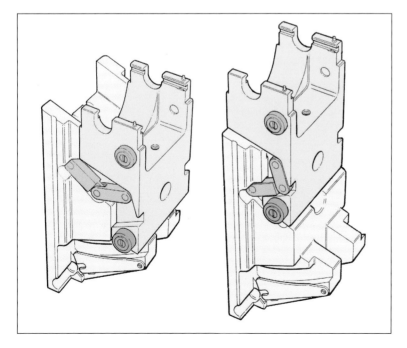

are chromium plated to give much greater wear characteristics – usually referred to as 'barrel life' – than its ancestors. At the top of the muzzle is a machined surface for the MRS mirror and protective shroud. The armament is mounted in a steel cradle, attached to the turret on either side by rotor pins, acting as trunnions and allowing the mounting cradle to be elevated and depressed using the elevation gearbox. The barrel passes through the heavily armoured mantlet, fitted to the front of the cradle. The mantlet also houses the TISH in an armoured box (the barbette) above the barrel and the MRS light source, as well as apertures for the co-ax MG and the GAS. Within the cradle are greased copper alloy liners, allowing the gun to slide forwards and backwards during recoil (rearwards) and run-out (forwards). Attached to the cradle are the components of the recoil system, which hold the gun in the fully forward position at all angles of elevation, and absorb recoil energy during firing.

The breech consists of a vertically sliding split breech block, which uses a neoprene Crossley pad-type obturator, rather than the large single-piece breech block with machined steel obturators of its predecessor, the L11 gun. Both upper and lower parts of the breech block are stepped in shape, and are joined by a hinged link assisted by rollers working within cam paths. A stainless steel loading tray

incorporating a charge retainer (to prevent the charge slipping rearwards when the gun is elevated and the breech open) is mounted on the top of the upper breech block. The breech is opened by the Breech Mechanism Lever on the left side of the ring. During firing the breech is opened automatically as part of run-out by a semi-automatic cam. Closing the breech is carried out either manually using the Breech Closing Lever, or, during an engagement, semi-automatically by pulling the loader's firing guard to the rear.

The recoil system is attached to the gun cradle and yoke; it is very similar to that used on the L11 gun – why change something that works perfectly well? It provides what amounts to an elastic link between the gun,

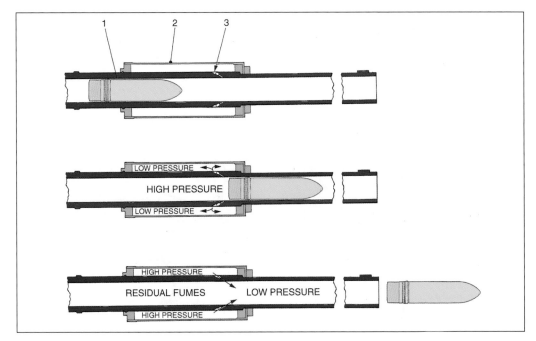

which can move fore and aft, and the cradle, which cannot. A hydropneumatic recuperator cylinder holds the gun in the correct fully run-out position even when the gun is fully elevated, and also returns the gun to run-out after recoil has been absorbed. This function is carried out by two oil-filled buffers which absorb energy and restrict the length of recoil to the correct amount. A replenisher accepts excess oil when the system heats up, and returns it to the buffer cylinders as it cools.

A cylindrical 289mm-diameter fume extractor is mounted at about the midpoint of the barrel. Two sets of thermal sleeves are fitted around the external parts of the barrel either side of the fume extractor to maintain accuracy as the barrel heats up during firing. Each set is made from a rigid phenolic resin reinforced with glass fibre. The two halves of each sleeve are sealed by silicone rubber strips and internal friction pads prevent movement fore and aft. A series of seven clamps hold the sleeves in place. The recesses along the length of each sleeve are there to add strength and rigidity to the assembly.

120mm ammunition

Members of the Royal Artillery have an expression which states that the weapon is not the gun, but the ammunition – and they are right. All of the money and effort that goes into design, development, buying the tank, equipping it with modern systems, training the crew and so on, is there with the intention of delivering (or indeed threatening to deliver) the ammunition carried on to the target as efficiently as possible. So it is worthwhile looking at the impressive family of ammunition used on Challenger 2 in some detail here – indeed VDS, in one of their presentational posters for CR2, made the claim that a projectile from the 120mm gun was the equivalent in energy terms to being struck by a 5-tonne elephant moving at 230kph!

Much of the ammunition used on CR2 originated from the L11 120mm gun fitted to Chieftain and then Challenger 1. This included the L31A7 HESH and L34A2 Smoke rounds,

120mm L30 data	
Length overall including ATL	6,987mm
Length of fume extractor	735mm
Weight overall including thermal sleeves	1,805kg
Weight breech block	71kg
Rifling	Right-hand, 32 grooves
Bore diameter	120mm nominal (119.38mm actual)

as well as the original training rounds known as DS/T and SH/P.[32] (Descriptions of the ammunition family for the L11 can be found in the Haynes *Chieftain* and *Challenger 1* Manuals.) The first type of Armour-Piercing Fin-Stabilised Discarding Sabot (APFSDS) ammunition used on CR2 was the L23A1 tungsten alloy projectile. This was originally developed in the days of Chieftain as an Operational Emergency (OE) ammunition, when it was realised that the existing L15 APDS projectile would be unable to defeat the new T64/72 series at battle ranges. Whereas T62 was fairly lightly armoured, the new T64 and T72 tanks were assessed to have much better protection and which caused a rapid investigation into the armour mounted on the new tanks, including the use of ERA. Assessments made in the late 1970s came up with the following figures:

	T62	T64/T72
Glacis	100mm RHA @ 60°	100mm RHA @ 68°
	(Equivalent pathway = 200mm)	(Equivalent pathway = 267mm)
Turret front	230mm	250mm

The in-service L15 APDS was quite capable of defeating such armour thicknesses, but by 1978 a reassessment of T64/72 increased the protection believed to be on the glacis to a new figure of around 400mm, which meant that L15 was rendered obsolete, and a new projectile was urgently needed.[33] This led to the production of GSR (OE) 3758, which was endorsed in January 1978, and which demanded the introduction of a projectile capable of defeating the frontal armour of T64/72 at a range of at least 2,000m. Fortunately, ROF Birtley had been working on a 105mm APFSDS projectile as a private venture. This was able to be scaled up and modified to make it suitable for three-piece ammunition, leading to the introduction of the L23 APFSDS projectile with L8 bag charge by late 1983 – an indication of just how complex and time-consuming producing new ammunition can be. The L23 penetrator was made of a compound of tungsten, nickel and iron. Even before the L23 was in service, in July 1980 another GSR (OE) was issued; this was numbered as 3851 and led to the development of the second-generation L26A1 APFSDS, using a DU core to increase its effectiveness and which was first used in anger (as was the L23) in the Gulf War of 1991. This again came about because of a reassessment of the threat. In this case it was the fielding of T80,

ABOVE Crews conducting the ever-popular physical labour known as ammo-bashing; a sea of 'Deep Saxe Blue' SH/P projectiles are laid on top of their storage boxes. *(Courtesy Andrew Totten)*

BELOW Bag charges are passed into the tank – it is the job of the loader to stow the ammunition correctly within the tank. *(Courtesy Andy Brend)*

believed to have a glacis thickness of 500mm of RHA, with an equivalent shot pathway of 577mm; it was introduced under the code name JERICO. L26, when fired from the older L11 gun on Challenger 1, was about 15% better in penetration terms than the L23, with improved consistency characteristics making it more accurate as well. When fired from CR2 using the higher-pressure L30 120mm gun, the increase was closer to 25%. Later still, the even more effective third-generation L27A1 APFSDS (with L16 or L17 bag charges) was introduced, and a training projectile known as the L29A1 was also brought into service in 2003;[34] in the fire order this is referred to as DS/T, the name previously given to the APDS training projectile which is no longer in service. The ammunition family developed specifically by Royal Ordnance for the L30 gun was known as CHARM (Challenger Armament) 3; as well as developing new projectiles, CHARM 3 also delivered a new, safer family of propellants used in the bag charges. Concerns had been raised over the volatility of the existing AX propellant used in the L8 bag charge in a turret fire, so a new design known as FX propellant was developed, leading to a much-reduced risk of explosion. Thus the L27 shot with the L16 bag charge is referred to as CHARM 3 ammunition, and with the L17 bag charge it is designated CHARM 3A1.

On the L30 the TVE (invariably referred to as the vent tube) is the TVE L4A2, a 13mm tube (as opposed to the larger 15.9mm TVE used on the L11 gun). The TVE is made of two metals; the forward part is of brass, needed to allow the tube to radially expand on firing to provide a gas seal in the breech, with an aluminium/bronze rear part screwed on to it which adds strength to the tube and allows it to be extracted without splitting and jamming the chamber. This replaced the original L4A1 TVE, which was made of beryllium-copper but which was found to present an unacceptable toxicity hazard when fired.

APFSDS and the long rod penetrator

A long rod penetrator is characterised as a projectile with a high length to diameter (l/d) ratio. Variants of the long rod have been developed for weapons with a calibre of 30mm upwards, with the most penetrative being utilised on the main gun of modern MBTs. The performance of the long rod penetrator is usually described in terms of the ratio of the projectile length to its penetrative performance against RHA. The performance of the long rod is dependent upon its l/d ratio, the density of the material it is made from, and the velocity at which it impacts its target. The l/d ratio is a critical factor in the design of the long rod. If the ratio is too low, the penetrator will lack kinetic energy, reducing its performance. If it is too high, the performance of the projectile is reduced as 'bending moments' on the rod will occur during shot travel and upon impact with the target; in other words the rod will flex as it moves. This will cause the rod to bend and possibly break upon impact.

The principal mechanism by which a long rod perforates armour is by producing a high kinetic energy density on the small contact surface

RIGHT The L23 APFSDS projectile sectionalised. The (grey) petals support the central core in the barrel, and the (green) fins that provide stability in flight are protected by the combustible protective case (red).

SHOT 120 mm Tk APFSDS L23A1

- NOSE TIP
- ALUMINIUM RING
- CORE
- CENTRING BAND
- TRI-SEGMENTED SABOT
- BUTTRESS THREADING
- BAND SEAL
- DRIVING BAND
- END SEALING RING
- TAIL FIN
- COMBUSTIBLE FIN CASE
- RETAINING SCREW

with the armour. The penetrative performance of the long rod has a greater correlation to the density of the projectile material rather than its strength, thus the most common materials used in long rod penetrators are tungsten alloys or DU, owing to their high densities. The performance of the long rod has been effectively approximated using hydrodynamic modelling, as plastic deformation of both the steel armour and the long rod is seen during the impact, although it is fair to say that the mechanism of penetration is still not fully understood. In broad terms the material within the rod is consumed as it penetrates through the armour thickness (rather than simply punching through), and the very high strike velocity means that the armour tends to flow out of the way of the incoming rod in a manner similar to hydraulics, hence the term hydrodynamic. Upon overmatching the armour of an MBT, significant heat is generated in the fragments and spall, which can ignite any flammable or energetic material within it (such as propellant or munitions stored in the vehicle). This can cause a catastrophic chain reaction within the vehicle which produces extremely high temperatures and pressures. This can result in the displacement of the turret, or in some cases complete destruction of the vehicle. It is this ignition of energetic material within the target vehicle, rather than any pyrophoric effect of the long rod material, that ultimately causes the catastrophic effect upon the vehicle.

In order to gain the maximum amount of kinetic energy density upon impact, long rod penetrators are designed to be a smaller diameter than the barrel of the weapon they are fired from. Typically, the velocities required have to be well in excess of 1.5km/s. In order to achieve these velocities, the long rods are fired using a sabot. The sabot provides obturation (gas sealing) between the projectile and the barrel wall of the weapon. This allows the expanding gases from the burning propellant of the main charge to accelerate the long rod down the barrel. To improve the stability of the long rod in flight, fins are attached to the rear of the penetrator. These stabilise the rod in flight in the same manner as the fins on an arrow. Upon exiting the barrel, the sabot will split and fall away from the long rod, to reduce drag on the projectile, allowing the long rod with its fins to stabilise in flight and move at very high speed to the target.

The stability of the long rod can be adversely affected by the spin imparted by a rifled gun, as too much spin is counter-productive – a projectile can only be spin- or fin- stabilised, not both. For this reason, most guns on MBTs are smoothbore. In the UK, the main gun on the Challenger 2 tank is rifled to improve accuracy with other munition types. Britain is one of very few countries (along with India) in the modern era to field an MBT to have been developed with a rifled barrel. To reduce the effect of the rifling, a slipping driving band is incorporated into the sabot. This is able to rotate around the sabot in the barrel, much reducing the spin imparted on to the long rod during its travel along the barrel and allowing it to fin-stabilise in flight.

High Explosive Squash Head (HESH) – a peculiarly British ammunition?

The British are often criticised by other nations for the insistence on retaining the HESH capability, which affects the choice of main armament used, whereas almost all other nations use HEAT as the secondary main armament round. The reasons for this are partly historical, as HESH was a British invention, developed by Vickers-Armstrong during the Second World War to defeat reinforced concrete fortifications, and it was found, more by luck than judgement, to be extremely good at penetrating armour plate. It was reintroduced into British service in the late 1940s after concerns that the in-service APDS ammunition could not defeat the frontal armour of the heaviest Soviet tanks, whereas HESH could. But aside from the historical – verging on emotional – aspect, the other reasons are much more practical, as HESH is a particularly versatile round. It is able to defeat a reasonable amount of armour, as well as producing high-explosive effects nearly as good as a dedicated HE round. Indeed, the Australians used HESH to great effect as an HE nature in the jungle during the Vietnam War.

Additionally, when engaging armour, even if HESH is not capable of destroying (penetrating) the target, it often damages sensitive equipment

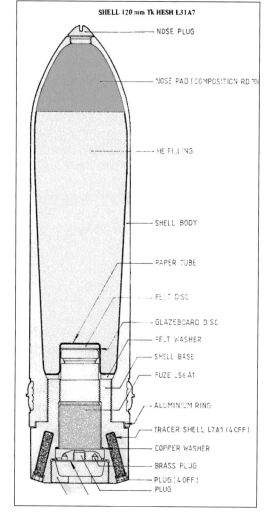

SHELL 120 mm Tk HESH L31A7

- NOSE PLUG
- NOSE PAD (COMPOSITION RD 19
- HE FILLING
- SHELL BODY
- PAPER TUBE
- FELT DISC
- GLAZEBOARD DISC
- FELT WASHER
- SHELL BASE
- FUZE L56 A1
- ALUMINIUM RING
- TRACER SHELL L7A1 (4 OFF)
- COPPER WASHER
- BRASS PLUG
- PLUG (4 OFF)
- PLUG

such as sights, radio items and delicate electrical components, as well as breaking tracks and damaging the suspension. And it has three other attributes that are not often realised. Firstly, its terminal effects are virtually independent of range, whereas with KE rounds the penetration characteristics drop off with increasing range. With HESH the penetration achieved at 5,000m is the same as at 500m. Secondly, because it needs to be fired fairly slowly for it to function correctly (as described below), it can be observed in flight and on impact, allowing corrections to be made if it misses the target, whereas with KE ammunition the high velocities generally mean that if the target is missed the gunner cannot identify where the round went in relation to the target. So, if the fire control system is damaged, or the gun/sight relationship is lost and cannot be restored, KE shooting is virtually pointless, whereas HESH can still be used. Lastly, it was designed to defeat concrete and is still extremely useful as an anti-structure round, particularly when supporting infantry in built-up areas.

The reasons for this are found in the way that a HESH round is constructed, and how it behaves when it hits the target. Externally it looks much like many other traditional explosive shells, although one feature distinguishes it from ordinary HE rounds, which is the lack of a nose fuse. This is one of its strengths, in that the fuse is inside the projectile at the base, and does not require complicated and time-consuming setting by the loader. The projectile is made up of a very thin-walled steel case which is largely filled with high explosive (HE); the walls are deliberately made as thin as possible – just enough to withstand the shock of firing and maintain the ballistic shape – in order for the shell to function correctly when it hits the target. The forwardmost portion within the curved ogive at the nose of the projectile is filled with an inert substance. The ammunition is fired fairly slowly, around 700m/s or less; this gives it a longish time of flight at battle ranges, 2 or 3 seconds, which means that it is much more susceptible to be affected by wind on its way to the target. The chances of a first-round hit are thus less than for APFSDS with its much flatter trajectory, although its slower speed and tracer means that its flight and impact can be seen by the gunner, allowing corrections to be made until the target is hit.

When attacking armour, the slow impact velocity and thin shell walls allow the projectile to rupture and 'pancake' against the armour, forming a roughly circular disc of explosive of about two or three times the diameter of the original calibre – when attacking armour the only function of the steel shell body is to contain the explosive and fuse and deliver it ballistically to the target; it forms no part of the defeat mechanism. It is at the point of impact that the need for the inert filling in the nose is apparent, as this prevents the shock of impact detonating the HE filling too early. As the projectile continues to pancake against the armour the base fuse is driven forward by momentum until it strikes the armour of the target, and at this point functions, starting the explosive train which detonates the main explosive pancake that is up against the armour – at the moment immediately before detonation looking very much like the most dangerous cowpat imaginable! The explosion causes a series of shockwaves to travel through the armour from outside to inside, and when the first of these passes into the void behind the inner face, a reverse wave is caused to pass back through the armour in the other direction, from inside to outside. When this reverse wave meets the next incoming wave, the crystalline armour structure fractures, and the impetus of the incoming explosive waves forces the fractured slab of armour to be propelled into the void where it flies around at speed, damaging or destroying all in its path until its energy is expended. This means that the internal systems inside the tank, including ammunition and the crew, are likely to be struck, with devastating consequences. Blast effects (overpressure) within the target are also significant. If the armour struck is fairly thin, as found on lighter AFVs such as APCs, the HESH will not pancake in this way but will simply penetrate the armour by brute force before detonating within the target, with devastating effects. When the attack on armour trials against prototype Challenger 2 turret shells were conducted, it was found that HESH was the one type of ammunition that came closest to damaging the turret structure, due to the violence of the explosion, although it could not penetrate it.

As a secondary round, it is desirable that the ammunition functions as closely as possible to a conventional HE round, making it useful when engaging non-armoured targets, including infantry. When a HESH round is used against a non-armoured target, the fuse operates in much the same way as described above, although in many cases the shell body will not rupture and pancake, but remains intact. When the fuse functions, the explosive fill detonates, splintering the steel shell body and the blast wave created spreads the fragments over a wide area. In fact, the blast effects of HESH are greater than a similarly sized HE round, although the splintering effects are less. Compared to HESH, the HE effects of a HEAT round used in this way are much less, although in very soft ground it is possible that the HESH will bury itself and either detonate deep in the ground or in extreme circumstances not detonate at all. Interestingly, during the Iraq operations conducted under the Operation Telic banner, it was found that the HESH training projectile, L32A6 SHP, could be used to knock neat holes through walls but without the explosive effects that went along with firing HESH, and so ammunition that had been designed for training was used on operations. In a typical media circus, some sources reported this as though the troops were being denied access to service ammunition, a gross distortion of the facts. At the same time, other tanks were fitted with another non-operational piece of equipment, the Live Fire Crew Training System (LFCTS). This is a sub-calibre simulator that is basically a bolt-action rifle that fires a .50in projectile down the main armament barrel, and which was used to engage snipers and pin-point targets, again in order to remove the problem of collateral damage.

Ammunition stowage

In line with British doctrine, all propellant bag charges, being easily combustible, are stowed below the turret ring in steel containers; a great deal of development effort has also gone into producing propellant mixtures that are less volatile when struck by fragments. In the turret, a number of projectiles can be stowed in the turret bustle of a standard gun tank. HCDR command tanks fitted with the Bowman UK VRC 340 High-Capacity Data Radio (HCDR)

RIGHT **Scots DG
crews stowing DS/T
charges from the back
of a Bedford MK 4-ton
truck.** *(Courtesy Andrew
Totten)*

can carry less, and the command tanks, which mount an additional HF radio set, have less again in this area. The inner liners of the projectile stowage tubes are fitted with slightly different designs, dependant on which ammunition is carried; one design is used with L23 APFSDS and DS/T, the other with L26 and L27 APFSDS.

Main armament engagement sequence

The following illustrates a basic engagement sequence firing APFSDS against a static target; there are many variations, caused by the different target types and ammunition used, whether visual or thermal sights are used and whether the full computerised system is working or has been degraded – one of the features that British tank design insists upon is that the tank must be able to sustain considerable damage and still be able to fight. This insistence leads to an increased training burden but does ensure that the tank and crew are able to operate in circumstances than many, perhaps most, other tanks could not.

■ The commander and gunner divide the arc of fire into two separate areas, ensuring that they overlap slightly. This allows for all of the ground to be covered while scanning quickly and efficiently.

■ The commander and gunner normally scan for potential targets in low magnification. When the commander (in this instance) sees a potential target, he selects high magnification to observe it in greater detail. If he decides to engage the target, he looks through the sight and, using his thumb controller, lays his CPS aiming mark on to the target. Continuing to maintain pressure on his grip switch, he presses and releases the Align switch on his control handle and issues the first part of the fire order: '**Fin, Tank**'. Pressing the Align switch causes the gun to be aligned with the CPS aiming mark, and the gunner's sight will switch to high magnification with the GPS aiming mark on the target.

■ Once alignment is complete, the commander waits for the gunner's response, to indicate that he can identify the target indicated.

■ Concurrently, the loader will complete the loading sequence and report '**Loaded**' when the gun is ready: this means that the breech is closed by pulling the loader's guard to the rear, the correct ammunition is selected and the next projectile is in his arms.

■ The gunner, having heard the fire order, engages the grip switch on his control handle (the commander's grip switch always overrides the gunner's) and checks that the correct ammunition type has been selected

by the loader by checking the display in the GPS. He reports '**On**' to tell the commander that he can identify the target to be engaged.

■ The commander will then release his grip switch; he can choose to either monitor the current engagement or, if there are multiple targets, will start to scan for the next target using the CPS in independent mode.

■ The gunner accurately lays his GPS aiming mark on to the centre of the observed mass of the target using his thumb controller. He then lases the target, which also tells the fire control computer to work out the ballistic solution for that target. He checks that the lased range is realistic and that his other GPS displays are correct, waits for the report of '**Loaded**', and announces '**Firing**' as he presses the firing switch. The gun will automatically move to the correct position according to the ballistic solution and fire as soon as it has achieved this, known as coincidence. As soon as the gun has fired it will move to a +5° angle of elevation to facilitate faster reloading.

■ If the projectile hits the target the gunner reports '**Target**'. If the commander considers that the target has been destroyed he will order '**Target Stop**', and the crew will

ABOVE Firing! The flash from the burning propellant at its maximum – this gives away the tank's position so choosing when to fire the first round is an important consideration for the tank commander.
(Courtesy Andy Brend)

LEFT A few milliseconds later, the flash has all but dissipated, the fume extractor has functioned and the discarded petals have struck the ground in front of the tank.
(Courtesy RWxY)

RIGHT Firing at night is always spectacular – the time of flight of the KE rounds is so short that the hard target here has been struck even as the flash is still burning at the muzzle. *(TM 7431-030)*

LEFT Inside the loader's station, as seen from the commander's position. All the available space is taken up with boxes for the NBC pack, loading panel, Bowman communications equipment or stowage. Despite this the loader has the most room of all four crewmen.

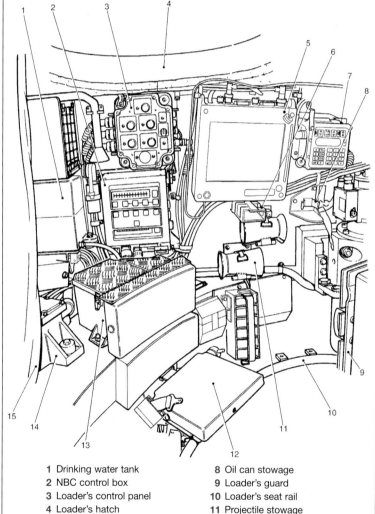

1 Drinking water tank
2 NBC control box
3 Loader's control panel
4 Loader's hatch
5 Vehicle User Date Terminal (VUDT)
6 TVE round storage
7 User Control Device (UCD)
8 Oil can stowage
9 Loader's guard
10 Loader's seat rail
11 Projectile stowage
12 Loader's seat
13 Ration stowage
14 Power distribution box
15 TVE shield

then continue to scan their arcs on low magnification. The loader will complete the loading sequence, reporting '**Loaded**' once it is complete.

■ If, however, the commander does not think that the target has been destroyed, he orders '**Target Go On**'. The gunner re-lays, re-lases and once again fires at the target as soon as the loader has confirmed '**Loaded**', reporting '**Firing**' as he does so.

■ If a round misses the target the gunner makes no report, but simply re-lays, re-lases and fires again. If after firing three rounds the target has still not been hit then the commander will order '**Stop, Disengage**' as this indicates that there is a system fault. The commander can change ammunition type, investigate the system to determine what is wrong, or wait for the target range to reduce to 1,000m or below to increase the apparent target size and thus the chances of a hit.

■ After completing an engagement, the gunner should check MRS through his GAS to ensure that accuracy is maintained; any adjustment made to the GAS automatically readjusts all the other sights at the same time.

LOADING THE 120MM GUN

The following sequence of images shows how the three-piece ammunition on CR2 is loaded in response to the commander's fire order, using Lt Matt Winters RTR as the demonstration loader on a Loader Drills Trainer – all RAC troop leaders are trained to be as proficient as gunners and loaders in these drills as the crews they command. The ammunition he is using is the Drill type, here representing APFSDS.

1 The loader checking the correct seating of the vent tubes before placing the magazine on the rear of the breech ring.

2 With the breech open, the loader selects the correct projectile as ordered by the commander.

3 He then places it on the loading platform on the top of the breech block and forms a fist with his right hand.

4 Using his fist, he rams the projectile as far forward as it will go – it will be pushed fully into the correct position by the bag charge.

5 He then opens the lid of a bag charge bin and using the handle extracts the appropriate charge – in this case APFSDS.

6 Handle first, the charge is pushed fully home into the chamber, which seats the projectile into the commencement of rifling.

7 The next APFSDS projectile is picked up and the breech closed by pulling the loader's guard to the rear.

8 He checks that the correct ammunition is selected on the loader's panel, and that the gun control equipment is live. He will now report 'Loaded!'

9 As the breech completes its full length of recoil, the loader's guard is 'tripped' – seen here as it flies forward under spring tension – and the breech opens during run-out, allowing the sequence to be repeated.

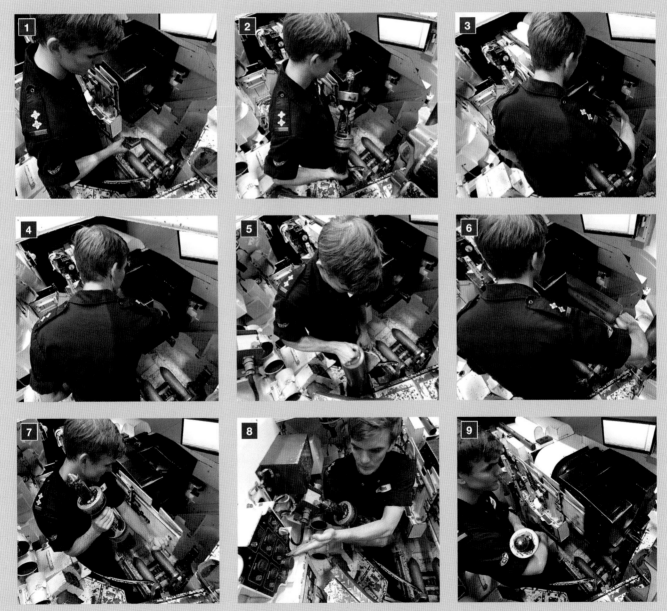

Sight alignment and the muzzle reference system

In principle, this operates in a similar manner to that described for both Chieftain and Challenger 1. However, on both of those tanks the main armament had to be depressed to a specific angle of depression in order to line up the components. On CR2, the main components (light source and GAS object lens) are mounted within the gun mantlet. This allows MRS to be checked and, if necessary, adjusted at any angle of elevation, speeding up readjustment and allowing it to be done during the loading sequence, when the gun is automatically positioned at a +5° angle to facilitate loading, known as the 'indexed loading position'. Adjusting the GAS automatically transmits data to the other sights, so that they are all kept correctly aligned.

But is it any good?

From the outset Challenger 2 was to prove that it was extremely good at hitting targets with its new L30 rifled gun. A firepower demonstration was conducted for the MGO on 24 June 1993 using prototypes V6, 8 and 9. During the rehearsal on the previous day and on the actual demonstration, a total of 73 rounds of main armament ammunition were fired, of which only two rounds missed; a hit rate of 97.3%. The mean engagement time for each target was less than 6 seconds. At another firepower demonstration conducted for the benefit of the Saudi Arabians in Warminster in November 1993, using V5 and V8, 25 120mm rounds were fired by demonstration crews with only a single miss, representing a hit rate of 96%. The Saudi Commander Land Forces was then coached through firing seven rounds of SH/P himself, and only a single shot missed, despite him having no tank experience and the ammunition being the most difficult to use. This was in part a demonstration of the essential accuracy of the gun control systems, but it must be acknowledged that it showed little of the realities of performing as a tank gunner in the stress of battle, concealing as it did the complexity of the gunner's job and the amount of time required to produce a fully trained gunner.

Engagement time was a specific area where everyone agreed that Challenger 2 needed to do much better than its predecessors, and these certainly compared very favourably with those achieved by Chieftain/Challenger 1 with their three-decades-old gun control equipment and 1970s fire control computer. The average Chieftain engagement static to static (ie from a static own vehicle engaging a static target) was 15 seconds, and Challenger 2 was able to halve that; indeed, it could halve that even if itself and its target were both moving! The overall standard engagement times from spotting a target to hitting it with the first round were reported as follows:

	Target static	Target moving
Own vehicle static	7s	8s
Own vehicle moving	8s	8s

These were of course averages, but give a good impression of just how much improvement had been achieved. An impressive record – which still stands to this day – was set by a Scots DG crew commanded by Sgt Colin Macintyre[35] in 1996 at Lulworth; during a firepower demonstration to the representatives of 42 nations at Lulworth, his tank hit six different targets at varying ranges in 26 seconds, an average of just over 4 seconds per hit, including acquisition and reloading time. The hunter/killer technique had come of age. However, demonstrating the capability of the tank in the most impressive way possible was not without its problems. Because it was possible for the gunner to lase a target which computed a firing solution, and then traverse off the target while retaining the solution within the fire control computer, someone came up with a bright idea of using this at the commencement of a firepower demonstration. Before the visitors arrived and took their seats, the tank was readied and a target was recorded as above, and the gun was then traversed over the rear decks towards the audience. As soon as the commentator finished his initial brief over the PA system, he would conclude by announcing 'This is Challenger 2!', and the commander would hit Align. The turret would immediately traverse at top speed to the front where, as soon as coincidence was achieved, the gun would fire and hit a hard target over a mile away, accompanied by a spectacular flash. Everyone

was massively impressed by this, until one day an astute spectator commented that surely this meant that the 120mm must be fully loaded when it was pointing at the audience, and was that really safe? Red faces all round, and future demonstrations took a more conventional, if less impressive, form.

Machine guns

The co-axial MG used is the L94A1 version of the US-designed 7.62mm Hughes EX34 Chain Gun; in the early stages of CR2 development it was commonly referred to as the HCG. (It is also sometimes referred to as the Long version, the L95A1 being a shorter-barrelled type not used on CR2.) The gun was designed for use on the M60 tank but was not adopted by the US military. It had already been in use for a considerable period as the secondary armament in the Warrior IFV before it was chosen for CR2, in part because it had already been fitted in the Vickers Universal Turret. As the chain gun is electrically driven, misfired rounds are able to be ejected without causing a stoppage as happens with gas-operated MGs. Additionally, toxic fumes are much reduced as they are expelled forward and out of the turret.

The gun is mounted to the upper left of the main armament breech, and takes its ammunition feed from the left side of the gun, with 1,400 rounds able to be linked up as ready ammunition; a transparent spent link chute takes the links from the breech into a container underneath the gun. A gun mounting bracket is bolted to the inside of the rotor, with an external barrel shroud protruding through the front of the mantlet. The rear of the shroud has a gun body mounting plate fitted with two plungers to allow the breech mechanism to be fitted

LEFT During trials the metal links that form the 7.62mm ammunition belt were found to be the cause of many stoppages on the chain gun, and improving the quality of these simple items solved many problems . . . but not before the gun had acquired a reputation for unreliability. *(Courtesy Nigel Atkin)*

and removed. The barrel has a Stellite lining to increase barrel life, and a spare barrel is carried in a stowage tube mounted alongside the gun; the barrel is changed after approximately 1,000 rounds fired to prevent overheating. A barrel shroud is mounted through the mantlet and protrudes through the front face; on the top of the shroud is the ejection tube, along which the spent cases are pushed in order to be ejected out of the turret. On the rear of the gun body is a coloured disc and a pointer, which acts as the gun condition indicator, allowing the loader to identify which part of the cycle the gun is in, and this will ensure that he can safely carry out the appropriate stoppage drill.

MG ammunition

The ammunition used with both the co-ax chain gun and the loader's pintle-mounted GPMG are the same – 7.62 × 51mm NATO ball and trace, supplied in boxes of 200 rounds. Many of the problems initially experienced with the chain gun and which led to its poor reputation initially stemmed from ammunition. The first was the way that the gun was turned about its axis in order to allow ammunition feed from the left side of the turret, and the other was more prosaic, although it took some time to identify. The 200 rounds in each belt are joined together by a disintegrating metal link; it was found eventually that the links, which were made overseas, were of an inferior quality, and it was these that were responsible for many stoppages. Improving the quality of the link removed the problem.

LEFT A CR2 loader manning his GPMG during a tactical refuelling operation – known colloquially as a replen – while on exercise. *(Courtesy Andy Brend)*

Survivability

Protection for the crew was uppermost in the minds of those responsible for selecting and building the tank. The success of Chobham armour meant that foreign competitors were hard-pushed to field an equivalent armour, let alone a better one, and the lesser protection on the Leopard 2, and indeed the M1 prior to the introduction of DU armour, meant that the crew of Challenger 2 would have great confidence in the ability of their tank to withstand even multiple hits. Even prior to the initial contract for the nine prototypes, VDS had begun to develop their Universal Turret design from the Mk 7/2 and turn it into the turret of Challenger 2; one major change that the MoD insisted on was the inclusion of a conventional 'facing forward' periscopic gunner's sight to replace the panoramic sight on the 7/2. Work started in early 1987 and was largely complete by August, allowing VDS to conduct their own 'firing-at' trials at some of the eight pre-prototype turrets they had decided to build. The results of these were spectacularly good. A wide range of different calibre ammunition, both kinetic and chemical energy, was fired at turret shells which withstood the attacks extremely well. The VDS Progress Report No 1 of March 1989 commented on the results of firings in November 1988 directed at the mantlet and rotor: 'Threat weapons can be defeated and the rotor bearings were still operational following multiple weapon attacks.' This was important, as historically many tanks with external mantlets have been rendered inoperative by a single strike jamming the mantlet – the place on the tank most likely to be hit. The cost of these trials were not insignificant: VDS put their own money where their corporate mouth was and paid out over £20 million to develop the tank prior to the award of the development contract, the equivalent of over two years' profit for the company.

The turret comprises a cast inner shell, with an outer covering of thin cosmetic plates. Sandwiched between the two is the main armour protection in the form of Dorchester armour 'slabs'. The rear of the turret overhang, or bustle, accommodates the two turret

BELOW Stowage rear left.

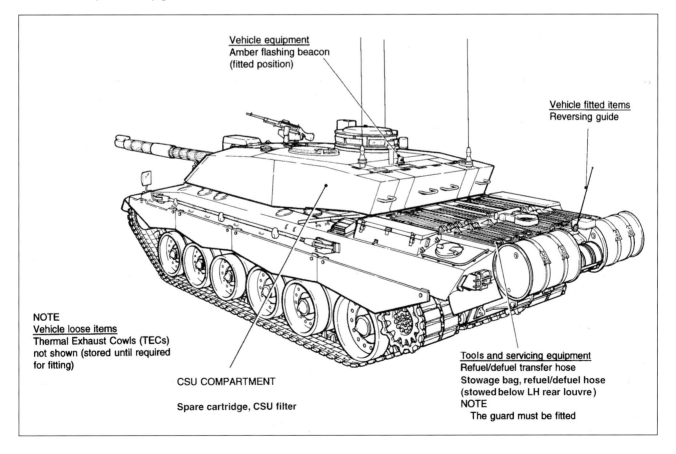

Vehicle equipment
Amber flashing beacon
(fitted position)

Vehicle fitted items
Reversing guide

NOTE
Vehicle loose items
Thermal Exhaust Cowls (TECs)
not shown (stored until required
for fitting)

CSU COMPARTMENT

Spare cartridge, CSU filter

Tools and servicing equipment
Refuel/defuel transfer hose
Stowage bag, refuel/defuel hose
(stowed below LH rear louvre)
NOTE
    The guard must be fitted

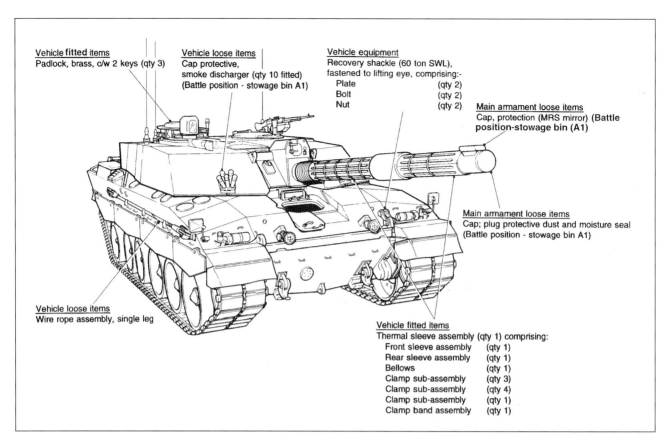

Vehicle fitted items
Padlock, brass, c/w 2 keys (qty 3)

Vehicle loose items
Cap protective,
smoke discharger (qty 10 fitted)
(Battle position - stowage bin A1)

Vehicle equipment
Recovery shackle (60 ton SWL),
fastened to lifting eye, comprising:-
Plate   (qty 2)
Bolt   (qty 2)
Nut   (qty 2)

Main armament loose items
Cap, protection (MRS mirror) (Battle
position-stowage bin (A1)

Main armament loose items
Cap; plug protective dust and moisture seal
(Battle position - stowage bin A1)

Vehicle loose items
Wire rope assembly, single leg

Vehicle fitted items
Thermal sleeve assembly (qty 1) comprising:
Front sleeve assembly   (qty 1)
Rear sleeve assembly   (qty 1)
Bellows   (qty 1)
Clamp sub-assembly   (qty 3)
Clamp sub-assembly   (qty 4)
Clamp sub-assembly   (qty 1)
Clamp band assembly   (qty 1)

ABOVE Stowage front right.

'radio' batteries, the cooling pack for TOGS, components of the GCE, the radio equipment, a drinking water tank, ammunition projectile stowage and the NBC unit. The hull also accommodates Dorchester armour slabs, and contains a fixed fire extinguisher system, used for combating powerpack fires. This incorporates two cylinders mounted in the left rear of the driver's compartment (cab), each containing 3.75kg of pressurised FM200 heptafluoropropane gas as the extinguishing agent. The cylinders are connected to perforated piping, which is arranged around the powerpack compartment. Discharging of one or both of the cylinders is carried out by operating red-painted handles; two are mounted adjacent to the cylinders in the cab, and one is found either side of the hull front for external use. A powerpack compartment fire warning system is also fitted, consisting of a sensing element loop around the compartment that sends an electrical signal to a control box when a certain temperature is exceeded. This causes both an audible and a visual alarm to be given to the crew, allowing them to take appropriate action.

External stowage appears very limited, particularly when considering the plethora of bins and baskets that adorned its predecessors. This is because the tank was designed to have the smallest possible radar cross-section, and the stowage boxes are all contained within the turret rear. There are in fact seven boxes, made from aluminium sheet for lightness, all providing dedicated stowage for particular items; they are identified as boxes A to G. The two side-most bins C and G are mounted on hinges, secured by pip pins; the remainder are rigidly mounted. Between the turret top and rear bins is the stowage position for the meteorological sensor for the fire control system, folded down and protected when not in use.

As well as the driver being able to produce a local smokescreen using the powerpack, the turret mounts two banks of No 18 Mk 1 dischargers either side of the turret front. These have five 66mm barrels, spread to cover an arc when fired simultaneously. L5 (white), L7 (green) and L8 White Phosphorous grenades can be used, the latter giving an almost instantaneous but shorter duration screen than the first two.

The NBC Filtration and Ventilation System

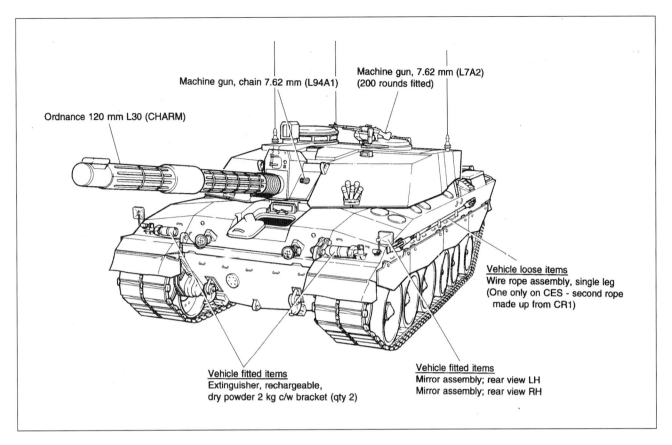

Ordnance 120 mm L30 (CHARM)

Machine gun, chain 7.62 mm (L94A1)

Machine gun, 7.62 mm (L7A2)
(200 rounds fitted)

Vehicle loose items
Wire rope assembly, single leg
(One only on CES - second rope
made up from CR1)

Vehicle fitted items
Extinguisher, rechargeable,
dry powder 2 kg c/w bracket (qty 2)

Vehicle fitted items
Mirror assembly; rear view LH
Mirror assembly; rear view RH

No 27 (aka the NBC pack) is mounted inside the rear of the turret bustle, with two main functions: to provide the crew with clean (uncontaminated) air when operating in an NBC environment, and to create an overpressure within a closed-down vehicle to prevent the ingress of any contaminated air. The air inlet and scavenge pump is located in the TOGS cooling

ABOVE Stowage front left.

LEFT A brand-new CR2 (in fact the fifth service tank built) demonstrates the diesel injection method of producing a rapid smokescreen from the exhausts. *(TM 5322C5)*

unit compartment behind the cupola, with the main pack (filters) in its own compartment to the right of the bustle on anti-vibration mountings. The control panel is mounted within the loader's compartment under the Loader's Control Panel, and air ducting is provided to each crew member individually. When operating, the pack main fan draws air in through the inlet louvre and then through an inertial separator and scavenge fan which removes larger dirt and dust particles, expelling them to atmosphere. The partly cleaned air then passes through two cylindrical composite filters and this completes the decontamination of the air, making it fit to be used by the crew without them needing to wear their general service respirators. Sufficient fan speed ensures that the volume of clean air generated is such that the pressure within the fighting compartment is always greater than outside the tank. This is known as overpressure, meaning that contaminated air from outside is prevented from entering the interior. It was recognised when designing the system that when operating in cold NBC conditions, the crew would be supplied with uncomfortably cold air; therefore a thermostatically controlled heater is included in the system, to warm the air before it reaches the crew.

Turret and armament safety features

A large number of safety features are included for the crew of Challenger 2. These include:

- The GCE safety switches prevent the powered GCE being used when any one of them is set to Safe.
- The firing circuits are isolated when the Loader's Control Panel is set to Safe.
- The main armament can only be fired if the loader's shield is pulled to the rear.
- Firing of all weapons (except using the emergency firing circuit and the smoke grenade dischargers) requires the use of two hands, to prevent inadvertent firing.
- The commander can override the gunner at any time.
- The main armament cannot be fired unless the breech block is closed and locked (sealed).
- After firing the main armament, the gun automatically moves to +5° to facilitate reloading.
- The main armament breech will not open until it is in the run-out phase.

RIGHT Another familiar survivability system used on British AFVs are the smoke grenade dischargers mounted on the turret. Here the White Phosphorous L8 grenades explode at about 10m above the ground and rapidly build up an effective screen. *(TM 5341E5)*

■ And last but not least . . . training. Safety is emphasised throughout all types of training, and care is taken to explain the safety features and to insist upon safe practices at all times.

Ergonomics

The Crew Temperature Control System (CTCS) must be considered as one of the most popular enhancements to the tank. Crews have complained about the working environment within the tank being too hot or too cold since the tank was invented, and despite a few – often half-hearted – attempts to rectify this, Challenger 2 is the first tank to build such a system into the design *ab initio*. The system, which is independent of the NBC pack, provides cooled, heated or indeed unconditioned ambient temperature air to each crew member; this improves the environment, making it easier to maintain human performance for longer. The system is effectively an aircon unit, and is controlled by the driver from switches on the DIP; the system evaporator unit is mounted to the right of the driver, with two levels of heat plus cool air, and two fan speeds. Using a vapour compression cycle refrigeration circuit, the system employs Forane R134a as the refrigerant. Ambient air for the CTCS is drawn in through an intake on the extreme right rear of the hull by an electrical motor unit located just forward of the intake. This drives the compressor mounted above it by two V drive belts. A condenser mounted adjacent to the left-hand ME radiator is cooled by the fan, resulting in cooling of the refrigerant by condensation. When heating is required, the compressor and motor are isolated, excluding the refrigeration circuit. One or both heating elements within the evaporator warm the air before passing it to the crew.

Another of the enhancements to ergonomics – again meaning better crew comfort – is the much-improved gunner's and commander's seats. The gunner's seat has six height positions, controlled by a hydraulic pump, and he is also provided with an adjustable chest pad in front of him, designed to hold him steady when moving at speed across country. This makes sighting and laying the gun much

easier. The commander's seat can be moved up and down over a range of 13in, and also move fore and aft nearly 6in. It can be set up either straight ahead or angled to the right by 22.5°. The backrest can also be angled to a 5° or a 17° reclined position. This means that the commander can adjust the seat for his own height and indeed preferences, making it much more comfortable over long periods of use. And finally on the subject of crew comfort . . . the humble loader's seatpad flips up to reveal a commode, designed to be used when the crew are confined to the tank for extended periods; this is seemingly a good idea, but I've yet to find a crewman who has made use of it![36]

ABOVE In conditions like this, the CTCS is a must! A Queen's Royal Hussars tank exercises in typical German winter weather. *(Courtesy QRH)*

BELOW Components of the CTCS shown in yellow, including the trunking that carries the hot or cold air to each crew station.

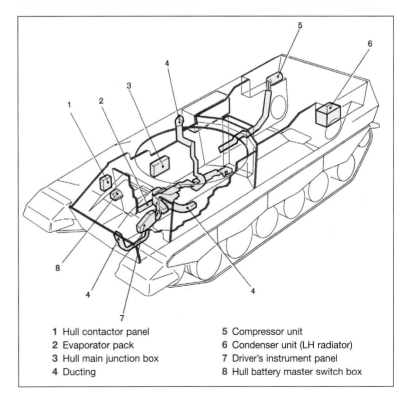

1 Hull contactor panel	5 Compressor unit
2 Evaporator pack	6 Condenser unit (LH radiator)
3 Hull main junction box	7 Driver's instrument panel
4 Ducting	8 Hull battery master switch box

Chapter Three

Challenger 2 walk-around

Before deploying Challenger 2 – or indeed any modern military vehicle – to a theatre of operations, consideration will always be given to ensuring that it is as well prepared as possible for the specific challenges and threats of that environment. The name given to this standard is the OES, meaning Operational Entry Standard. This defines all the modifications and enhancements required, without which the vehicle will not be allowed to serve in that theatre.

OPPOSITE Megatron looks very different from a 'vanilla' tank when covered by the mobile camouflage system – somehow it always seems to make a very large tank seem considerably smaller. *(Tank Museum)*

Megatron, as the ATDU OES tank, therefore represents the latest thinking in MBT survivability, lethality and mobility, and although it may not be exactly the same version as that deployed on the next operation, whenever and wherever that is, it certainly provides an excellent start point, particularly when time is short.

The tank illustrated here is DT18AA, the current Megatron tank used by ATDU. Officially, it is the Challenger 2 Operational Entry Standard tank, or CR2 OES. This reference tank is held by ATDU in order to continue to develop and refine the various new systems and sub-systems required to make the tank as effective as possible. Sometimes such enhancements might be very small and seem routine or even humdrum, for example a new type of seat belt or a slightly modified Boiling Vessel. In other cases they are more visual and more dramatic, for example a new type of appliqué armour, an improved ammunition or better mobility. Illustrated here is the OES tank as photographed by Matt Sampson in May 2017, with the kind permission of CO ATDU. All of the images are in the Tank Museum range 10391 and 10392, except where uncredited, in which case they are mine (clearly identifiable by the much lower quality . . .).

RIGHT Front right, with the Remote Weapon Station on the turret roof – this is a very obvious difference to the tank in the standard training configuration. *(Tank Museum)*

RIGHT The additional under-belly armour can be glimpsed in this image, a necessary improvement to add protection to an area in which all tanks are traditionally vulnerable. *(Tank Museum)*

LEFT The tank 'gun front', demonstrating how the additional equipment necessarily changes the silhouette – and overall dimensions – of the tank.
(Tank Museum)

LEFT Megatron is probably the most reliable tank in the fleet, despite its high mileage; it is a truism that tanks benefit from being operated rather than sitting unused in hangars or in storage.
(Tank Museum)

LEFT The left side, with the MCS covering the side armour packs (unlike the earlier Barracuda system which did not). The rear side bar armour has been covered with scrim, as has the armour over the rear half of the turret bustle.
(Tank Museum)

ABOVE The rear camera is fitted alongside the first-aid box, which itself is mounted above the box containing the defuel/refuel pump controls and the infantry tank telephone.

ABOVE L/Cpl Nathan Keys RTR demonstrates the MCS attachment using Velcro, and also the silver heat reflective inner surface of the system.

RIGHT Without knowing that this is a CR2, it might be difficult to work out which tank we are looking at, which of course is part of the reason for the sophisticated camouflage system. *(Tank Museum)*

RIGHT The rearmost bar armour is suspended from an articulated mounting to prevent it being damaged when moving over complex terrain. *(Tank Museum)*

ABOVE Right side, looking sleek and menacing. One of the advantages of the MCS is that it can be delivered in the pattern needed for a specific environment, without needing to repaint the tank underneath. *(Tank Museum)*

LEFT Front right, with all sights including TOGS and GAS open. *(Tank Museum)*

LEFT Although the turret roof looks cluttered, the systems are designed to be operated from under armour. *(Tank Museum)*

ABOVE Looking inside the powerpack, with the front engine deck raised rearwards on its torsion bar to reveal the filter banks and the large yellow oil dip/filler neck. *(Tank Museum)*

RIGHT Looking from the left side of the hull into the engine; accessing the compartment is made more difficult when the side appliqué armour is mounted to the turret. *(Tank Museum)*

BELOW The fuel injection system for the 12 cylinders necessitates some complicated 'plumbing'. The large box on the right of the photo is the air cleaner. *(Tank Museum)*

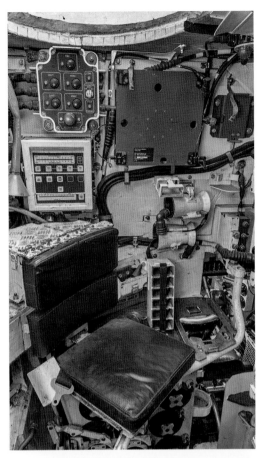

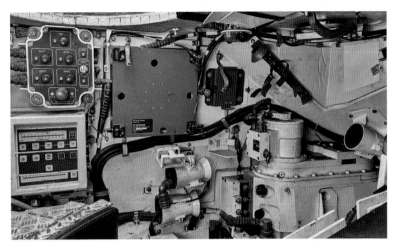

LEFT Getting inside the tank, this is the loader's side as viewed from the commander's seat. The 'ladder' box next to the seat is for stowing the vent tube magazines. *(Tank Museum)*

ABOVE The left side wall of the turret, with the loader's panel and NBC control box towards the rear; the bracket for one of the internal fire extinguishers is empty, which officially makes this tank illegal to be used on public roads. Three individual stowage collars for APFSDS projectiles are also in view. *(Tank Museum)*

BELOW The breech ring and blocks of the 120mm L30 gun dominates the loader's compartment. *(Tank Museum)*

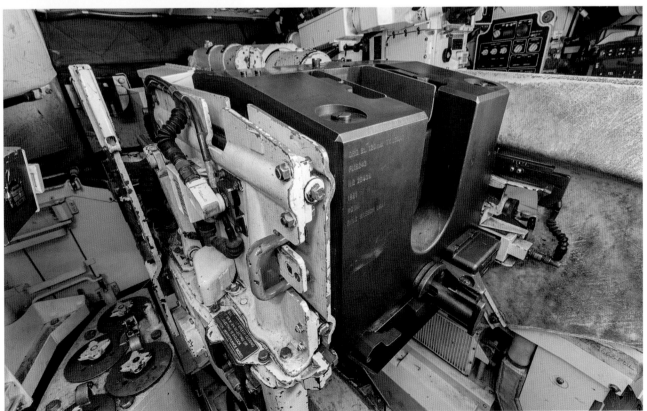

ABOVE Looking over the top of the breech towards the gunner's space; the block mounted to the underside of the turret roof is a depression stop, physically limiting the depression of the main armament when the driver has his head out of the hatch, and which is removed when he is closed down.
(Tank Museum)

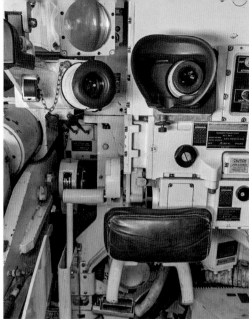

ABOVE The gunner's view of his position, with the various sighting eyepieces for the GPS, GAS and TOGS at the top, his control handles below, and the adjustable chest pad in between.
(Tank Museum)

LEFT With the gun slightly elevated, the top of the (closed) breech block can be seen, with the recoil system replenisher and one of the recoil buffers visible: it is the white cylinder at the front.
(Tank Museum)

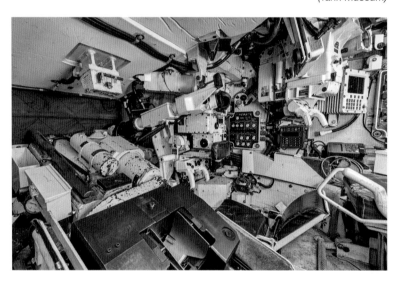

BELOW The commander's control handle under the CPS can be raised and locked out of the way to allow the gunner to enter and exit easily.
(Tank Museum)

BELOW The gunner's control handle, with various switches for selecting day or night systems, the sight magnification, the laser firing button, armament selector, aided lay and the thumb controller with which he controls the movement of the gun and turret. The manual traverse handle is to the right.
(Tank Museum)

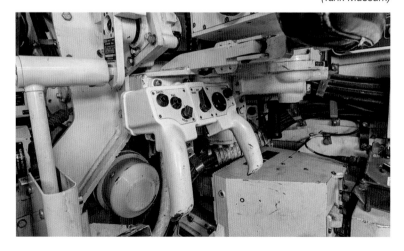

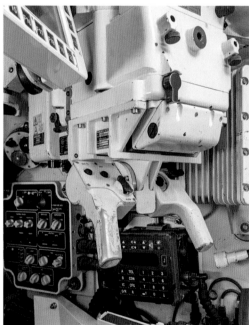

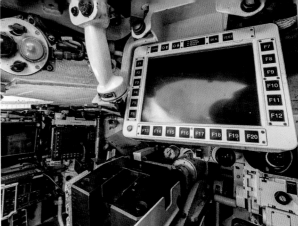

ABOVE The commander's view of the bottom of his CPS and control handle in the down (operating) position, with control panels and keypads both left and right of the sight, interrupting his view of the gunner. He can monitor the gunner adequately through the use of tell-back displays, however. *(Tank Museum)*

ABOVE RIGHT The addition of Bowman added more capability but more complexity – and boxes – to the tank, making the commander's job a very responsible one. It certainly demands someone who can multi-task! *(Tank Museum)*

RIGHT The bustle stowage looking directly rearward, with the capacity to stow 16 of the projectiles in this place; all the bag charges are kept in armoured bins below the turret ring. *(Tank Museum)*

BELOW The half-moon discs on the bustle projectile racks are rotated in order to either secure all four APFSDS rounds (in the position shown here), or to release one at a time when required for loading. *(Tank Museum)*

RIGHT Ammunition projectile stowage can also be found under the gun, but has to be transferred into a more convenient stowage position during a lull in battle – known as the replenishment of turret stocks.

And hot off the press are images of two RTR tanks (DR42AA and another one . . . ever noticed how crews always stand in front of markings when the cameras come out?) painted in July 2017 in Tidworth in a version of the Berlin Camouflage scheme. As the RTR were heavily involved in conducting urban warfare exercises (known in unofficial British army parlance as FISH, Fighting In Someone's House) on Salisbury Plain, the CO Lt Col Simon Ridgway decided to dip into the past and re-create the scheme. And very fetching it looks too!

ABOVE, RIGHT AND OPPOSITE PAGE The newest oldest thing: the Royal Tank Regiment's two Challenger 2s freshly painted and looking good in the Berlin urban camouflage scheme in summer 2017.

Chapter Four

Challenger 2 in service

After years of development and testing, Challenger 2 finally entered service about four years after it was scheduled to do so, in 1998. Unusually for a service tank, this meant that the regiments received tanks that were mostly free of defects and annoying faults; as a result they were unanimous in their praise for the fighting qualities of the tank, as well as its reliability. In this respect Challenger 2 probably represents the peak in British tank design and production, and has set the exemplar for how a tank – or indeed any other complex military equipment – should be brought into service.

OPPOSITE The Commanding Officer of 2RTR, Lt Col Paddy Allison, commands callsign 11B Nomad on the BATUS prairie; 2RTR were the second regiment to convert to CR2 and within four years had conducted operational tours of the Balkans and Iraq. *(Courtesy RTR)*

The most tested tank in the world

It was a proud claim of VDS that when it entered service, Challenger 2 was without doubt 'the most rigorously tested main battle tank of all time'. This was no idle boast. Although in ideal circumstances of course the tank should have entered service four years earlier than it did, the series of trials allowed a host of problems – large and small – to be ironed out, and which under normal circumstances would have only come to light when it entered service. In order to illustrate some of the many minor but still important enhancements that resulted from the trials period, L/Cpl Jim Elgar 2RTR was one of the trials crewmen, and recalled three specific examples when the trials crews were able to insist on changes. Firstly, on the original design there was no cover over the object (external) lens of the GAS, meaning that the lens quickly became obscured with mud and dirt. This meant that not only could it not be used in an emergency, but also that the MRS could not be used to check and adjust the sights; some VDS staff suggested that no modification was needed, as the crew could simply wipe the lens clean every time the tank stopped! In part this was because fitting an external flap was more complicated than it sounds, as a cable or other opening/closing device had to be fitted through the armoured mantlet. Secondly, part of the original commander's hatch mechanism was mounted immediately behind the commander's seat, meaning that not only would his jacket frequently snag on it when entering the tank, but also it became extremely uncomfortable, even painful, very quickly. Lastly, there was no ×1 window for the gunner to look out of, restricting his view to the inside of the tank or through the magnified sights only, which often led to the gunner getting severe motion sickness when travelling at speed – not pleasant for him, or indeed the rest of the crew. These points – and others – were frequently raised by the trials crews who sometimes felt that they were getting nowhere, but they were delighted when the first production tank appeared at Bovington, as the defects had all been remedied, with a GAS flap fitted, the commander's hatch modified and the ×1 Gunner's Unity Vision Periscope incorporated.

Into service with the British Army

The In-Service Date (ISD) was originally intended to be when the 74th production tank had been accepted into service, allowing enough tanks to equip (nearly) two complete regiments. This was later changed to become when one regiment of 38 tanks was trained and equipped, and it was belatedly achieved in June

RIGHT The official signing-over ceremony at Chelsea Barracks by Sir Colin Chandler of VDS and Defence Secretary Malcolm Rifkind in 1994 marked an important stage in the story of Challenger 2, but the tank was not to enter service for another four years. WO2 (later Lt Col) Norrie Robertson BEM Scots DG, who was a key figure in the trials, is standing alongside the tank. *(Courtesy Norrie Robertson)*

1998 when the Royal Scots Dragoon Guards[37] received their final tank, as all the crews had already completed their training. Scots DG were based in Wessex Barracks, Fallingbostel, Germany, as one of the two tank regiments within 7th Armoured Brigade. Two selected crews from the regiment had received the first production tanks as early as 25 July 1994 in order to allow complete crews (as opposed to ATDU crewmen) to conduct in-depth user trials at Bovington and Lulworth, but it was not until late January 1998 that the regiment received its first eight genuine service tanks, replacing the Challenger 1s which the regiment had been equipped with for a decade. Lt Col Andrew Phillips was the Commanding Officer for this period, and, in his foreword to the regimental journal, had this to say:

It is my privilege to convert the regiment to the British Army's new and formidable main battle tank, Challenger 2. Currently I am halfway through my conversion course and can report that this has been the most demanding but enjoyable tank course that I have ever done. The associated training equipment is superb – for the Chieftain and Challenger 1 old sweats amongst you, we now have double the number of loader trainers as well as a six-fold increase in gunnery trainers. In addition, we have a troop trainer that can be used for gunnery, map reading and tactics training. Challenger 2 is the most tested and proven main battle tank in the world. It is very different from its predecessor. The most radical differences are in the turret. Not only is CR2 better protected but, more importantly, it has been designed around the crew. With its heating and air-conditioning systems, the turret is now a comfortable place to be and it is obvious that a lot of thought has gone into its ergonomics. The fire control system is a world beater. Thanks to the stabilised sights, both the commander and gunner can fire accurately on the move at moving targets. ... The engine is most reliable [and] the driver can tension the track whilst closed down at the flick of a switch. With another flick of a switch, he can inject diesel into the exhaust to produce a most effective smokescreen.

In summary, CR2 is radically different from its predecessors but has kept its fightability. This, together with the superb training package will undoubtedly make it the most formidable tank in the world.

A year later the same CO was able to look back on the regimental conversion training period, noting that 'We have found the reliability of CR2 to be excellent, with only four litres of engine oil being used by the two tanks on the Driving & Maintenance course vehicles that drove 2,000km during training.' The regiment was very impressed by the precision, fidelity and availability of the new training equipment, including the gunner's Part-Task Trainer (PTT), the Loader Drills Trainer (LDT) and the Troop Gunnery Trainer (TGT). These allowed each gunner and commander to carry out over 600 simulated engagements before live firing twice on Hohne ranges near Hanover. Lt Col Phillips again:

The gunnery test exercises place a very strong emphasis on firing on the move at top speed. Tanks fire with the main armament over the sides as well as over the front, and also fire in reverse. The high standard of gunnery attained during the firing periods showed that the synthetic training and live firing balance is pitched at the right level.

BELOW CR2 FOP (First Off Production): 61KK68 on fielding tests at Bovington. She incorporates the modifications identified during the prototype trials, but still has the disliked D-ring MG mount. *(Courtesy Jim Elgar)*

RIGHT No 61KK68 drains water as she negotiates a water obstacle on the Bovington training area; note how the front mudguard has been flipped upwards on its hinge. The unprepared fording depth is officially set at 1.07m.
(TM 7431-015)

At the end of the first range period the regiment in the shape of C Squadron conducted a demonstration of CR2's capabilities on

RIGHT A newly produced CR2 leaves VDS Leeds on a civilian transporter in April 2001.
(Courtesy Neil Bolton)

Range 9 at Hohne to personnel from 1st (UK Armoured) Division, as well as many visiting VIPs including German tank crews. Sir Colin Chandler, Chairman of VDS, was also present and somewhat belatedly marked the official handover of the tanks to Scots DG. At first the regiment only had three small squadrons of 12 tanks each, plus two in Regimental Headquarters (RHQ) – what the CO referred to as 'the unworkable Type 38 armoured regiment'. Fortunately the Strategic Defence Review of 1998 changed the establishment back to a Type 58, giving the regiment four squadrons of 14 tanks, again with two in RHQ. B Squadron was the first to be fully equipped, carrying out intensive conversion training from January until June 1998 using both real tanks and the brand-new synthetic training equipment, which all crews realised was at least two generations better than the previous versions used with Challenger 1. The squadron was then ready to be used as the In-Service Reliability Demonstration (ISRD) squadron, being detached to Bovington and Lulworth from August until December 1998 with its 12 tanks (four troops of three tanks, one of which was SHQ troop) for the task. The structure of the ISRD was similar to that used on the User Trials and PRGT, with BFDs as the benchmark, the main differences being that 'normal', newly trained crews were used, mounted on 'normal' production standard tanks operating as a complete squadron. The intention was that ISRD was just that, a demonstration that the standards of reliability shown to be attainable by 'expert' crews on the carefully husbanded prototypes could be transferred across to in-service tanks and crews. In many respects, therefore, it was a more demanding and realistic trial, and in some ways tested the crews as much as it did the vehicles. Each tank was required to complete seven BFDs, totalling 84 for the squadron: this involved driving nearly 5,000km, 60% of which was cross-country, and firing the 120mm guns nearly 3,000 times.[38] The demonstration was passed 'with flying colours', the crews learning an enormous amount about their new charges (or should that be 'chargers' for a cavalry unit!) and leading to the in-service standard being set at a very high level.

RIGHT Scots DG crewmen shackle down their tanks on railway flats, the usual method of moving the tanks long distances over land. The turrets have all been camouflaged using woodland camouflage nets with green and brown plastic 'scrim'. *(Courtesy Andrew Totten)*

BELOW Sunset at BATUS; this tank is carrying the TES (Tactical Engagement Simulation) equipment used during the force-on-force phase of the exercise. Callsign 22 comes from Armoured Squadron Two, identified by the white surrounds to the callsign backings and the Zap Code 208. *(Courtesy Andrew Totten)*

BELOW Zero Bravo identifies this tank as the mount of the squadron leader, a major. The Zap Code of 101 and the plain callsign backings tell us that this is Armoured Squadron One. The introduction of CR2 into BATUS caused some of the safety procedures to be revised, in order to allow the hunter/killer technique to be practised safely. *(Courtesy Andrew Totten)*

The next regiment to receive its tanks was 2RTR, based in Lumsden Barracks, Fallingbostel, and which was the other armoured regiment in 7th Armoured Brigade alongside Scots DG. The first eight examples were received on 29 July 1998, allowing the regiment to train the required 38 crews between 10 August and 18 December of that year, by which time the remaining tanks had arrived. Again, crewmen used to Chieftain and Challenger 2 were delighted with the new tank. Cpl Stu Flackett wrote in 1998:

Well, Challenger 2 is just plain better! Right from the first day when we deployed to ranges we didn't have to slave-start any of the beasts, which makes them 100% better already. The whole squadron drove out of the back gates and arrived at the range under their own steam. The 'new toys' Vickers has supplied us with are living up to their advertising. Every tank has passed Live Firing Exercise (LFX) 1 with no hassle, because the hunter/killer gunnery system is so much quicker and more accurate than Challenger 1's

ABOVE The officer commanding Armoured Sqn 1 (from Scots DG) at BATUS. *(Courtesy Andrew Totten)*

BELOW The Scots DG battlegroup show off their organisation during the first BATUS deployment using CR2. Two squadrons of 14 tanks flank the two RHQ tanks, with an infantry company in Warriors behind. *(Courtesy Andrew Totten)*

IMPRESSIONS OF CHALLENGER 2

by Lt Matt Smith B Sqn 2RTR

As one of the last officers to complete a Challenger 1 troop leader's course, but not so long in the tooth to have grown fond of it, I am considered well suited to compare the two tanks. Well, to be quite honest about it, there is NO comparison, because CR2 simply surpasses CR1 in all respects. The conversion course was thorough and at the end of it I felt that I was familiar with the tank. The course culminated in three weeks of Turret Gunnery Simulator (TGT) work to train both commanders and gunners together. The TGT can do so much more than any of the CR1 training aids ever could, replicating the right-hand side of the turret . . . but no amount of simulation can ever supplant the atmosphere, excitement and reality of the turret on open ranges. The main advantage of CR2 over its predecessor is its ability to fire on the move accurately at both static and moving targets.

There are now nine live firing exercises (LFX) on ranges, with LFX 6 being the Annual Crew Test (ACT), and LFX 9 the Annual Troop Test or ATT. LFX 6 consists of a brief static shoot of both main armament and co-ax, and then firing on the move at a presentation of seven targets, finished off with a final static shoot. That is what it is, and this is what it is like to do: the driver sets off at a rate of knots (personally I think the faster the better) and the first pair of targets pop up. 'DST Tank' – the gunner is onto the first whilst the commander acquires the second through his sight. There is a brief but nail-biting pause whilst the gunner gets a perfect central aided lay, followed by 'Firing!' – BANG – 'Target Stop'. The commander screams the next fire order (he's very excited by now!): 'DST Tank . . . aligning'. Another age, in reality a second or two, whilst the loader gets clear of the traverse, and then press the Align switch to lay the gun onto the next target. The loader completes the loading sequence, 'Loaded', followed immediately

by another 'Firing!' – BANG – 'Target Stop'. And so this continues until all those nasty little (much smaller than a real tank) targets are dead, and no longer a threat to our fine nation. Throughout the ranges crews were regularly getting four or five rounds off within a minute when firing on the move . . . the hunter/killer capability is truly deadly, the only thing slowing us down is the speed of loading.

During our second range period we progressed onto troop firing, after practising on the linked-up TGTs in barracks, something else that couldn't be done on CR1. We again completed LFX 1 to 6 in a matter of days, and moved onto Troop-level Fire and Movement Exercises (FMX). CR2 has greatly increased the firepower of the troop, let alone the squadron, and seeing three tanks firing on the move together is really quite impressive. All the troops passed the Annual Troop Test and our two range periods convinced everyone that what had been claimed of Challenger 2 was indeed correct. It does everything you want it to, and it is reliable too. Even the cursed Chain Gun began to be tamed after the loader's learned how to deal with its idiosyncrasies. CR2 is incomparable with CR1 and gives the regiment an awesome capability. One thing that is desperately needed though is a commander's independent TI sight – the result of this omission is the loss of the hunter/killer capability at night. There are some other things that would be on my list in case Father Christmas is reading this: a built-in GPS, and perhaps some more stowage space. But Challenger 2 is a brilliant tank, not only effective but also great fun to be in, and to command. No longer do we have to make do with unreliability, but we know that we are in a really excellent tank. Everyone feels confident of their own and their tank's capabilities, and by the end of the coming training year feel we'll be ready for anything.

dinosaur fighting systems. By the end of the first day the squadron was well into LFX 3; with the old tanks we would still be trying to get through the preliminary Confirmation of Accuracy by Firing (CABF) procedure. The same three-piece ammo is used but the set-up is different, enabling us to be faster and fire rounds quicker than before, and definitely quicker than any auto-loader!

The following year Cpl Flackett's young troop leader, Lt (now Lt Col) Matt Smith wrote a detailed description of his first impressions of the tank for the regimental journal, and reproduced here as it tells us much not only about the tank but also the crews and the training systems used.

No 2RTR deployed to Iraq as a regiment on Operation Telic in 2003, and Egypt Sqn returned in 2007 on Operation Telic 9, with Badger and Cyclops squadrons both on Telic 10. In addition to Scots DG and 2RTR, five other RAC regiments have operated CR2. These are, in order of seniority, the Royal Dragoon Guards, the Queen's Royal Hussars (QRH), the Kings Royal Hussars (KRH),[39] the Queen's Royal Lancers, and 1st Royal Tank Regiment (1RTR).[40] At the time of writing the army has three operational CR2 regiments: QRH, KRH and RTR. In addition, the Royal

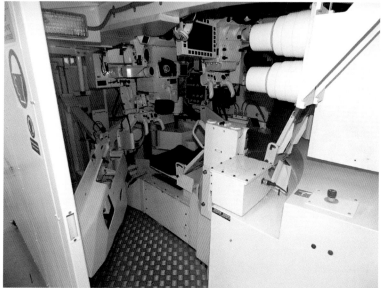

CENTRE The Turret Gunnery Trainer accurately replicates the gunner's and commander's positions in the tank, including the movement of the gun shield, seen hinged open on the left to allow the crewmen to enter/exit their seats.

LEFT However high-fidelity the simulation is, nothing compares to the thrill of firing real ammunition on a range. (Courtesy Andy Brend)

RIGHT It is time for the Yeomen to fire DS/T, the training ammunition that simulates the APFSDS natures; both projectile and two bag charges (with the training blue ends) can be seen. *(Courtesy Andy Brend)*

BELOW The proof of the training is in the firing: the RWxY are the only Army Reserve unit who are trained as CR2 crewmen, and this tank proudly carries their 'broken spur' symbol on the side of the TOGS barbette. *(Courtesy Andy Brend)*

LEFT AND BELOW RWxY having fun on an urban exercise, reducing a car to scrap in a couple of seconds. There is a real military point to this – roadblocks in towns have to be really substantial to stop a Challenger 2! *(Courtesy RWxY)*

ABOVE RDG crews top up their tanks – in both senses of the phrase – on exercise. CR2 carries a maximum of just over 2,000 litres of diesel fuel, including 410 litres within the two external tanks. *(Courtesy Andy Brend)*

Wessex Yeomanry, an Army Reserve (formerly Territorial Army) unit, has the mission of training replacement crews for a number of AFVs, including CR2. When eight crews used CR2 on a gunnery camp at Lulworth in May 2001, it was the first time that a reservist regiment had fired on tanks since the 1960s.

The Royal Dragoon Guards (RDG) completed their conversion in 2000 and were to be key to the development of CR2 – including and unbeknown to them at the time, to the desertisation modifications required – because of their participation on the now infamous Exercise Saif Sareea[41] II – see below. The regiment also participated in the prolonged series of operations around the Basra area after the Iraq War, with the first deployment on Operation Telic 5 from November 2004 until the end of April

EXERCISE SAIF SAREEA II – EXTRACTS FROM THE REPORT

The National Audit Office

The Challenger 2 MBT was originally designed and procured for use in north-west Europe during the Cold War. This decision, taken in 1987 and re-endorsed following the 1991 Gulf War, was taken on the understanding that additional measures (including additional air conditioning and extra cooling systems) would be necessary for the vehicle to be capable of operations in more extreme conditions. The Strategic Defence Review recognised the need for equipment to operate globally. As a result funding was assigned in 1999 (some £23 million) to include 'desertisation' modifications for some 30 tanks (two squadrons). One of these modifications included the skirt plate which involved the incorporation of new seals, dust strips and trackguards: this was costed at £464k for four battlegroups, or 116 CR2s. However, this funding was subsequently delayed and ultimately deleted in May 2000. (The Royal Army of Oman operates a specially desertised version of CR2.)

In July 1991 Permanent Joint Headquarters (PJHQ) directed, despite concerns raised by HQ 1 (UK) Armoured Division and 4th Armoured Brigade, that the A3 climatic conditions predicted removed the need for CR2 modifications prior to deployment to Oman.[43]

The nature and quantity of the dust led to the tanks' air filters becoming clogged at a rate much faster than anticipated. The fine nature of the sand and its tendency to solidify led to significant clogging, [which] led to a daily consumption of 46 filters for the 66 vehicles. Soon after the beginning of the first exercise, Desert Warrior, it became clear that CR2 was encountering difficulties in Oman. The problems did not occur because of the extreme heat (which exceeded the A3 limits considerably and climbed on occasion to A1), but rather because of the amount and peculiar nature of dust being thrown up. Large quantities of dust and sand are thrown up by the roadwheels and track of the tank. This enters the air filters; if the filters fail, the result is serious engine damage and failure. If the filters become blocked the engine is starved of air and stalls. The effect is exacerbated by the airflow behind the rank, with a vortex effect created by the forward movement. The urgency attached to these consumables meant that they had to be transferred to theatre by air, [which with a combined weight of] 55 tonnes, prevented the supply of spares for other vehicles. Two squadrons were removed from the exercise, [but] in all other respects the tank performed well.

2005 in which two CR2 squadrons deployed with 4th Armoured Brigade, A Sqn going to Al Amara and B Sqn into Basra itself – this tour included the regiment producing their version of the now famous 'Is this the way to Amarillo?' song, which is proof positive of the flexibility of the British tank crewman! On a more military note, on Operation Telic 11 (December 2007 to June 2008) B Sqn deployed as part of the Scots DG battlegroup, with Sgt (now WO1 RSM) Chris Richards winning the Military Cross, believed to be the first MC won on a battle tank in action since the Korean War; his story is told later.

Exercise Saif Sareea II represented the largest UK deployment overseas since the Gulf War of 1990–91. It took place from September to November 2001 in the extreme environment of the southern Omani desert 5,000 miles away from the home base; 66 CR2s were deployed in five squadrons, the majority came from RDG, with a squadron from the Queen's Royal Lancers. By the time of the exercise RDG had completed conversion training plus a series of exercises culminating in exercises in Poland and Canada. Aside from the extreme heat they encountered, the ubiquitous fine sand and dust proved to be the biggest problem, working its insidious way into all the systems, and causing numerous breakdowns, many of which were novel to the crews and the REME supporting them. The air filters, which normally lasted for many months in Europe, required changing on average every 30 hours or so, despite the best efforts of the crews to prolong their life by frequent cleaning; the filters would be completely clogged after only 4 hours of desert motoring. Other equipment also suffered – roadwheel rubbers, trackpads and sensitive electronic components. The demands on the suppliers and maintainers, not to mention the crews, were enormous, and the level of breakdowns effectively rendered the tank non-operational. On the final day of the exercise, only half of the CR2 fleet were classed as operational. Unfortunately this led to observers – some with a particular axe to grind – to take the opportunity to decry CR2 and ask why it had been selected, even though every other major equipment used suffered similar troubles.[42] What they failed to understand, or chose not to, was that the tank had never been specifically designed for those conditions, and although the modifications that were required for desert operations were well known (and in a lot of cases already designed), the money was not made available to allow them to be fitted to the tanks as a money-saving measure; the tanks were not even allowed to be painted in desert camouflage paint! The results were entirely predictable and were not an accurate reflection of the tank and its crews. However, the failings identified (which culminated in a National Audit Office inquiry and report – see separate box) provided a relatively short-term benefit; within 18 months desert-modified CR2s had operated very successfully in the Iraq War and the subsequent operations, proving conclusively that the fundamental design of the tank was not at fault.

BELOW Sand ingress into the engine was a problem identified during the prototype trials – here V9 creates a typical sand and dust cloud as it negotiates desert country. (Courtesy Pete Breakspear)

LEFT Although the problem of dust ingress into the engine was known to the MoD, the solution was not funded for the RDG tanks on Saif Sareea II, leading to many unnecessary and expensive, not to say embarrassing, failures. (Courtesy RDG)

RIGHT The very fine Omani dust wrecked many an engine, but the same problems were not encountered in Iraq as the money was made available to introduce the modifications needed to overcome the problem. *(Courtesy RDG)*

ABOVE AND RIGHT A CRARRV and a Warrior repair vehicle attend to CR2 casualties on Saif Sareea II – note the blue recognition symbols used on that exercise. *(Courtesy Pete Breakspear)*

ABOVE It is **NOT** meant to look like this. Despite their reliability Challenger 2s do, of course, break down, and this tank needs some serious attention. *(Courtesy Andy Brend)*

ABOVE RIGHT The CRARRV is designed to recover MBTs, and this Challenger 2 has been hitched up and is in the process of being recovered to a location where it can be quickly repaired. *(Courtesy Andy Brend)*

RIGHT QRH crews working on their tanks; these CR2s carry the black pig design used by D Sqn QRH, as well as 20 Armoured Brigade, QRH regimental, and the New Zealand silver fern devices fixed to the TISH barbette.
(Courtesy Andy Brend)

The Queen's Royal Hussars (QRH). QRH completed CR2 conversion in 2000, and deployed one squadron on CR2 to KFOR in Kosovo during 2001. Three CR2 deployments were conducted in Iraq, all as part of 20th Armoured Brigade: Telic 3 (November 2003 to April 2004); Telic 8 (May to November 2006);

RIGHT Officers of the Queen's Royal Hussars wear the unique Tent Hat that the regiment adopted from the 8KRIH via the QRIH; the many amalgamations of cavalry regiments over the last century have led to an interesting and often confusing array of uniforms and regimental insignia. *(Courtesy Andy Brend)*

and Telic 13 from December 2008 until April 2009. QRH are expected to return to UK from Sennelager around 2018, moving to Tidworth but remaining as a CR2 regiment.

The Kings Royal Hussars (KRH) are one of the three regular regiments still operating Challenger 2, having received their first six tanks in Tidworth in December 2000, starting the conversion of crews to the tank in January 2001 but not completely finishing until spring 2002, owing to other commitments. Driving and Maintenance (D&M) conversion took two weeks but the completely new turret took longer, at six weeks. They were, however, lucky enough (some involved might take the opposite view) to be the first regiment to have their Challenger 2 fleet converted to the brand-new Bowman communications system in 2003, a lengthy and at times frustrating process, as it interfered with them getting to grips with the new tank. During the conversion process an anonymous author from C Squadron commented that the gunnery training introduced them 'to some incredible concepts, like actually hitting things on the move!' The Commanding Officer was startled

to realise that one of the gunnery test exercises required him to engage five targets in 65 seconds . . . while on the move, an impossible task for its predecessors. From April until November 2005 the KRH deployed on their first and only operational tour on CR2, on Operation Telic 6 in Iraq. Two small tank squadrons were used, A Sqn with seven tanks in Al Amarah and B Sqn with three troops working for a Danish battlegroup in Shaiba.

The QRL reported their experience on the tank thus:

We converted to Challenger 2 in 1999. B and C Squadrons saw active service in 2003 deploying to Kuwait under command of the 1st Royal Regiment of Fusiliers battle group (BG), part of 7th Armoured Brigade. On 21 March 2003, amongst the first tanks into Iraq were those belonging to B Squadron in its initial role as the brigade's bridgehead force, crossing the border obstacles and establishing a strong presence inside enemy territory in order to allow the rest of the brigade to pass through. Both squadrons were involved in the fighting for the brigade

objective of southern Basra; sadly, on 25 March Cpl Steve Allbutt and Tpr Dave Clarke of C Squadron were killed in action.[44] Once the city was secured, both squadrons were faced with the complex problem of Peace Support Operations including prisoner of war handling, stabilisation activity and security patrolling – at the time these were uncommon activities for armoured soldiers. As a result of the two squadrons' involvement in Iraq, the regiment was awarded the Al Basra battle honour. Less than a year later, and following a period of relative calm in Iraq, the Mehdi Army's challenge to the authority of the Iraqi police grew to the point where British soldiers in country were re-tasked from routine security activity to frantically preparing equipment for possible war-fighting. As part of Op Telic 4 in the second half of 2004, the other two tank squadrons in QRL reactivated the Challenger 2 fleet to support efforts against the growing insurgency. D Squadron were tasked, amongst other things, to protect the principal bridges into Basra, whilst A Squadron supported the Princess of Wales' Royal Regiment BG's efforts to loosen

ABOVE AND BELOW A King's Royal Hussars CR2 comes ashore from a Royal Marine-operated landing craft; tank crews practise all types of mobility and movement, including crossing tank bridges and amphibious exercises. *(Courtesy KRH and Andy Brend)*

LEFT A TES-equipped CR2 (DR47AA) of A Sqn 1RTR moves at speed on a road on the Salisbury Plain Training Area (SPTA), nearly 400km² of MoD-owned land in central southern England. *(Courtesy Andy Brend)*

the insurgency's grip on Al Amara. The Challenger 2 and its crews prevailed, despite 50° heat (upwards of 60° inside the turret even with the CTCS running at full pelt), a tenacious enemy and the ever-present threat of being mobbed by hostile crowds; it more than proved its worth in complex operations. The squadrons returned to the UK in October 2004 and QRL then changed role, converting to Formation Reconnaissance in 2005, thus bringing to an end the regiment's extremely busy period of service on Challenger 2.

LEFT The same tank seen from the rear; the fuel drums and mountings are not fitted to this tank, nor is the rearmost bazooka plate, common practice to prevent mud building up around the sprocket. *(Courtesy Andy Brend)*

BELOW Tank commanders boresighting their own tanks (Confident, Cossack and Chanter) at BATUS in 2016, using extension leads to allow them to talk to the gunner using I/C (intercom). The jerrycans give them a little extra height to reach the boresight in the muzzle if necessary. *(Courtesy QRH)*

A Squadron 1RTR operated CR2 in the demonstration role on Salisbury Plain Training Area and was equipped with some from the last batch of Challenger 2s produced, having received its first tank in 2000 and its final one in April 2002. The remainder of the regiment had converted to the specialist CBRN role in late 1999, and A Sqn was detached to provide the means of demonstrating CR2 capabilities to visitors, as well as often providing the Opposing Forces (OPFOR) for units exercising on the Plain. For this reason their tanks were painted in the 'BATUS' scheme of Light Stone and NATO Green, usually seen on the vehicle fleet in Canada (although since 2010 the BATUS fleet has used a plain single colour based on Light Stone).[45]

Training the individual crew members

The training of the individual crew members on CR2 followed a familiar pattern to those of previous generations, with one notable difference – the provision of high-fidelity training simulators, as will be explained later. Soldiers are trained initially as drivers at Bovington, having completed their recruit training. The driver's course includes not only driving the tank on roads and cross-country, but also involves learning a multitude of maintenance tasks. He also begins training on radio systems and procedures at this stage of his career. After a period as a driver, a crewman then completes his gunnery course and the second part of the radio training, allowing him to be used as a gunner and later, with a little more experience and seniority, as the loader/operator. After a number of years and having been promoted to corporal, selected crewmen attend the armoured crew commander's course at Bovington and Lulworth, which includes both technical and tactical elements. At about the same stage he will also qualify as an instructor in one of the three trades: gunnery, driving and maintenance (always referred to as D&M) or radio.

Officers, on the other hand, attend the armoured troop leader's course shortly after commissioning as 2nd lieutenants from the Royal Military Academy Sandhurst. This course consists, in effect, of certain elements of the D&M, radio, gunnery and the

crew commander courses, as attended by the soldiers, but with a lot of emphasis on commanding a troop in the field. Apart from becoming the officer equivalent of an instructor in one of the three trades – known as Regimental Gunnery Officer (RGO), Regimental Signals Officer (RSO) and Regimental D&M Officer – the officer will next receive tank-specific individual training when he is about to become a squadron leader as a major.

What makes these courses different for the CR2 crewmen compared to their predecessors is the range, complexity and fidelity of the training equipment used, particularly for the gunnery courses. While CR2 was being developed, a suite of Precision Gunnery Training

BELOW Gun barrels are still cleaned in the old-fashioned way, using an oiled brush attached to wooden staves; there is no high-tech kit here. This would be familiar to crewmen from Centurion onwards. (TM 5012C3)

BELOW A KRH tank commander leans across to retune one of the Bowman radios – they are placed in the most convenient position in the turret for both the crew commander and the loader.

LEFT Inside the Loader Drills Trainer, which allows the loader to learn and practise all drills including misfires and stoppages on both the main armament and the chain gun.

Equipment (PGTE) was developed concurrently, and which represented a major step forward in quality, being based on the then-new affordable computers which had appeared in the late 1980s and into the 1990s. In brief, the gunnery courses use the following equipments:

■ **CBT**. Computer-Based Training uses a number of instructor-controlled PCs, one per student, to allow the crewman to complete theory and information lessons in a structured way, complete with periodic and final tests. An advantage of this over the traditional lesson format is that the brighter students can complete the material faster, which is more efficient and allows the instructor to spend more time with the slower class members.

■ **LDT**. The Loader Drills Trainer replicates the loader's side of the turret, complete with a main armament that simulates firing and recoil/run-out. The loader uses durable representations of the 120mm ammunition to learn and practise all the drills and procedures, including misfires, which are set up by the instructor using the menus on the control computer. Chain gun drills can also be incorporated. While one trainee is acting as the loader, the other five members of his crew observe his performance from outside, which increases the learning experience as they are expected to spot errors and omissions.

■ **PTT**. The Part Task Trainer is a simplified gunner's station, allowing the gunner to become familiar with some of the main elements of his controls, including his firing

CENTRE Turret bustle APFSDS ammunition stowage in the LDT.

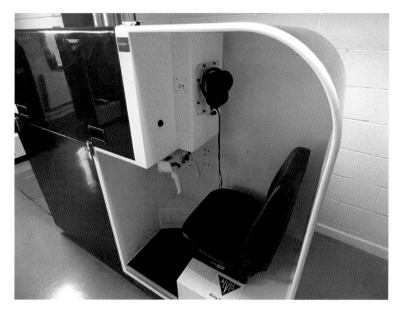

LEFT The Part Task Trainer (PTT) allows the gunner to complete many shooting exercises prior to progressing on to the TGT.

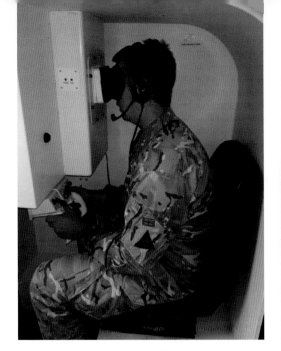

handle and sight picture. Again under the close supervision of the instructor, who monitors six students simultaneously, the trainee will work his way through a series of gunnery exercises, which gradually become more complex as he progresses. Should he fail to achieve the standard, he cannot progress until he achieves it, which may include additional remedial training as determined by the instructor. The PTT also has an 'Arcade' mode, a simplified though still accurate version which is intended to encourage the trainees to continue to hone their skills out of working hours.

■ **TGT**. The Troop Gunnery Trainer replicates in great detail the right-hand side of the turret, allowing a commander and gunner to work together in very realistic environments, which include all sighting systems. The TGT also includes a moving component that represents the right side of the main armament, which increases the fidelity. All crewmen who have used the TGT agree that the standard required is very high, and that it is an excellent simulator which prepares the crew for live firing. Up to four TGTs can be linked together into a TFCT, or Troop Fire Control Trainer, allowing procedures within the troop to be practised, with the crews travelling over the same virtual terrain.

■ **SADT**. The Small Arms Drills Trainer allows trainees to conduct the full range of chain gun drills, including stoppages, in the classroom before progressing on to the LDT and live firing.

ABOVE LEFT A trainee gunner practices engagement sequences in the Part Task Trainer (PTT). *(Courtesy RWxY)*

ABOVE A Yeomanry crew inside the TGT, which, as well as being very realistic and a lot of fun, also puts the two crew members under a lot of pressure, as everything they do is recorded for analysis and critique. *(Courtesy RWxY)*

BELOW The SADT is a stand-alone computer-controlled replica chain gun, used to practise drills and stoppages on the co-axial machine gun.

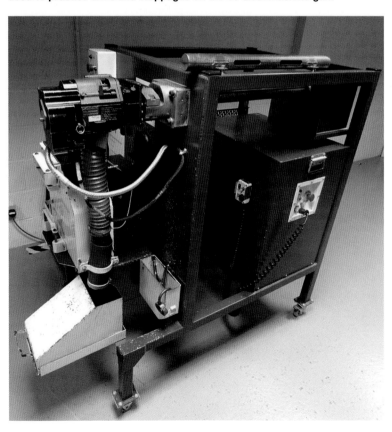

THIS PAGE Woods provide perfect places for tanks to conceal themselves, using thermal sheeting to defeat TI devices and camouflage nets for the IR and visual spectrums. No 22B is the tank belonging to the regimental 2IC. *(Courtesy Andrew Totten)*

Training the squadron

The training of a squadron of 14 tanks follows a similar pattern to that familiar to generations of Royal Armoured Corps crewmen: troop and squadron training using training areas in UK, Germany and/or Poland, followed by an intensive series of live-firing and force-on-force exercises in the British Army Training Unit at Suffield, Canada. What is different in the modern era is the impact of WFM, or Whole Fleet Management, introduced in the early 2000s. WFM came about as the result of the realisation that the manner in which tanks were allocated to regiments was, from the financial point of view, inefficient. Previously, each tank crew 'owned' its own tank, and was responsible for maintaining it in every respect, assisted of course by the REME. Therefore a Type 58 regiment possessed 58 tanks, and used them for training including live-firing and tactical exercises. While this promoted pride of ownership and individual responsibility, as well as increasing their deep knowledge of the tanks' systems through daily contact with them, it also meant that the crews were very much tied to their tanks as the maintenance routines were almost never-ending, preventing them from conducting other training. It was also extremely expensive, as more usage led to more spares being required, along with huge amounts of fuel and other consumables. It was therefore decided to introduce WFM, meaning that instead of holding all its tanks, a regiment

LEFT Many bridges cannot cope with the weight of an MBT; the Scots DG wisely chose to drive alongside this wooden structure. *(Courtesy Andrew Totten)*

CENTRE BATUS; the tank has the frequently seen striped antennas, and the side of the CPS has the coloured squares used by the range safety staff to watch where the commander is looking. The right side is bright green, the left side fluorescent orange or red. *(TM 5947A3)*

would only own a small number which would be passed around the squadrons as necessary to allow training, with the remainder held in special environmentally controlled storage. Popular as this was with the budgeteers, it is much less popular with the crews, who still yearn for the opportunity to 'own' a tank that belongs to them alone.

Registrations

The British Army production CR2s were ordered in two batches, with blocks of registration numbers allocated to them; from these it is easy to determine which batch a given tank came from. Batch 1, ordered on 21 June 1991, was for 127 tanks and was in the range of Vehicle Registration Marks[46] (VRM) 61KK68 to 62KK99 (132 tanks). Batch 2 used the latest registration system which had been adopted on 27 September 1993. The format of the registration changed, from the previously used format of two digits, two letters, two digits, to two letters, two digits and two letters. This new system allowed for around 45 million vehicles to be registered . . . only 254 of which were CR2s. These were in the range DP70AA to DT23AA. The 386 British Army MBTs were built at both the Leeds and Newcastle plants, although the Omani tanks were all constructed in Newcastle.

RIGHT FOP 61KK68 demonstrates deep fording in Bovington; taking it slowly is advisable unless the crew fancy getting wet. . . . *(TM 4901D4)*

Batch	VRM	Number
1	61KK68 – 61KK99	32
	62KK00 – 62KK99	100
2	DP70AA – DP99AA	30
	DR00AA – DR99AA	100
	DS00AA – DS99AA	100
	DT00AA – DT23AA	24

The camouflage system can be used in open country, which does not prevent an observer from seeing that there is something there, but makes it more difficult to work out exactly what it is. *(Courtesy Andy Brend)*

LEFT A plain green CR2 drives on exercise without any of the equipment used on operations or on TES exercises; such tanks are sometimes referred to as the 'vanilla' variety. *(Courtesy Andy Brend)*

Chapter Five

Challenger 2 on operations

The only true measure of a tank's worth is when it is used operationally. On peace support operations in the Balkans, but more importantly in the heat and dust of Iraq, Challenger 2 delivered what it was there for, time and again. Expertly handled by the brigades and battlegroup staff, and crewed by well-trained and highly motivated professional soldiers, again and again it lived up to its reputation as a tank that could 'do what it said on the tin'!

OPPOSITE An up-armoured Challenger 2 of the Queen's Royal Lancers in full Operation Telic rig, *c*2004, with the dust mitigation skirts attached under the side armour, and the TECs fitted over the exhausts. The CIP/TIP thermal recognition panels have not been mounted but an extemporised wire cutter has been fitted to the left front of the turret. *(TM 6388A5)*

RIGHT A grubby 2RTR CR2 in Bosnia, carrying the Stabilisation Force marking on the bazooka plates – the appliqué armour packs have not been deemed to be necessary. *(TM 5922B4)*

LEFT Scots DG were the first regiment to receive CR2 and to take their tanks on an operational deployment, Op Agricola 3 in Kosovo. This tank is only carrying the side armour packs, but the crew are clearly in 'prepared-to-warfight' mode as the turret and gun are camouflaged with netting. *(Courtesy Andrew Totten)*

The Balkans

Operation Agricola 3 to Kosovo was the first operational deployment of Challenger 2. B Sqn Scots DG, the same squadron that had conducted the ISRD and which was therefore probably the most experienced CR2 sub-unit available, was deployed to assist in the peacekeeping and stabilisation operation in Kosovo in 2000; before then Challenger 1 had been used. Following its use in Kosovo, the most kinetic operation being undertaken in the Balkans, it was also deployed

LEFT No 11B (One One Bravo), the CO's tank of 2RTR on duty as part of the peacekeeping force in Kosovo; tensions remained high in the area after the NATO intervention in 1999, and it was thought appropriate that the tanks should be protected with the additional appliqué armour packs. *(Courtesy RTR)*

RIGHT A typical Balkan scene – life goes on while a 70-ton tank driven by an 18-year-old carefully picks its way through the traffic.
(Courtesy Andrew Totten)

with the Stabilisation Force or SFOR in Bosnia, which was a slightly more stable situation and known as Operation Lodestar. Typically each armoured regiment would only deploy one squadron of MBTs, the other squadrons converting to a mixture of light armour using CVR(T) (Combat Vehicle Reconnaissance (Tracked)) and infantry, reflecting the versatility of the RAC crewman. Although the CR2s did not have to fire their main armaments in anger during the operations, their mere presence was often enough to calm down a potential flashpoint and bring belligerents to their senses; on more than one occasion the CR2s were used in firepower demonstrations for the warring parties, in order to make clear the capability that the international community could call upon if required.

RIGHT As well as a perfect view of the top of the tank, a prize to anyone who can work out what is going on here – look very carefully and it is possible to make an educated guess . . .
(Courtesy Andrew Totten)

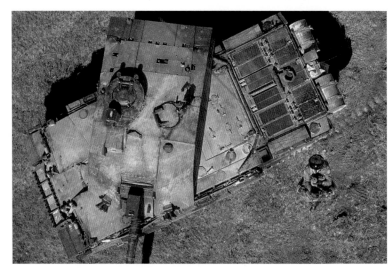

ABOVE . . . it is a CASEVAC exercise using an RAF KFOR Puma to extract simulated casualties from a simulated minefield. *(Courtesy Andrew Totten)*

BELOW AND RIGHT Scots DG troopers starting the task of fitting the support frame to the side of a Challenger 2; alignment frames are used to ensure that the upper and lower mounting rails are correctly aligned before the armour packs are fitted. *(Courtesy Andrew Totten)*

ABOVE All tank crews who were on standby to deploy to the Gulf as part of Operation Telic went through a preparatory range firing package in Germany before leaving; here two of 2RTR's CR2 fleet are seen on a firing point. *(Courtesy RTR)*

Operation Telic – Iraq

In 2003 116 Challenger 2 tanks in eight squadrons were deployed on Operation Telic (the invasion of Iraq from Kuwait) in early 2003, with the majority of the crews coming from Scots DG, 2RTR and two squadrons from QRL. The tanks and their crews had time for a short but intensive training package in Germany before being shipped over to Kuwait, arriving in early March 2003. The composition of the units, which were 'battle-grouped' as combined arms organisations, was as follows:

- **Scots DG BG**
  30 × CR2 (RHQ, B and C Squadrons)
- **2RTR BG**
  30 × CR2 (RHQ, Cyclops and Falcon Sqns)
- **1BW BG**
  28 × CR2 (A Sqn Scots DG, Egypt Sqn 2RTR)
- **1RRF BG**
  28 × CR2 (B and C Sqns QRL).

RIGHT No 2RTR vehicles being loaded up in the ship that will take them to war in early 2003. *(Courtesy Tank Magazine)*

ABOVE An incongruous sight: 62KK12, a CR2 of 4 Troop A Sqn Scots DG resplendent in its new Light Stone paint, being driven in the snow in Fallingbostel, prior to being shipped to Kuwait.

ABOVE Before and after: two Challenger 2s of Cyclops 2RTR as they are prepared for war, with appliqué armour, dust skirts, TECs and the recognition devices. *(Courtesy RTR)*

LEFT A close-up of the TECs and the rear of the armour packs and skirts. *(TM 6388B6)*

A number of modifications were also required – everyone remembered the experience of Exercise Saif Sareea – to ensure that the tanks were ready for combat in the extremely harsh climate of Iraq, where temperatures above 50°C were common, and the sand was as fine and ubiquitous as that found in Oman. Aside from the side and nose armour packs, the tanks needed modifications to keep the dust ingress to a minimum, to shield the thermal signature from the side-mounted exhaust cowls and to assist in recognition. Major Cliff Allum was one of the trials staff officers at ATDU who was deeply involved in the work.

As mentioned by Maj Allum, fitted to the tanks in the Kuwait desert in early March 2003

LEFT Ready to go: callsign 21 of A Sqn Scots DG in full rig and ready for action, which was only days away. *(Courtesy 'Monty' Montgomery)*

ABOVE Bombing up: Egypt 2RTR preparing the ammunition that they will soon be using. Note the mixtures of desert and temperate combat uniforms. *(Courtesy RTR)*

RIGHT Bombing up: SHQ A Sqn Scots DG with their L26 APFSDS ammunition – the arrival of 'Fin' caused much excitement but also made the crews realise that war really was imminent.
(Courtesy 'Monty' Montgomery)

LEFT Cyclops 2RTR completing their final sight adjustment and systems checks in March 2003; not all of the tanks have had their CIPs fitted.
(Courtesy RTR)

LEFT Digging shell scrapes was a feature of life, something to be done every time the tank was halted for any length of time; note that this tank is still carrying its peacetime oil drip tray, albeit sprayed in Light Stone! *(Courtesy RTR)*

BELOW LEFT Going to war: 2RTR crossing the border into Iraq. *(Courtesy RTR)*

BELOW The frequent dust storms did not cause the engines many problems due to the modifications, but made life very unpleasant for the crews and negated the advantage of the TOGS system. *(Courtesy 'Monty' Montgomery)*

URGENT OPERATIONAL REQUIREMENTS

Maj Cliff Allum MBE, RTR

The Transition to War (TTW) activities in preparation for Operation Telic were considerable, and not least in the Armoured Trials and Development Unit (ATDU) in Bovington. The Unit, commanded by Lt Col Nigel (Noddy) Stafford 9/12L was charged with bringing the armoured fleet to combat readiness and with trialling and perfecting various Urgent Operational Requirements (UOR) and finding answers to the many questions raised by taking AFVs designed for operations in north-west Europe to a Middle Eastern theatre of operations. Chief among these questions was the knowledge that the CR2s on Exercise Saif Sareea in Oman had been unable to operate

at their optimum performance because of the talcum powder-like sand of the desert. Tanks moving at speed through the sand created a dust cloud which swirled up and over the turret and then straight down into the main engine air intake. This had the effect of quickly clogging up the air filters and frequently brought the tank to an embarrassing – and in conflict potentially fatal – halt. Within ATDU the Weapons and Heavy Systems office, headed by myself as the SO2 Weapons and ably assisted by WO1 (RSMI) (later Major) Wolfie McKendrick RTR, were charged with devising and trialling a solution to this and other requirements as part of the now-urgent TTW. Working closely with BAE Systems,

RIGHT A Royal Engineer (still wearing temperate DPM) guides Challenger 2s and Warriors over a tank bridge, used to cross the Iraqi border defences. *(TM 10354-003)*

were three devices to aid recognition, both from the ground and the air; these were CIPs, TIPS and an IR beacon. The Combat Identification Panels (CIPs, pronounced sips) were designed to allow friendly forces with thermal imaging devices to recognise each other quickly. For CR2, all of which were fitted with them, they consisted of two types: two flat panels fitted to the sloping fronts of the tanks either side of the main armament, and a number (usually four) of 'venetian blind' panels mounted around the turret sides and rear. These panels were made up of metal louvres angled up towards the sun and fitted into brackets, coated with a special grey thermal tape designed to show up in TI displays. If required, they could be reversed to angle them downwards and prevent them

RIGHT Trooper Rarawa, a gunner in Egypt 2RTR, gives a confident thumbs-up at the start of operations; he is wearing the recently issued one-piece flameproof coveralls. Note also the S10 respirator conveniently positioned to his rear. *(Courtesy RTR)*

the team developed two complementary solutions. BAE Systems had already started work on a new air filter that would handle any of the fine dust that found its way into the engine. At the same time other work began on a 'back of a cigarette packet' plan to change the shape of the air vortices swirling over the turret. The solution was to hang rubber skirting below the existing skirting (bazooka) plates in order that air, and consequently dust, rushing over the tank would be held lower long enough to allow the AFV to avoid the damaging cloud. Frenzied design meetings with BAE and long discussions with other manufacturers led to hurried field trials conducted both at ATDU and

also by Cyclops Sqn 2RTR in BATUS Canada (where the prairie can be almost as dusty as a genuine desert). These proved successful and all the CR2 on arrival in theatre were retrofitted with both the new air filter and the skirting fitted to the appliqué armour side panels. None of the tanks that crossed the line of departure in Operation Telic suffered air filtration issues. In addition to the air filtration issue, the ATDU team also sourced, trialled and deployed Thermal Recognition Panels and lights, as well as Combat ID solutions and a number of other improvements which remain classified; these were fitted with the assistance of a forward ATDU team deployed to Kuwait.

being seen – if, for example, it was believed that the Iraqis were using TI systems. Additionally, fluorescent air recognition panels called Thermal ID Panels (TIPs) were attached, typically to the top of the turret rear bustle, to provide both visual and TI identification to friendly aircraft. Lastly, the IR beacons, so small that they are invisible in most images, consisted of a flashing bicycle safety lamp with an IR filter over the bulb. Again mounted on the rear of the turret roof behind the cupola, these provided a flashing indication of a tank's position.

Aside from these methods which were coalition-wide, other recognition markings were used on the CR2s, which allows us to differentiate between the various regiments and squadrons. The system used was as follows:

SQN	TACTICAL SYMBOL AND CALLSIGN	THERMAL SLEEVE	FUME EXTRACTOR BODY	TROOP RINGS ON FUME EXTRACTOR	NAMES	REMARKS
RHQ SCOTS DG	Black diamond	Light Stone	Light Stone	Not used		Large black callsign on front of hull side armour
A Sqn SCOTS DG	Black triangle	Light Stone	White	Not used	Informal names in black on hull sides front	Large black callsign on front of hull side armour
B Sqn SCOTS DG	White square	Light Stone	Light Stone	Black		Large white callsign on front of hull side armour
C Sqn SCOTS DG	Black circle	Light Stone	Light Stone	Black		Large black callsign on front of hull side armour
RHQ 2RTR	Black diamond	Light Stone	Light Stone	Not used	CO's tank c/s 11B Nomad	
Cyclops 2RTR	Black square	Light Stone	Light Stone	White	Begins with C	Black single eye below TISH door. Large black callsign on front of hull side armour
Egypt 2RTR	Black circle	Light Stone	Black	White	Begins with E	Sphinx emblem on TISH sides
Falcon 2RTR	Black rectangle	Light Stone	Light Stone	Black	Begins with F	Black falcon head on turret front sides. Large black callsign on centre of hull side armour, small version on front
B Sqn QRL	Black square	NATO Green	Light Stone	Not used		Large black callsign on front of hull side armour
C Sqn QRL	Black? Circle	NATO Green	Light Stone	Not used		

Both Scots DG and 2RTR, belonging to 7th Armoured Brigade, painted the famous Red Rat symbol on their tanks; locations varied, but most seem to have painted one on the TISH door on the front of the TOGS barbette above the barrel. Four-inch squares of thermal glint tape were frequently stuck to the turret sides to allow callsigns to be seen at night-time, arranged in patterns that allowed the callsign to be interpreted by those in the know. Scots DG tanks all used Scottish saltire devices on the lower front turret sides, and some tanks, including the COs, had a Scottish lion rampant in black on the middle of the turret sides. No 2RTR tanks had their vehicle names painted in black on the hull sides, and often used individual squadron symbols, for example Falcon used a falcon head sign applied using a stencil. QRL tanks often displayed their famous 'Or Glory' motto on the front or side of the TISH barbette, although at

ABOVE Target Stop! An MT-LB burns – 120mm HESH dual-purpose ammunition would easily destroy the lighter armoured vehicles, leaving the APFSDS for tanks. *(Courtesy RTR)*

RIGHT Inside Iraq, callsign 32 of A Sqn Scots DG – note how this squadron used squares of glint tape on the turret sides to indicate the callsign through thermal imagers. Three pieces of the dust skirt have gone missing in action. *(Courtesy 'Monty' Montgomery)*

BELOW Cyclops 2RTR in a typical scene from southern Iraq, where the infrastructure was in a terrible state even before a major war was fought over it. *(Courtesy RTR))*

ABOVE Centaur, aka callsign 40 of Cyclops, is the subject of respectful attention from these Basra residents. *(Courtesy RTR)*

least one version looked more like a pirate skull and crossbones than the actual badge!

Of course, aside from the invaluable work performed by ATDU and others, the crews themselves had a multitude of tasks to complete, from refreshing individual and collective training skills to painting the vehicles and fitting new equipment. Sgt Brian Maddams was an experienced Troop Sergeant in 2RTR who fought throughout the 2003 campaign and who is well placed to take up the story:

BELOW The squadron leader's tank of B Sqn QRL being used as a makeshift platform to allow a senior US officer to address the 1BW BG. *(TM 10354-004)*

PREPARING FOR WAR

Sgt Brian Maddams 2RTR

DS16AA callsign 21 of 15 Troop was the Challenger 2 that my crew and I took to Iraq in 2003 as part of Operation Telic.[47] Our squadron, Falcon, belonged to the Second Royal Tank Regiment and we deployed as part of the 2RTR Battlegroup.

Preparations for war began at our Fallingbostel base in Germany in early 2003. There was of course a myriad of administration and training required to prepare the individual soldiers, but this was nothing compared to the work required to get the tanks ready. These Goliaths that took all available time to keep them maintained when they were not even being used now had to be prepared for war! I am sure it is still the case today but almost without exception all our tanks carried faults or required spare parts. These spares would miraculously become available when we were about to carry out an exercise or live firing and this was no different. There was also an increased sense of urgency and concentration regarding maintenance as this was for real and the tanks had to be fully ready.

What was different was the requirement to paint the tanks for the desert. We had to go from the standard north-west Europe black and green to desert yellow; I am sure NATO has a better name for the colour but I can't remember it.[48] Painting our own vehicles was something that, apart from minor damage repair (aka patch painting), just wasn't done by units; we used to spray our own vehicles in the late eighties and early nineties but this was stopped due to health and safety flexing its muscles. There were, however, enough 'old sweats' left that could still remember how to use a spray gun and compressor, and there was certainly enough enthusiasm by everyone else to complete the task. This enthusiasm soon faded as people discovered (or rediscovered) what a pain it is to spray-paint a main battle tank, made worse by unreliable spraying equipment. . . . However the job got done, and I will never forget the moment when the three freshly painted

15 Troop tanks were driven out into the daylight, only to reveal that, along with hundreds of gallons of desert yellow that the squadron had been supplied, had been a few tins of another colour which was distinctly pink! While an SAS 'Pinky' Land Rover festooned with machine guns would have looked the part in that colour, my Troop Leader's tank most definitely did not. It was unfortunately too late to do anything about it and so the 'Pink Panther' had to go as it was! The only saving grace was that this paint was not nearly as durable as the proper stuff on the tanks and after a few days in the desert had pretty much worn off.[49]

The preparation period is pretty much a blur now, but we did it in time (just!) and the tanks went on a train to move to the post for embarkation, and the crews went on by aircraft to be reunited in Kuwait. While the men and machines are metaphorically in transit I will explain a bit about my own tank. According to the practice of the Royal Tank Regiment, the Troop Sergeant's tank of the second troop in the fourth Armoured Squadron is named 'FEROCIOUS', and that is what we stencilled back onto our handsome new desert livery. Not a bad name really when you look at the others in use: FANNY for example might have cut it in 1917 but not in 2003! That tank had been 'mine' for the best part of four years, and I was also fortunate to have the same driver for all that time in Tpr Tony Lee. For the war I had Tpr Neil Bozier as the Gunner, with L/Cpl Scott Greene as the Loader/Operator. The crew were good, Ferocious was great, and most importantly, it was the right colour!

We finally arrived in Kuwait, and spent a few days staying in large Bedouin-type tents until the tank transporters arrived carrying our tanks from the port. One tank of course was much easier to spot than the others with its pink tinge. As anyone familiar with tanks will know they require regular maintenance even if they have done nothing, so quite a bit of time was spent getting the vehicles ready again and then we were off into the desert.

We spent a week or so carrying out 'beat-up' training and getting generally familiar with operating in the desert. This culminated in Live Fire Exercises and FIN commissioning, which is the set-up procedure for the fire control

ABOVE Ferocious, Sgt Brian Maddams' tank, that gave him such great service during the war. *(Courtesy Brian Maddams)*

systems and gun to fire the DU APFSDS ammunition. Rumours were rife about the radiation hazard that this ammunition could pose, not helped by the issue of personal dosimeters, which I am sure was just a precaution and probably was more to do with the presumed threat posed by the Iraqi forces. I distinctly remember Scott (my loader) gently placing the first DU round we fired into the breech as if it were a priceless Ming vase!

BELOW The crew of Ferocious, with Brian 'Mads' Maddams sitting atop the cupola. Both the headlamps are wearing goggles, and the Multi-Barrelled Smoke Grenade Dischargers (MBSGDs) are loaded with L8 smoke grenades! *(Courtesy Brian Maddams)*

The next activity was to head to a vacated Kuwaiti army barracks for the fitting of the Urgent Operational Requirements or UOR as they are known. This is best described as 'pimp my tank'! I will point out at this stage that there was some concern as to how the tanks would perform in the desert as during a previous exercise in Oman CR2 had problems due to massively high oil consumption caused by the inability of the air filter system to deal with sand. Our tanks did suffer clogged air filters but that problem was about to be solved for good.

The first step in the process was to check the hydrogas suspension units on each tank to make sure that they could cope with the additional weight of the add-on armour that was about to be fitted. This was a nervous time as a failure meant that the vehicle and crew went to the back of the queue to wait for spares to solve the problem. However, Ferocious passed and we were introduced to a team of civilian engineers from Alvis[50] that would fit our modifications. I will never forget them cooing like proud parents as our powerpack had run for 400 hours without requiring a base overhaul – the leader of the team working with us even dragged other teams over to have a look!

The first items fitted were additional armour packs. This was nothing new and not really a UOR, as they had been fitted to CR1 in the First Gulf War. I won't go into details but basically a frame is fitted to each side and a nose cone to the front, onto which is attached additional armour suitable to defeat the expected threat. (We did not get the turret armour packs that were fitted on later TELIC operations.) Fitted as part of this were Thermal Exhaust Cowls (TECs) which fitted onto the existing exhaust and routed the exhaust gas rearwards instead of straight up; this design was supposed to reduce the thermal signature of the vehicle. I don't think the enemy had any thermal imagers but it certainly made us feel that things were being done to protect us. What the TECs also did was divert the unpleasant exhaust fumes and heat away from the turret which was a bonus. My crew were so keen to get the TECs fitted that we worked into the early hours of the morning without Alvis's help to fit ours . . . only to be told in the morning that they were upside down!

The real winner that we had fitted in Kuwait was the new air filter system, comprising a new filter hopper and scavenge unit with a new type of filter element. To say this was a great improvement is an understatement, and we conducted the whole campaign on only one filter. Even with the weight of the extra armour and all the other gear we were carrying, Ferocious clocked 78kph (approx. 50mph) one night, which is a great testament to the effectiveness of the new system. Due to the previous experiences already mentioned, every tank was carrying masses of spare oil and filters in case of blockages but in the event none were needed. Heavy duty canvas skirts were also fitted that helped to minimise the dust thrown up by the tracks. Due to the efficiency of the new air filters I think these helped more to reduce signature but again were a welcome addition, although they gave the impression that we had some sort of 'hover tank'. I cannot remember the exact mileage we did but Telic was the only time in 23 years' service that I carried out the 1,000km/one yearly major service on a tank because it had driven 1,000km rather than because 12 months had elapsed!

We were also given camouflage nets that were made of a thicker hessian-type material that just did not snag on anything, unlike the traditional string camouflage nets used in Europe. For the unfamiliar I will explain that putting up a camouflage net over a tank is like pulling a giant piece of Velcro over it – the net catches on absolutely everything! These new nets hardly caught at all and could just be pulled over the tank without snagging. Being thicker they were also more wind-resistant which proved useful as the dust storms could be, like my tank, ferocious (although this did lead to some pretty spectacular scenes if they were not firmly secured and the wind picked up . . .).

There were also dozer blade kits on offer, which our squadron did not have fitted; I think this was because we had already fitted our nose cones which would have had to be removed, and we did not have time, although to quote Tony my driver 'If we have one of those we'll be expected to dig holes for everyone' which I think was an astute observation, and I was happy not to have one fitted. The Alvis guys also welded studs to the turret to fit the Combat ID Panels (CIPs). These were basically panels with louvres on them which could easily be identified through a thermal imager. In 2003 every tank commander had their own privately purchased GPS receiver. Usually this was a little handheld Garmin or the like, designed for outdoor sports but quite suitable for use on tanks, and to be honest, invaluable. The problem with these on tanks was that it was impossible to get a signal when you were closed down under armour with the hatches shut, a situation that would be common in the coming days and weeks. The Alvis guys solved this and fitted each tank with an issued Garmin

GPS to the right of the commander's station, powered from the vehicle and with its own external antenna so it would work closed down. This was best described as a 'result' and was a real asset. All in all these modifications greatly enhanced the capability of what I think was already a potent MBT. To quote an American M1 Abrams commander who looked over Ferocious: 'This mother sure looks like it knows how to fight!'

Ferocious only let us down once during the war. She was bested neither by clouds of dust nor a lack of spares, but by German mud! Unbeknown to us this had clogged the air intake of the CTCS (air conditioning for those not in the know). It was ironic that mechanically the tank performed flawlessly despite the harsh environment and high mileage, only to suffer problems with overheating turret systems (crew included) caused by a blocked air intake! After the war and as we left to return to Germany, Ferocious remained in Iraq as part of the in-country fleet. I have no idea what happened to her but no doubt she was well used, fitted with even more UORs, given numerous paint jobs (hopefully not pink) and new names by the units that used her. I am sure she served well under whatever colours, and hopefully now sits in storage somewhere – an old veteran probably looking a bit tired and shabby but with a real soldier's heart, waiting to be called up again!

LEFT Soldiers always do their unwitting best to obscure vehicle names in photographs! No 40 of A Sqn Scots DG entertains a couple of visitors as her tracks are changed for brand-new ones. *(Courtesy 'Monty' Montgomery)*

153

CHALLENGER 2 ON OPERATIONS

Operation Panzer, also known as the Fourteen–Nil engagement, was in many ways the ultimate demonstration of what CR2 was capable of when handled by determined and professional soldiers. On 27 March 2003 the fourteen CR2s of C Sqn Scots DG, operating as two half-squadron groups, intercepted a similar number of Iraqi T55 tanks and other AFVs south of Basra moving towards the Al-Fawr peninsula, and destroyed them all without loss. Colin Macintyre, who had been heavily involved in the trials of CR2, was then the Squadron Sergeant Major of C Sqn, and he recalled the difficulties that the tanks faced in getting into action. He noted how quickly the squadron were given brief orders to move about 50 miles to join up with 40 Commando Royal Marines, in order to give them much-needed firepower as an Iraqi armoured assault upon them was thought likely. The squadron had never worked with the Commandos before. The move out was done at night, made much more difficult by the lack of maps, as only the squadron leader and his 2IC had one each and led their respective half squadrons, comprising 2nd and 3rd Troops and 1st and 4th Troops respectively.

Crossing the major water obstacle of the Khawr Abd Allah, a wide estuary of the Shatt al-Arab river, was a hugely difficult task, the tanks having to drive down what felt like vertical slippery banks in order to cross the water using RE-operated M3 ferries of 23 Amphibious Engineer Squadron. Led by recce cars from the Queen's Dragoon Guards, the tanks moved into the city using the best routes they could find in the marshy ground – the sand-covered oil pipelines that were clear of obstructions and were thus used as a road, although whether the pipes could bear the weight of a CR2 was the cause of some uncertainty . . . they did. The 3rd Troop made the initial contact with the enemy tanks, and C Squadron let the APFSDS and HESH do their talking for them, excited and yet in control at the same time. Avoiding but also using co-ax MG fire to engage and clear a surface-laid minefield, the tanks of C Sqn manoeuvred and engaged enemy T55 tanks and MT-LB personnel carriers, as well as dismounted infantry, RPG teams and bunker positions. In only a few minutes the final tally

was seven tanks, six APCs, two fortified bunkers and any number of infantry – leading one to question where the media-inspired fourteen–nil came from. What was not in doubt was the performance of the crews and their tanks.

Another demonstration, this time of the survivability of Challenger 2, came outside Basra on 6 April 2003, involving B Sqn and in particular callsign 30 belonging to the troop leader. As the regimental journal recounted:

Captain De Silva's crew were taken aback to discover that a previously abandoned T55 fired a [100mm] round which hit them squarely on the nose. A good shot from the T55 but sadly its last as some stunned seconds later the whole troop responded by firing back and destroying the enemy tank.

Other incidents were recalled:

The enemy still proved determined and one man, on a suicide mission, emerged from a bunker to throw a grenade into Cpl Smith's tank; he was promptly cut down by machine gun fire from the rest of the forward tanks. . . . We came under fire from heavy machine guns mounted on the bridge of a boat that had been held in dry dock. It was hit with main armament HESH . . . USMC Super Cobra attack helicopters flew in front of our arcs whilst we were firing in order to engage and destroy two enemy AFVs. . . . The infantry investigated some bodies at the entrance to a complex; the 'dead' miraculously rose up and fired RPGs at the armoured congregation! One unfortunate met his end as a result of a 25m HESH engagement and another was crushed under a wall as he rose to fire his RPG. . . . Most of them were foreign nationals who had come to fight for Saddam; none were able to use the return portion of their airline tickets.

Away from the Scots DG BG, A Squadron Scots DG was detached (along with Egypt from 2RTR) to support the 1st Battalion Black Watch (1BW) infantry battlegroup. Sgt 'Monty' Montgomery was a troop sergeant with the former, and offers this account of his war:

BELOW A poor image, but this shows where the 100mm round fired from a resurrected T55 hit Captain De Silva's tank – the ERA operated as designed and there was no other damage. *(Courtesy Scots DG)*

Sgt William 'Monty' Montgomery Scots DG (1BW BG)

On arrival in Kuwait, one of the first tasks we needed to complete was to ensure the tanks were ready to fire the 'Fin' APFSDS round. Each tank varies slightly and therefore its gunnery system needs to be adjusted individually. A makeshift range was set up in the Kuwaiti desert and members of the AFV Gunnery School and the Armour Training Advisory Team had been sent from the UK to ensure the ranges were conducted correctly and to ensure that each CR2 sighting system was correctly adjusted according to how it fired. Most of the squadron had only ever seen 120mm training ammunition and we were surprised at the length of the actual round itself compared to the DS/T training round we were used to. There was a definite excitement across the tank crews when handling and using this ammunition, and I think that it was at this point that the situation began to feel very real. The ranges went very well and we left with a high degree of confidence that the tank would fire accurately in the desert. It was no real surprise as by this stage most of the crews had fired the tank regularly on the ranges in Germany and Canada and knew what the tank was capable of.

After ranges were complete, our next task was to move the tanks to the Kuwaiti army camp in which they would be up-armoured and 'desertised'. Other than spraying the tanks with their desert colours before leaving Fallingbostel, little else had been done in order to make them fit for desert conditions. It had only been 2 years earlier, during Exercise Saif Sareea II, that CR2 had received a pretty bad press on its performance in similar conditions in Oman. It was accepted at the time that this wasn't really an issue with the vehicle as it just hadn't been properly prepared. Lucky for us, these lessons had been learned and we were due to receive a number of modifications. The work to up-armour and modify the CR2s was pretty tough. Vickers [sic] had sent teams of engineers direct from the factories in Newcastle and Leeds to assist in carrying out the work. The extra armour was extremely heavy and required two men with specialist lifting equipment to get it on. We also fitted upgraded air filters, which would greatly assist in the reliability of the engine . . . [and] various items which would assist in recognition of friendly forces by both day and night. The square strips of paper often

BELOW 'Monty' in the cupola with his crew, looking relaxed despite their youth. He ascribed this to their training and confidence in the unit and the tank. (Courtesy 'Monty' Montgomery)

seen on the side of the turret could actually be seen through thermal imaging and were laid out in a way to identify each particular troop of the squadron. The extra armour brought about extra confidence in the tank. What was already a formidable vehicle now looked almost indestructible. What was also comforting was the fact that although a lot of weight had been added, the performance of the tank didn't suffer too much. From here, we moved to another location in Kuwait, which acted as the Forming-Up Point (FUP) for the entire Battlegroup (BG) and here we also carried out final checks and maintenance whilst we waited for the order to advance into Iraq.

The journey into Iraq itself was more straightforward than most imagined. 1RRF BG had already broken through but we were still not sure what to expect. I seem to remember that there was more a feeling of excitement than fear and we were pleased that we weren't waiting around in the sandstorms of Kuwait any longer. Already, my high confidence in the tank was growing ever more. The vehicle was driving extremely well and coping with any obstacles that we came across. At this stage, we thought it may still be an open desert, tank on tank, type of battle. However, that was not to be the case and it would actually turn out to be the more difficult urban warfare on the streets and roads of Al-Zubair and Basra. During April 2003, A Sqn Scots DG took part in what at the time was the deepest raid into enemy-held Basra, which I shall endeavour to describe. The squadron was allocated three targets, which comprised of a Fedayeen stronghold, a symbolic monument, and for my troop along with SHQ, we would target the main TV mast.

The mast was being used to transmit across the city and its destruction would assist in halting the spread of Saddam's propaganda.

The squadron formed up in the early hours of the morning and, despite having been subject to a BM-21 multi-barrelled rocket attack only a few hours earlier, I was amazed at how calm my crew was. As I looked around the turret making final checks and studying my map, the others were sitting quietly having a brew and reading a book or magazine. It was a scene I'd witnessed countless times on exercises in Germany and Canada but the fact we were about to go into an extremely dangerous situation, not knowing if we'd return, made it quite surreal. We weren't sure if we'd face enemy armour but we knew they'd be prepared, well defended and have access to anti-armour weapons in the form of RPGs and guns. The order came to move and we crossed over a bridge and down Route Red, which was a main dual carriageway into the city. The CR2s were quickly at full speed and scanning for signs of trouble ahead. As I had done many times before on the tank ranges of Germany, I scanned my arcs for enemy through the commander's sight but also kept an eye through the cupola periscopes as to the position of the other tanks within the squadron. Being a TV mast, the target was pretty easy to spot in the distance and I laid my gunner onto the target. At this time it was out of effective range but I wanted to give him some situational awareness.

As we moved closer into the city it became very apparent that our presence had been noticed. As I looked through the sights, I was faced with an incredible scene of both incoming and outgoing fire. It reminded me of the final scene in *Star Wars* when Luke Skywalker is flying across the Death Star and there is a huge blaze of fire and light. This was the early hours and there was still a level of darkness, which enhanced the lines of tracer fire coming from both sides. Both main armament and co-axial fire was coming from the CR2s whilst on the move. Eventually, we arrived at a point where my troop could put down effective fire on the TV mast. At each corner of the compound was a sentry tower and I've often wondered what must have been going through the minds of the Iraqi soldiers guarding the installation – if indeed they were prepared to hang around and find out. These towers were quickly neutralised. The effort then focused on bringing down the mast.

Although we knew this was our ultimate objective and required HESH, I had ordered the loader to initially load Fin prior to the assault in case we needed to deal with any enemy tanks on the way in. This was ineffectual against an open metal structure, but we fired at it anyway as we needed to clear the chamber in order to load HESH. At this stage we had considered it safe to go static: CR2 fires on the move very effectively but a static shoot would be far easier and we also needed to hold this position. Within a very short period of time, the tower came crashing down. We heard from the other troops that they'd also successfully destroyed their targets and were making their return. The squadron then had to make its way back down Route Red. No tank commander would ever bare the rear of his tank to enemy fire so the first part of the withdrawal was carried out in high-speed reverse. CR2's reversing speed is impressive and it got us out of the danger zone very quickly whilst the gunners could still engage targets if necessary. Once clear, we were able to turn the tanks around and drive forwards for the rest of the way.

On return, the squadron was in a jubilant mood. It was 'mission complete' and we'd suffered no casualties or major damage to the tanks. This was incredible considering the amount of firepower that had poured down on us. I think this was a real turning point. We were already extremely confident in the tank's abilities but this just brought it home. For the remainder of the war, whenever I was in my tank, I felt that I could take on anything. What struck me most about being a troop sergeant during Op Telic was the attitude and performance of the men in my troop. Most of the soldiers were very young and my tank, callsign 31, comprised of an 18-year-old driver, a 19-year-old gunner and my operator/ loader was only 21. Probably, just like myself, there were times when they were scared or feeling anxious but they never really showed it. I believe that this was because they were confident in their leaders, their training and also in the tank itself.

Within a few short but intense weeks of combat Basra had been secured and the war appeared to be over, only for a period of relative peace to be followed by an upsurge in violence as different insurgent groups fought for control. This led to a series of 12 roulements, each lasting six months and in which all the various CR2 regiments deployed. The list of these roulements shows the regiments and, where identifiable, the discrete squadrons deployed, although it should be noted that not all of these were 'in-role' on CR2. Demonstrating the exceptional flexibility inherent in the Royal Armoured Corps, many CR2 crews deployed on other vehicles, from Snatch Landrovers and CVR(T) to Warrior, and many were employed in the dismounted role as infantry.

Telic 2	July–October 2003	No MBT component
Telic 3	November 2003–April 2004	QRH
Telic 4	May–October 2004	A & D/QRL
Telic 5	November 2004–April 2005	RDG
Telic 6	May–October 2005	KRH
Telic 7	November 2005–April 2006	B/KRH
Telic 8	May–October 2006	QRH; D/SCOTS DG
Telic 9	November 2006–April 2007	QRL; B/SCOTS DG; Egypt 2RTR
Telic 10	May–October 2007	KRH
Telic 11	November 2007–April 2008	C/SCOTS DG
Telic 12	May–October 2008	SCOTS DG
Telic 13	November 2008–April 2009	QRH

The same operational name, Telic, was used for these roulements within Iraq. The limited number of armoured regiments and squadrons available meant that each regiment would return two or three times over the next years, and although there were fewer tanks deployed (often as a single squadron), and the war-fighting was officially over, this did not mean

Cpl Stew Baird KRH

On 19 September 2001 I was finishing my first ever BATUS exercise in Canada on Challenger 2, the regiment having completed the conversion to the new tank earlier in the year. Exactly four years to the day later in Iraq, two undercover British SAS soldiers were captured by insurgents, and taken to the notorious Al-Jameat prison in Basra. During the subsequent (first) attempt to release them, a violent protest had taken place by a crowd armed with small arms and RPGs, which they directed at the British troops who were using Warrior infantry fighting vehicles. This culminated in one Warrior being set on fire by petrol bombs and having to be abandoned; at least three soldiers became casualties and the whole event was filmed, making worldwide news.

At 1715 hours I was largely oblivious to this, and was preparing for the daily squadron orders group. At this stage in my career I was a corporal acting as the troop sergeant, based in the Shaiba Logistics Base to the west of the city. I was in the *de rigueur* off-duty dress of flip-flops, shorts and squadron T-shirt (but carrying my body armour and helmet inside my daysack) when I was approached by a warrant officer I had never seen before asking how he could 'get hold of some tanks'! I directed him to squadron headquarters whilst I grabbed a quick brew; we

were due to go out in Snatch Land Rovers that night. However, on arrival at the O Group I was told to get 'a pair' ready (meaning two tanks) as things had changed – I hadn't seen the news all day so I was completely oblivious to the rapidly escalating situation in Basra. We parked the two tanks, callsigns DW60 and DW61,[51] outside the gate ready to go. (By the way, my tank, DW61, was known by its nickname 'Big Punisher', written in marker pen on the front of the hull sides; this was unusual as we didn't officially name our tanks in the KRH. I had named mine after the first US M1 Abrams to get into Baghdad, though whenever asked I would always reply that it is called that because it is, and it does!).

The squadron leader arrived and told us to get out our Basra maps; after much rummaging around the turret, we eventually found them. We were part of the Danish BG operating north of Basra and we had never actually been into the city. With only scant available information about the situation we were going to face, we set off; the troop leader volunteered to lead, with me check-navigating behind. He got us directly to the RV, where we dismounted and set about finding out just what we were there to deal with. We were directed to the back of a Warrior, accompanied by the loud announcement that 'the Challies are here', much to my annoyance as a bugbear of mine was that I always referred to them as Challengers! We were then brought up to speed with what was happening, and then given a quick 'bonnet brief' (a map spread on the bonnet of an available Land Rover) with a few aerial photos. After being told of our part in the plan, within only a few minutes it was time to mount up and go, followed by a very fast move from the RV to Al-Jameat. Our task was to breach the prison walls by smashing through them, allowing the Warriors which were carrying a scary-looking bunch of SAS guys in the back to enter the prison and rescue their mates.

There was a pause whilst the final attempt at obtaining their release through negotiation was tried (and failed), and then, with a fast approaching H-Hour, all the lights around us suddenly went out. This did nothing to calm my nerves, even though it was just one of the

BELOW Cpl Stew Baird and his crew immediately after the operation to rescue the SF soldiers – the front of Big Punisher is still covered in rubble from destroying the walls. *(Courtesy Stew Baird)*

LEFT Big Punisher, covered in bits of walls but still fully operational. *(Courtesy Stew Baird)*

regular power cuts in the city; still, I took that as my cue to close down. As soon as H-Hour was reached we had the command 'GO, GO, GO!' I had been tasked with breaching three of the outer walls of the prison and, given the level of the RPG threat, I chose to go in gun-front, presenting my strongest armour to the enemy and allowing me to fire my weapons. Unfortunately we hadn't gone in quite straight and so we only breached the first two walls; by now my driver was driving blind as a lot of rubble had fallen onto the tank, blocking his periscope. It was only when I felt the nose of the tank take a sudden dip downwards that we stopped. I was more than slightly disorientated by this unusual manoeuvre – we had never driven through walls before as it is not the sort of thing that you do on training! [Author's note: a Royal Marine SF helicopter pilot observing the action through night-vision equipment commented that the walls appeared to ripple as the tank tore through them!] I decided to open up and take a look at what was going on with my head out. Only then did I realise that we were parked inside a building! I grabbed a bit of handy 4 × 2 timber off the turret (which wasn't normally stowed there but came courtesy of the unusual method of entry) to sweep the debris off the driver's sight, and then moved Big Punisher into a position to provide over-watch where I could support the SAS troops dismounting. What they hadn't mentioned during the bonnet brief was they

were using explosive method of entry – to them it was probably so obvious that they needn't mention it! This made one hell of a bang that had me scanning like mad looking for the bad guys! It soon became pretty evident that the prisoners were not there, so we pulled out and had a rapid regroup before trying another area of Basra. I took up position in the rear of the convoy, and then a crowd began to build up behind us. I'm not sure if CR2 was ever designed with crowd control in mind, but it certainly worked, they were not keen on getting too close as they were staring down the gaping muzzle of a 120mm gun!

We pulled into an over-watch position at the Shia Flats (which was the second location) and soon the two prisoners had been released, allowing us to return via the initial RV and then back to Shaiba. On our return we were greeted with cries of 'You two have just been on *Sky News!*' However, my new superstar status didn't last long as we were ordered to refuel immediately in order to be on standby to go back out if needed! To conclude, and this is going to sound odd, but that night I believe that Big Punisher knew that she was needed, the vehicle almost understood my own sense of urgency. I genuinely believe that a vehicle can have a soul as she performed faultlessly all night; and both the crew and the Iraqis could feel the power emanating from her, giving us total confidence and them good reason to avoid the sort of punishment that she could clearly deal out.

RIGHT A view from a later Telic, as the Barracuda camouflage system bears witness. The tank is acting as a very effective roadblock. *(Courtesy RTR)*

RIGHT This is a QRH tank fully prepared to be shipped out to Iraq in 2008; this was the regiment's third Telic tour. Camouflage painting of the vehicles was not necessary by this time, as a different kind of war was being fought. *(Courtesy Jim Elgar)*

RIGHT The rear of the QRH tank, showing the arrangement of the bar armour used to protect against RPGs. *(Courtesy Jim Elgar)*

that they stood idle. Quite the contrary, the tanks proved their worth over and over again in the counter-insurgency that followed the war. The experience gained from the nature of the conflict fought increased and led to a number of additional protective survivability measures being taken with the tanks, particularly to counter the two main threats of short-range hand-held anti-tank weapons (mostly of the RPG family), and extremely large buried explosive charges, known as Improvised Explosive Devices – the now-infamous IEDs. Under-belly armour was modified, new side appliqué armour packs were developed, including for the turret sides, and Electronic Countermeasures (ECM) packages brought into service. Bar armour was also used as an anti-RPG measure and fitted to the hull rear sides and rear. Cpl (now WO2) Stewart Baird was a tank commander in the King's Royal Hussars whose first experience of war was to come on one such deployment, in 2005.

Postscript

Challenger 2, much to the chagrin of many observers and almost all tank crews, was not deployed to Afghanistan. This was not because it did not have utility there in a pure military sense – as was proved by the Canadian and Danish Leopards deployed there – but rather because of the logistical and support difficulties, and therefore the enormous costs involved. This infuriated the RAC, who could

see that an opportunity to provide immediate and devastating direct support to the infantry, one of the two prime tasks of armour, had been denied them. Having to rely on other nations' tanks was a bitter pill, particularly for the hundreds of Challenger 2 crewmen deployed to Helmand province on other vehicles and who knew just how effective their beloved 'Challies' could have been . . . however, even as this book goes to print, a number of Challenger 2s from the Queen's Royal Hussars are deployed in Estonia, as part of the UK contribution to NATO operations in support of the Baltic states. The utility of the tank continues to be demonstrated, although it is to be hoped by a passive rather than an active demonstration of its range of capabilities.

ABOVE A Remote Weapon Station was fitted to replace the loader's GPMG, allowing the loader to engage targets from inside the turret without exposing himself to enemy fire. *(Courtesy Jim Elgar)*

LEFT A protective and alarmed security blanket was developed to provide security in transit, hence the addition of numerous welded loops for the straps all round the tank. *(Courtesy Jim Elgar)*

Chapter Six

Challenger 2 versions and variants

From the outset it was intended that the basic hull of CR2 would be used for a number of variants of the MBT, allowing the benefits of commonality of production, maintenance and repair and training to be realised. In the event, only three versions have been produced for the British Army: the Driver Training Tank or DTT, and two engineer variants, Trojan and Terrier, totalling 88 vehicles.

OPPOSITE Megatron, the unofficial name given to the ATDU Challenger 2 reference vehicle in what used to be referred to as the Iraq Theatre Entry Standard (TES) guise, is probably the most well-known and photographed Challenger 2 in the fleet. This is DT22AA, the second-last CR2 built. Challenger 2 was used to provide the basis of a number of specialised variants, including engineering vehicles and the MBT version developed for Oman, as well as a specially developed but ultimately unsuccessful export version. *(Courtesy Andy Brend)*

The Driver Training Tank

The Driver Training Tank (DTT) variant was developed from the earlier Challenger Training Tank (CTT) used to train drivers on Challenger 1. Externally very similar, with the turret replaced by an all-weather crew cabin, the DTT was modified to reflect the new (still under development) automotive systems used on Challenger 2, plus other alterations to suit the tank's training purpose. The main modifications from the CTT were:

- TN54 transmission.
- P4108 APU.
- The Digital Automotive Systems Control Unit (DASCU) to replace the Main Engine Control Unit (MECU).
- Lighter and unarmoured hull – achieved by using thinner plates.
- Double-pin track.
- External lights.
- Scalloped skirting plates.
- External fuel drums and brackets.
- Modified driver's compartment.
- Ballast weight to replicate MBT mass and performance.

LEFT There is usually no need for the DTTs to carry the external fuel drums, but a CR1 rear turret bin is used to stow personal kit behind the control cabin. *(Courtesy Andy Brend)*

- LRUs grouped on RH hull wall to facilitate easy replacement.
- Improved engine deck design including a torsion bar system.

Full development started in December 1991, with the first DTT prototype 62KK96 being built between July 1992 and September 1993, and it was then used for development trials by both VDS and the MoD, which concluded in January 1994. Vehicles 2–13 (the first batch of 13 had been ordered in June 1991) were then built at VDS Newcastle between October 1994 and May 1995. Eventually 22 DTTs were built for the British Army. As well as its primary training role, DTT has a number of potential secondary operational roles such as dozer tank, mine plough tank or ARV without winch, although these have never been required (or it seems, tested).

The Royal Engineer variants: Trojan and Titan

With the introduction of the Trojan and Titan engineering vehicles,[52] for the first time in decades Britain was operating a range of specialist engineering tanks that were on the same chassis as the in-service battle tank. Some 33 of each type were bought, the Trojan as an engineering support vehicle (but more commonly referred to using the familiar title of Armoured Vehicle Royal Engineers or AVRE), and the Titan as an armoured vehicle-launched bridge (AVLB). Both were developed from the hull of the CR2 MBT, but have a number of improvements fitted to them that stem directly from the work done on the Omani and CR2E variants, including an improved engine cooling system.

Originally known as the Future Engineer Tank project, the contract for Trojan was awarded in 2001, and 33 vehicles were made using the registration range ECxxAB, with AK36AB as the prototype. The first vehicle was trialled by the Royal Engineers Trials and Development Unit (part of ATDU Bovington) in early 2004. The main role of Trojan is to assist the Royal Engineers in their battlefield task of enabling movement through complex terrain and when faced with obstacles – both man-made and

natural – known officially as the mobility and counter-mobility roles. It is used in the minefield-breaching role, clearing and marking safe lanes, as well as being capable of enabling the crossing of short gaps using the fascine system, which is wide enough to allow CR2 to pass over it. It can also assist in the preparation of defensive positions and in creating obstacles to hinder the movement of enemy forces; on the front (as FEE – Front-End Equipment) it can be fitted with either a dozer blade (the BEMA(I) or Bulldozer Earth Moving Attachment

ABOVE Trojan moves at speed: not surprising really, as the hull is based on the current CR2 Main Battle Tank and shares similar characteristics. This Trojan has been equipped with an earth-moving blade on the front. *(Courtesy Andy Brend)*

BELOW A sapper guides a Trojan across a bridge; the FEE (attachments that can be fitted to the front, here another FWMP) mean that extra care has to be taken when manoeuvring in tight spaces. *(Courtesy Andy Brend)*

(Improved)), or a Pearson full-width mine plough – an improved version known as FWMP(I); this can be used with a Hard Surface Device (HSD) to clear mines from roads, runways, tarmac and so on. A rocket-propelled explosive minefield-clearing hose called Python can be towed in an L9 four-wheeled trailer and fired forward of the vehicle, the hose exploding on contact with the ground and the 1½ tonnes of explosive in it clearing a 7.3m-wide by 200m-long safe lane through a minefield. This can then be marked from under armour using the on-board Obstacle Marking System (OMS).

Trojan mounts a hydraulic excavator arm with a digging bucket and which is also used as a crane to lay the Midi pipe fascine that can be carried on the rear of the vehicle. The excavator is a militarised version of the Caterpillar 315

ABOVE The wheeled L9 trailer carries the Python minefield-breaching equipment, and can clear a 200m-long lane through a minefield in a few seconds. *(Courtesy Andy Brend)*

RIGHT Another trailer that can be towed is the AVRE trailer, used to carry a range of additional stores, in this case extra fascines. *(Courtesy Andy Brend)*

RIGHT The author took this image of a Trojan on operations in Afghanistan in 2011 where it was used to breach IED belts using Python. These vehicles were (obviously!) fitted with the genuine side armour panels, rather than the training versions usually carried on exercises.

model, and is controlled by the operator using a thumb controller. The bucket has a level capacity of 0.82m², and can lift 5.5 tonnes at a reach of 4.1m. An overhead remote weapon station mounting a 7.62mm GPMG gives the Trojan a close-range defensive capability, and it can also generate smoke using the engine or by the multi-barrel smoke grenade dischargers. An AVRE four-wheeled trailer can be towed by Trojan, which has a capacity of 8.25 tonnes of engineer stores on eight NATO pallets, or a midi pipe fascine, or a BEMA(I) or a FWMP(I) or two rolls of Class 70 trackway, making it a very useful addition to Trojan's capability at the expense of presenting a slightly incongruous appearance. The Trojan has a crew of three and weighs around 62 tonnes. Unlike the MBT variant, in 2009 Trojan was deployed to Afghanistan.

Trojan characteristics

■ Length (no FEE fitted)	9.45m
■ Length with mine plough fitted	12.87m
■ Width	4.2m
■ Width with mine plough fitted	5.27m
■ Height to commander's hatch	3.04m
■ Military Load Classification (MLC)	85 tonnes
■ Training weight	57,550kg
■ Combat weight	65,048kg
■ Combat weight with FWMP(I) fitted	68,468kg
■ Max speed (road)	59kph
■ Max speed (road, towing AVRE trailer)	30kph
■ Vertical obstacle	0.9m
■ Trench crossing	2.8m
■ Shallow fording (no preparation)	1.07m.

Titan is the AVLB version based upon a CR2 hull. It is capable of carrying and launching three different types of combat support bridge, known as the Nos 10, 11 and 12. These bridges can all be used to cross both wet (rivers, etc.) and dry (trenches, etc.) gaps up to a maximum crossing width of 24.5m with a single bridge. As with Trojan, FEE can also be carried, consisting of either BEMA(I) or the track-width mine plough (TWMP). The OMS can also be carried. The No 10 bridge

RIGHT This is called over-bridging: laying a No 10 bridge (in this case) over an existing structure in order to increase its safe carrying capacity. This combination will be able to carry MBTs in a few minutes more. *(Courtesy Andy Brend)*

is a maximum of 26m long overall, and can bridge the widest gap, up to 24.5m. It is a single-fold scissors bridge, hinged in the centre and constructed from a number of aluminium panels, allowing a slightly shorter 22/20.5m version to be constructed when required. The No 11 is a 16m-long, 14.5m-span bridge, and the No 12 is a 13.5m-long, 12m-span bridge; both Nos 11 and 12 bridges are of the up and over type. Spare bridges for Titan – 1 × No 10 or 2 × No 12 – can be carried on a Unipower 8 × 8 Tank Bridge Transporter. In order to span wider gaps than these, a Trestle Adaptor Set allows a second No 10 to be placed under the far end of the first bridge, enabling it to cross a much wider gap, up to 46m.

Titan characteristics

■ Length (no bridge)	11.7m
■ Length (with No 10 bridge)	14.4m
■ Length (with No 11 bridge)	16.35m
■ Length (with No 12 bridge)	14m
■ Width	4.2m
■ Height to top of superstructure	3.04m
■ Height (with No 10 bridge cross-country)	4.4m
■ Military Load Classification (MLC)	83 tonnes
■ Training weight	65,987kg
■ Combat weight	73,520kg
■ Max speed (road)	59kph
■ Vertical obstacle	0.9m
■ Trench crossing	2.8m
■ Shallow fording (no preparation)	1.07m.

RIGHT Camouflaging both the Titan and its bridge requires a really big net – breaking up the distinctive box shape at the rear will be this crew's next task. *(Courtesy Andy Brend)*

LEFT VDS converted prototype V9 into the correct configuration for the Omani tanks, including the different rear hull design which was part of the enhancements to the powerpack cooling system. (TM 4632E2)

Challenger 2 in Oman

During the 1990s the Sultanate of Oman placed two orders with VDS for Challenger 2 MBTs to equip a single armoured regiment. In June 1993 18 MBTs were ordered as part of a contract worth around £140 million. A second contract for another 20 MBTs was placed in November 1997, worth around £100 million. Ordered at the same time as the first contract were two Driver Training Tanks and four Challenger Armoured Repair and Recovery Vehicles. The two DTTs were to be used by the Armour School to train drivers and the CRARRVs would be split, two to 1MBTR and two to the Command workshop. The DTT and CRARRV would use the same cooling system, fuel system and track as the MBT, as described below.

The First Main Battle Tank Regiment or 1MBTR was chosen to receive the new equipment, Oman operating two regiments of tanks. At that time 1MBTR was equipped with 29 Chieftain tanks that had been supplied in the 1980s. The new regiment was originally conceived as a Type 43 with three tank squadrons and a headquarters squadron. Each tank squadron was to have 14 tanks and the RHQ would have had one for the commanding officer. Subsequently, the order was reduced by five, as some of the money was diverted in order to buy a large number of Panhard armoured cars instead. The 38 Challengers that were eventually delivered formed three squadrons of 12 with two vehicles in RHQ. Deliveries commenced in early 1995 and were complete by late 2000.

Training equipment supplied included three Turret Gunnery Trainers (TGT); six Part Task Trainers (PTT); one Loader Drills Trainer (LDT); and a Secondary Armament Drill Trainer or SADT. A full training package was also supplied by VDS which consisted of a Training Needs Analysis and all the courseware that was required to teach the pilot courses. An additional LDT was supplied during 2008. All training systems, courseware and publications were provided in dual languages, Arabic and English. The original intention was that the Oman MBTs would only be delivered after all relevant modifications identified as necessary from the UK Reliability Growth Trial had been incorporated into the Oman build. However,

BELOW One of the Omani CR2s; externally the first clue that this is not a British Army version is the loader's .50 MG, but look closely and the single-pin CR1-style tracks are another giveaway. (Courtesy Peter Breakspear)

because the UK RGT was delayed and the Oman vehicles were already in production at Newcastle, a number were delivered before the UK RGT was concluded. It was subsequently agreed that all the relevant modifications would be incorporated when the vehicles were in country after delivery, the cost borne by VDS. These modifications, along with other Oman-specific changes, were implemented by a team from VDS and took several years to complete, ending in 2003.

The differences between the Omani MBT and the UK Challenger 2 were largely dictated by the high ambient temperatures experienced in the Sultanate; temperatures exceeding 50°C are not uncommon, as well as the ever-present problem of dust. The main differences are as follows:

■ The vehicle uses the same single-pin 'dead' track as used on CRARRV and the older Challenger 1 tank. The new double pin 'live' track was not adopted for Oman; this seemed to be a good decision when, during Exercise Saif Sareea II in late 2001, no Omani tanks shed tracks, whereas many British tanks with double-pin tracks did, although this can be attributed in part to the Omani drivers having greater experience in the conditions.

- Large full-height skirting plates similar to those used on Challenger 1 are fitted to help mitigate the dust problem.
- A larger air-conditioning unit is fitted. This is positioned within the space usually taken up by the right-hand No 3 fuel tank, meaning that 1,321 litres can be carried internally, 271 litres or 17% less than in the UK vehicle. Two extra fuel fillers were fitted above the No 2 tanks on both sides to enable faster refuelling. The pannier bags in the fuel tanks were replaced by a sealed compartment system similar to that used in aircraft; this system was subsequently adopted for the Titan and Trojan Engineer vehicles for the British Army.
- Two external approach-march fuel containers can be carried as on the UK vehicle, giving an additional 360 litres. Because of the different airflow for engine cooling, these are stowed on top of the transmission decking rather than at the rear of the tank as in the UK build; they are designed to be discarded easily after use if required.
- The ME and GUE, although basically the same as the UK vehicle, have more efficient cooling fitted to cope with the conditions. The airflow is drawn through larger radiators and after circulating is expelled through large louvres on the rear of the hull. The modified airflow, described by one user as being of 'hurricane force', reduces the problem of dust being drawn up on to the engine and transmission decks when the vehicle is at speed. The three main engine fans are powered by a hydraulic pump driven from a power take-off from the gearbox, rather than using the belt-drive system. The transmission has a larger heat exchanger fitted. The GUE originally had a high-capacity five-bladed fan operating at a higher speed, with a thermal switch to cut off the fuel should the drive to the GUE fan fail, but was subsequently converted to an electric motor drive to improve reliability.
- The loader's pintle-mounted machine gun is a Browning .50in M2HB with a quick-change barrel. Hull stowage was changed internally to allow for five of the larger ammunition boxes to be stowed where the BV is carried (when out of use) on the British version, alongside the TVE magazines.

- Two RACAL Jaguar VRQ 316 secure radios were fitted with a radio harness for the crew; two antenna mounts are attached to the right side of the turret roof. A Garmin GPS navigation system is installed in the commander's station.
- More water stowage was required so two jerrycan holders are fitted to the turret front, one either side of the smoke grenade

ABOVE How to tell an Omani version from the CR2E: the Omani tanks have this distinctive chevron-shaped grille on the rear, as opposed to a rectangular version on the 2E. *(Courtesy Peter Breakspear)*

BELOW The front of the hull with the gun in the clamp. The biggest giveaway here apart from the scheme and the tracks is the RACAL Jaguar antenna mount, looking not dissimilar to the UK Bowman type. *(Courtesy Peter Breakspear)*

ABOVE The Royal
Oman Land Forces
also use four versions
of the CRARRV as
their tank recovery
vehicle; two DTTs
were also purchased.
*(Courtesy Peter
Breakspear)*

dischargers. Tools and equipment that on
the British version are mounted on the hull
rear are repositioned along both sides of the
hull, including the towing frame and spare
track links.

The soldiers of the Royal Army of Oman
were – at first – sceptical of the complexity of
Challenger 2, having been used to the much
simpler Chieftain and M60, but over the ensuing
years as they have gained confidence and
experience they have used the vehicle in a very
aggressive and confident way. Possibly one
of the reasons why the Omanis took to CR2

was that when the tanks were commissioned
on the ranges, the targets they used were the
old Chieftains that they had been operating
previously, and which did not stand up well to
the L23 APFSDS used by the Omanis.[53] Most
shooting on the ranges is done while on the
move, with very little from a static firing point –
Omani drivers seem to be completely fearless
when at speed, so always make the best use of
Challenger 2's excellent mobility.[54]

Looking for other export markets – the development of Challenger 2E

Saudi Arabian Army personnel were briefed
by VDS in November 1991, and were still
interested enough to have a bespoke firepower
demonstration laid on for them two years later,
as noted in Chapter 2. Kuwaiti officers were
also briefed in late 1991, and earlier that year
VDS had visited Sweden to brief them on the
tank's capabilities, but then decided not to even
offer the tank to them, in large part as it was
seen as a possible distraction from getting the
British order right at a time when the tank was
in its early stages of development. At one point
around 2000 it looked as though the Australians
might be interested in Challenger 2
as a replacement for their ageing Leopards,
but they opted for refurbished M1s from the
USA instead. Qatar also expressed an interest
in CR2E – see below for details of the 2E
version – but no orders were forthcoming. So
it can be seen that none of these campaigns
came to anything, much to the disappointment
of the MoD, the Treasury and most of all VDS.
In part of course this was because each of the
customers had their own view of what they
wanted the tanks for – in other words, they
were looking at how closely the contenders
met their doctrine. CR2 had been built with a
particular set of priorities, with survivability at the

LEFT V1 was converted to CR2E (export)
standard after it was no longer needed for British
Army trials, and now stands duty outside the
BAES facility in Telford. *(TM 5986C1)*

top of the list, and of course it carried a rifled gun. As not everyone viewed the world like this, it was always going to be an uphill task to convince potential customers that their doctrine and priorities were, in effect, wrong.

This can be illustrated by looking at the Greek MBT competition. In the mid-1990s the Greek Army began exploring a partial replacement for its fleet of 105mm armed Leopard 1 tanks, some of which had been purchased from Germany and others donated by the Netherlands. Competitive firepower trials were conducted in late 1998 involving CR2E as well as Leclerc, Leopard 2A5 (in the Swedish Strv 122 configuration), M1A2, plus T80U and the Ukrainian T84. The Leopard 2 was the clear winner, followed by the M1A2 and Leclerc within a hair's breadth of each other, and then CR2E just a little behind. Details of the exact nature of the trials are not clear, but as everyone knows, it is quite easy to set up a test that favours the competitor one most wants to win, and the Greeks already knew and liked Leopard, as much for its simplicity and ease of training as anything else.[55] They cannot really be criticised for this. CR2E was certainly hampered in the firing trials by the speed of loading; as quick as it was, it could never compete with single-piece ammunition unless the engagement was prolonged, and in particular it was disadvantaged when nobody was interested in looking at the survivability

RIGHT The redesigned
engine deck, with the
gun clamp between
the two louvres.
(TM 4975F5)

ABOVE CR2E in a typical export scheme moves at speed during a
demonstration at Bovington; at this time the smaller scalloped bazooka
plates are being used, rather than the full-depth versions usually seen.
(TM 10380-001)

BELOW This is CR2E as used on the Greek Army MBT competition, with
the appropriate camouflage scheme and additional dust-mitigation skirting
under the nose and bazooka plates, as well as the SAGEM sights. (Courtesy
Peter Breakspear)

advantages gained by the British design. In 2000 the Greeks announced that they would buy 170 Leopard 2A6 HEL.

Even while the tank was being perfected for British Army service, VDS realised that certain aspects of CR2's design and performance caused concern to potential export customers, and decided to develop a version of the tank to rectify some of these concerns, hence the suffix of E for export, first used in the late 1990s. The start point was the modifications requested by the Omanis, and which made sense as most of these potential export customers were to be found in the Middle East, including Saudi Arabia, Qatar and the UAE, as well as Turkey and Greece, where heat and dust were the main concerns. The major and most obvious modification was the replacement of the powerpack. Instead of the CV12/TN54 combination used on the service tanks, the 2E used a transverse MTU MT883 V12 1,500hp diesel, linked to the Renk HSWL 295 TM transmission; in this configuration it was often referred to as the EuroPowerPack. The powerpack was mounted on a rail system, allowing a quick change by dropping the hinged rear hull louvres. One key reason for using the MTU unit was that it is very small, about 60% of the volume of a Leopard 2 engine, and thus allowing much more fuel (or ammunition) to be carried within the hull, which can increase the range by about 100km. In the driver's compartment a half 'go kart' steering wheel was adopted in place of the steering tillers, and a forward driving camera was fitted. While the L30 gun remained the same (although VDS would have been receptive to customers who wanted another main armament mounted), the fire control system was updated. The commander was provided with a panoramic stabilised day/night sight, as was the gunner, both sights being made by SAGEM, finally, CR2 had been given what the crews had asked for during the trials – a true day/night hunter/killer system. Although the CR2E was clearly a more capable tank than its base version, as we have seen it was not selected for the Greek Army – or anybody else – and in 2005 development and marketing ceased. Which elements of the CR2E might make their way on to the Life-Extension Programme (LEP) remain to be seen.

TRIGAT missile tank

An attractive and unusual design was proposed in the late 1980s for using the hull of Challenger 2 to mount a TRIGAT missile system capable of dealing with a massed tank attack at ranges of up to 2,400m. In May 1989 a sketch was produced that showed the CR2 hull mated to a Krauss-Maffei-designed hydraulic hinged mast, on the top of which was a box containing the sighting system plus 12 TRIGAT missiles. A further 12 missiles were to be carried as an immediate reload on the engine decks. It was thought that both UK and Germany (mounting theirs on a Leopard 2 hull, unsurprisingly) might require up to 225 platforms each, with an in-service date of 1998. The fall of the Berlin Wall prompted the so-called peace dividend, allowing the NATO countries to reduce defence expenditure, and the project remained a paper one only.

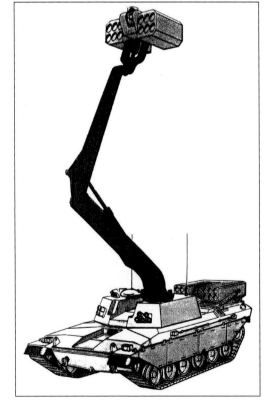

ABOVE The .50 HMG was fitted to the CR2E as this was most likely to be the weapon required by potential export customers, using the same pintle-mount used on the Omani version. *(TM 4977E2)*

LEFT The brochure illustration of the concept of a TRIGAT-armed CR2 missile tank, 12 missiles on the articulated arm and a reload on the engine decks.

Megatron

Megatron is the unofficial but frequently used name given to a tank operated by the Armour Trials and Development Unit at Bovington which is fitted with a full suite of add-on capability enhancements, designed to make the basic tank even more potent and ready for specific operational threats. This tank is probably the best-cared for tank in the fleet, and in the words of one of its crew members, is 'ultra-reliable . . . it hardly ever breaks down', despite being in constant use. The official designation of the tank is the Operational Entry Standard (OES) tank, as opposed to the 'vanilla' tanks, those in training configuration.[56] The tank can be configured in a number of different states, designated OES 1, 2, 3 and so on, which allows it to be customised to reflect the threats faced on specific operations. In general terms, though, the tank as shown here features the following enhancements over a vanilla tank:

- Armour upgrades include a Dorchester Level 2i (i for improved) appliqué system.

This includes a new one-piece nose cone to replace the previous CR1-style nose armour. Additional armour packs known to the crews as biscuits can be fitted to the sides of the turret, and bar armour, designed to protect from RPG HEAT ammunition, is added to the hull and turret rear. (Fitting the bar armour on the hull sides prevents Thermal Exhaust Cowls being used, and the nose cone prevents recovery from the front.)
- Additional under-belly armour to protect the crew compartments.
- Mobile Camouflage System (MCS). Two types of MCS are being trialled, both of which are fitted to reduce the external electromagnetic signature of the tank. One of these is the Saab Barracuda system secured to the tank using Velcro patches, the other the Rheinmetall Solarshield system, which is attached using magnets. The former system reduces the thermal signature, the latter both radar and thermal. As well as reducing the signature, the systems allow different camouflage patterns to be used without repainting the tank, as well as breaking up

the unnatural shine from the numerous flat surfaces (which were intentional as they aid in reducing the radar signature, an illustration of just how complex designing tanks really is!).

■ Cameras are fitted to the hull front and rear, making manoeuvring easier for the driver. The driver may not use the rear camera without the commander's assistance during training, but on operations can reverse the tank unaided, allowing the turret crew to concentrate on the threat and possible engaging targets.

■ Extended mud/dust flaps are fitted front and rear. (The dust reduction flaps that were used

below the earlier DL2 side packs are not fitted with DL2i).

■ A Remote Weapon Station can be mounted to the loader's roof, and controlled from inside the turret. The RWS fitted currently is the Rafael/Selex Enforcer 1 non-stabilised system which can mount a 7.62mm MG, the .50in HMG, or a 40mm Grenade Machine Gun. In the future an ATGW missile might be fitted, and the Enforcer 2 stabilised version can also be mounted. The RWS is controlled from a panel and joystick used by the loader to avoid overloading (no pun intended) the commander.

■ A threat-specific suite of ECM can be fitted to the hull and on to the 'bird table' fitted to the turret rear. Details of these items are of course highly classified.

Overall Megatron, with all the bells and whistles, weighs in at 74.8 tonnes. As it is a command tank 42 rounds of all types of main armament ammunition are carried, plus 4,200 rounds of 7.62mm. The current tank (as at spring 2018) bears the registration DT18AA, which replaced the previous original Megatron DT22AA when it had to undergo a full base overhaul – no surprise considering the extremely high mileage that it put on while at ATDU.

BEMA – the bulldozer

Challenger 2 uses the same BEMA, or Bulldozer Earth Moving Attachment, as its predecessor CR1. The BEMA comes as a self-contained kit which includes the blade, the powerpack and the necessary hydraulics; there is also an electrical harness and, mounted in the driver's cab, the control unit. The unit, with a joystick to control the blade, is mounted in the right side of the driver's compartment immediately above the rear of the battery housing. With the blade fitted, the tank has to be reversed on to a tank transporter, and can only be recovered from the rear. The blade is an easy item to use and drivers can be trained to employ it effectively very quickly. The 3.78m-wide blade is capable of digging a tank scrape in approximately 10 minutes, allowing a tank to adopt a hull-down position in areas where there is little natural cover. Spotting a BEMA attached to a CR2 is something of a rarity, as whole fleet management and the rotation of tanks through armoured squadrons means that they are not often fitted, although some older soldiers who understand the capability provided tend to bemoan this as a missed opportunity.

RIGHT The front of the BEMA, showing the steel cutting edge mounted below the main aluminium blade. *(Courtesy Andy Brend)*

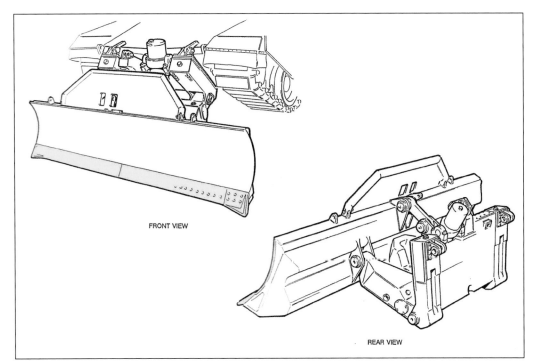

FRONT VIEW

REAR VIEW

Looking to the future – the Challenger 2 MBT Life-Extension Programme (LEP)

In order to modernise the CR2 fleet for service into the mid-2000s, two programmes were originally envisaged, the CLIP (Challenger Lethality Improvement Programme), and the CCSP (Challenger Capability Sustainment Programme). Neither of these was funded and both were replaced in 2015 by the LEP – the Life-Extension Programme. It was decided that the existing CR2 fleet needed to be modified, for two main reasons: firstly, some of the existing sub-systems were difficult to support, as some of the sub-contractors who supported specific items were no longer in business or the technology used was obsolete;[57] and secondly, to enhance certain capabilities, to allow the tank to remain competitive until 2035, its current expected out of service date (OSD). Included in the latter are expected to be such items as independent electronically cooled TI for both the gunner and commander, giving redundancy but more importantly the true day/night hunter/killer capability that was desired but not funded in the mid-1990s. Other items expected to be changed are an updated fire control

computer with peripherals, a modern electronic architecture to replace the current databus, a new commander's station, provision for the Bowman replacement radio system and work on ergonomics. All of these it will be realised are concentrated in the turret, but what of the hull? Improvements to the suspension, engine and transmission might be affordable within the publicised £700 million budget, but a brand-new powerpack might be a step too far.

In order to achieve the best value for money and to encourage commercial competition, over 20 initial bidders were whittled down to six, and then to two: BAES Land Systems UK, the Design Authority who took over the product responsibility from VDS in 2004 (working with a number of other companies), and the German Rheinmetall Land Systems, RLS. In December 2016 the MoD announced that £23 million each had been awarded to the two companies to begin the competitive assessment phase. A final decision on the winning bid is not expected before 2019, with the modified tanks, totalling an estimated 227, becoming available from 2025, remaining in service until 2035 – and possibly beyond. The designation of the new tank is not yet clear, although in a blast from the past, BAES are referring to the tank as the 'Challenger 2 Mark 2 specification', the same name used by VDS in the late 1980s.

Abbreviations

ABRO	Army Base Repair Organisation
ACTOC	Air Cooled Transmission Oil Cooler
AFV	Armoured Fighting Vehicle
APC	Armoured Personnel Carrier
APDS	Armour Piercing Discarding Sabot
APFSDS	Armour Piercing Fin-Stabilised Discarding Sabot
ARMCEN	Armour Centre
ATDT	Automated Target Detection & Tracking system
ATDU	Armour Trials & Development Unit
ATGW	Anti-Tank Guided Weapon
ATL	Automatic Tube Loader
ATR	Automotive Test Rig
AVLB	Armoured Vehicle-Launched Bridge
AVRE	Armoured Vehicle Royal Engineers
BAES	BAE Systems
BAOR	British Army of the Rhine
BATUS	British Army Training Unit Suffield
BEMA(I)	Bulldozer Earth Moving Attachment (Improved)
BFD	Battlefield Day
BG	Battle Group
bhp	brake horsepower
BICS	Battlefield Information Control System
BITE	Built-In Test Equipment
CABF	Confirmation of Accuracy by Firing
CAT	Canadian Army Trophy
CBRN	Chemical, Biological, Radiological & Nuclear
CBT	Computer-Based Training
CCP	Commander's Control Panel
CE	Chemical energy
CH	Chieftain
CHARM	Chieftain/Challenger Armament
CHIP	Chieftain Improvement Programme

CIP	Combat Identification Panel
CLIP	Challenger Lethality Improvement Programme
CPS	Commander's Primary Sight
CR	Challenger
CR1	Challenger 1
CR2	Challenger 2
CR2E	Challenger 2 Export
CRARRV	Challenger Armoured Repair & Recovery Vehicle
CTCS	Crew Temperature Control System
CVR(T)	Combat Vehicle Reconnaissance (Tracked)
DA	Design Authority
DESO	Defence Export Support Organisation
DF	Direct fire
DTT	Driver Training Tank
DU	Depleted uranium
EM	Electromagnetic
EMA	Ease of Maintenance Assessment
EPC	Equipment Policy Committee
ERA	Explosive Reactive Armour
FCE	Fire Control Equipment
FMBT	Future Main Battle Tank
FST	Future Soviet Tank
FTMA	Future Tank Main Armament
GAS	Gunner's Auxiliary Sight
GCE	Gun Control Equipment
GPMG	General Purpose Machine Gun
GPS	Gunner's Primary Sight/Global Positioning System
GSR	General Staff Requirement
HEAT	High-Explosive Anti-Tank
HESH	High-Explosive Squash Head
HCG	Hughes Chain Gun
HP	High-pressure
ISD	In-Service Date
ISRD	In-Service Reliability Demonstration
KE	Kinetic energy
KRH	King's Royal Hussars

LDT	Loader Drills Trainer
LP	Low pressure
MA	Main Armament
MBT	Main Battle Tank
MBT 80	Main Battle Tank for the 1980s
OAP	Operational Armour Pack
PC	Prime Contractor
PGTE	Precision Gunnery Training Equipment
PTT	Part-Task Trainer
QRH	Queen's Royal Hussars
QRL	Queen's Royal Lancers
RARDE	Royal Armament Research & Development Establishment
RB	Rifled bore
REME	Royal Electrical & Mechanical Engineers
RGT	Reliability Growth Trial
RHA	Rolled Homogeneous Armour
RO	Royal Ordnance
RTR	Royal Tank Regiment
RWxY	Royal Wessex Yeomanry
SB	Smoothbore
SH/P	Squash Head Practice
SR (L)	Staff Requirement (Land)
ST (L)	Staff Target (Land)
TI	Thermal Imager/Imaging
TMS	Turret Maintenance Simulator
TOGS	Thermal Observation Gunnery System
TTW	Transition to War
TVE	Tube Vent Electric
T2	Titan and Trojan
UOR	Urgent Operational Requirement
USMC	United States Marine Corps
V-A	Vickers-Armstrong
VDS	Vickers Defence Systems
VRM	Vehicle Registration Mark
WFM	Whole Fleet Management
WMR	War Maintenance Reserve

Challenger 2 technical data

NOMENCLATURE	
Designation	Tank Combat 120mm Gun Challenger 2

DIMENSIONS	
Length overall (gun front)	11.753m
Length overall (gun rear)	9.806m
Height (to top of commander's sight hood)	3,038m
Width (over tracks)	3.370m
Width overall (including skirting plates)	3.554m
Ground clearance (nominal)	0.512m
Width between tracks	2.17m
Length of track in contact with ground	4.79m
Weight Combat (loaded with ammunition, fuel, toolkit and crew stowage, excluding crew and DL2 armour)	64 tonnes
Weight Training (as above less ammunition)	62.5 tonnes
Bridge Classification (training)	70
Mean ground pressure (training)	276kPa
Track width	0.6m
Number of links (new track)	80

MOBILITY

Maximum road speed	60kph
Maximum road speed reverse	38kph
Vertical obstacle	0.9m
Maximum gradient (moving vehicle)	58%
Trench crossing	2.8m
Unprepared fording	1.07m
Range	450km, or 550km using external 350-litre fuel drums

POWERPACK

Main engine	Perkins CV12 TCA 1200 No 3 Mk 6A. 60° Vee, liquid cooled four-stroke compression-ignition
Capacity (swept volume)	26.11 litres
Idling speed	550–650rpm
Governed speed	2,300rpm
Rating (gross)	1,200bhp (895kW) @ 2,300rpm
Generator output (nominal)	500A DC
Generating unit engine	GEC 4.108 or 404C-22
Governed speed	2,850rpm (GEC), 3,100rpm (404C)
Generator output (nominal)	350A DC
Gearbox	TN54 No 2 Mk 1. Epicyclic 6 forward and 2 reverse gears

CAPACITIES

Main engine overall	91 litres
Fuel	1,592 litres under armour. 410 litres in external tanks. Total 2,002 litres
Coolant (main engine only)	81 litres
Coolant (complete powerpack)	136 litres

LETHALITY and SURVIVABILITY

Main armament	Ordnance Breech Loading 120mm Tank L30A1
Elevation and depression	+20° (356 mils), –10° (178 mils)
Rate of fire	8 rounds in one minute; 20 rounds in 4 minutes
Main armament ammunition	Gun tank: 50 rounds (33 APFSDS, 17 HESH/Smoke); HCDR Command (SHQ) tank: 45 rounds (29 APFSDS, 16 HESH/Smoke); HF Command tank (RHQ): 43 rounds (27 APFSDS, 16 HESH/Smoke)
Co-axial machine gun	Machine gun chain 7.62mm long L94A1
Turret machine gun	Machine gun 7.62mm L7A2
MG ammunition	4,200 rounds

KEY DOCUMENTATION

AESP 1230-C-100-711	Weapons Control & Optronics systems
AESP 2350-P-050-711	Armour
AESP 2350-P-102-201	Operating Information
AESP 2350-P-102-302	Technical Description
AESP 2350-P-102-601	Maintenance Schedule
AESP 2350-P-102-741	Illustrated Parts Catalogue
AESP 2350-P-102-741	Complete Equipment Schedule
AFV Technical Training School	Armoured Engineer Equipment Precis

Appendix 3

Bibliography

Davidson, Graeme and Johnston, Pat, *Modelling the Challenger MBT* (Osprey, 2006)

Dunstan, Simon, *Challenger MBT* (Osprey, 2007)

Dunstan, Simon, *Challenger 2 MBT* (Osprey, 2006)

Edworthy, Niall, *Main Battle Tank* (Penguin, 2011)

Foss, Christopher and McKenzie, Peter, *The Vickers Tanks* (Keepdate, 1995)

McKenzie, Peter, *The Barnbow Story* (Longhirst, 2000)

Suttie, William, *The Tank Factory* (History Press, 2015)

Various, *Eagle & Carbine*, Vols 27, 28 (Scots DG, 1998–99)

Various, *Tank Magazine* (RTR, 1995–)

Appendix 4

Endnotes

1 Hot on the heels of the cancellation of the collaborative FMBT project which had started in 1972.

2 Which with the low weight had the potential to make MBT 80 very fast indeed.

3 However, it did prepare the way for the same concept to be authorised for use on CR2, thus saving time and angst.

4 The hulls used for the two ATRs look very similar to the Shir 2 design, which they were based upon. They were not, however, Shir 2 development hulls, but were built specifically for the MBT 80 project.

5 One of ten FV4211 turrets made in the early 1970s. The project was cancelled in 1972.

6 This compared very favourably with the equivalent amounts mounted on Challenger 1: 315mm on the glacis and 430mm on the turret front.

7 See the explanation of the 'Survivability Onion' in the Haynes Manual *Challenger 1*, page 82.

8 From spotting the target to it being destroyed by a first-round hit.

9 It is important to note that these figures included Chieftain without Chobham or the later Stillbrew; whether T64 was calculated as carrying ERA is not shown.

10 One MoD source states 17, VDS figures give 21.

11 Challenger Improvement Programme and Challenger Automotive Improvement Programme.

12 Sometimes called the Challenger 2 Mk 2, just to add more opacity! And as if that was not confusing enough, the MoD insisted on referring to it as the Challenger 2 (Plus).

13 VDS estimated that the CR2 would cost £1.373m per tank, with the CR2/2 coming out at £1.437m. Within 15 months the price for the latter had risen to £1.745 million, an increase of over 20%.

14 H5B2 was the codename given to a modified Challenger 1 hull used to mock up the new hull systems.

15 A series of 120mm gun and ammunition projects called CHARM, Chieftain/Challenger Armament, had commenced in the late 1970s to replace the L11 gun and ammunition fitted to those tanks.

16 Excluding the training fleets in UK and Canada, and the repair pool.

17 The regiments were (in order of seniority): Scots DG, RDG, QRH, KRH, QRL, 1RTR (one squadron only), 2RTR.

18 Keeping going with Chieftain, however much improved, was never a real prospect. It should be noted, though, that using the status quo as the start point is a frequently used method when examining potential change, and allows comparisons to be made between what is and what might be.

19 CHIP was to feature a new fire control system, ICSS; a modern fire control computer; improved elevation gearbox; and a new cupola and target acquisition system.

20 The major review was the completion of Milestone 3 in September 1990, when the decision to proceed with CR2 – or not – was to be made.

21 This was known as GFE or Government Furnished Equipment, and included such items as radio equipment, the Boiling Vessel, some tools, and the machine guns.

22 Since the Second World War and the early days of the Cold War the nature of the threat against tanks had changed, with the introduction of anti-tank guided missiles. The British assessment was that only 40% of hits on tanks would come from the enemy's tank guns firing KE projectiles, with a lot of attacks coming instead from HEAT warheads on missiles.

23 The French GIAT Leclerc was also considered and had some innovative features including an autoloader and an exceptionally small silhouette, but was never as well thought of as the US and German competition; in any case, it was not believed to be available until 1996 at the very earliest. Subsequently the French government formally requested that Leclerc was reconsidered, which it was.

24 The author was shown the top-secret firing trials video while serving at the RAC Gunnery School, Lulworth, and remains impressed by the results to this day.

25 For an example of the problems found on brand-new CR1s, see the Haynes Manual *Challenger 1*, page 46.

26 Official publications use the term GUE, as opposed to the APU or Auxiliary Power Unit adopted on CR1.

27 At one point the option of rebuilding some of the existing CR1 hulls into CR2 standard and replacing the turrets was considered, but this was technically demanding, involving a lot of modifications, and was also very expensive, being estimated at £349 million for just the turret conversions for 370 tanks; it was not proceeded with, and the hulls for CR2 were all brand-new builds.

28 Early versions had five and then six periscopes, which were found to be inadequate.

29 The changeover appears to have happened around the build of 62KK20.

30 Standing for 'Experimental Land Model One'. The XL28 was the gun originally intended to be used on the MBT 80, but at some point (probably around late 1979) this was superseded by the XL32 design.

31 The gun is fitted to the MBT 80 held at the Bovington Tank Museum.

32 HESH, Smoke and SH/P all use the same L3A2 bag charge filled with NQ propellant.

33 On both Chieftain and Challenger 1 the L15 APDS was known as sabot in the fire order. With CR2, as L15 is not used, L23 ammunition is referred to as sabot, and L27 as FIN. L29 is called DST.

34 This was often referred to as C3TR, for CHARM 3 Training Round.

35 I have some small pride here, as I had trained Colin on his gunnery instructor's course in 1992.

36 The prototypes also had an item known as a Beresford funnel in the loader's side, to be used for urination . . . none of the British crews thought it was necessary and for cultural reasons it horrified the Omanis, and so it was deleted.

37 Please! *Never* call them RSDG or SDG – the correct abbreviation is Scots DG!

38 Special 120mm water shot was often used which replicated firing and exercised the gun and recoil mechanism fully, but which greatly reduced the enormous safety template required with 120mm ammunition. It consisted of a water-filled fibre tube which replaced the normal projectile, and produced a bang which was much louder than any service ammunition!

39 KRH converted to CR2 from late 2000 into early 2001.

40 In August 2014 1RTR and 2RTR amalgamated to become the Royal Tank Regiment (RTR).

41 Arabic for 'Swift Sword'; Exercise Saif Sareea I had been conducted in 1986.

42 Aside from CR2, over 480 other armoured vehicles deployed on the exercise.

43 NATO standard climatic conditions define A3 in average temperature terms as a daily range between 28 and 39°C, whereas A1 (and known as 'Extreme Hot Dry') is between 32 and 49°C.

44 In DS59AA.

45 The year 2009 was the final one in which the Medicine Man exercises, run since 1972, were conducted. From 2010 the exercises were altered to reflect the contemporary operating environment and renamed Prairie Thunder.

46 Often but incorrectly called VRN – the registration is made up of both letters *and* numbers!

47 Historically there was no 13 Troop as it was considered unlucky, so the fourth squadron numbered its troops 14–17.

48 It is actually called No 361 Light Stone.

49 He is referring to paint No 380, named confusingly as Desert Sand and mainly used by the RAF as a Temporary Camouflage Coating (TCC) for application on aircraft!

50 On 30 September 2002 VDS were acquired by Alvis plc, who took on responsibility as Prime Contractors.

51 B Sqn KRH were working as part of a Danish battlegroup, so c/s W61 (troop sergeant 6th troop) used a D prefix to denote this.

52 An easy way of remembering which is which, is that the name TiTan has two letter Ts which support a bridge!

53 L23 APFSDS is the only KE ammunition used, DU ammunition is not supplied to Oman. Omani Chieftains were not fitted with the Stillbrew appliqué turret armour.

54 I am indebted to Mr Pete Breakspear, ex-17/21L and a former Lulworth gunnery instructor, for this information and accompanying photographs.

55 There was a suggestion that French commercial interests had interfered with some of the trials.

56 This term has replaced the previously used Theatre Entry Standard (TES) designation.

57 A lot of these issues would have been tackled had CLIP or CCSP been completed.

Index